MW01137981

AGAINST THE ODDS

By the same author

THE COAL-SCUTTLE BRIGADE
BLACK SATURDAY
STRIKE FROM THE SKY
THE GOLDEN WRECK
HMS BOUNTY
THE FRIENDLESS SKY
FROM MERCILESS INVADERS
CAEN: ANVIL OF VICTORY
GORDON OF KHARTOUM
VIMY RIDGE
FARMING THE SEA
HISTORY UNDER THE SEA
THE RACE FOR THE RHINE BRIDGES
KING HENRY VIII'S MARY ROSE
DEATH RAFT
THE QUEEN'S CORSAIR
ICE CRASH
INTO THE BLUE
DRESDEN 1945: THE DEVIL'S TINDERBOX
HOW WE FOUND THE MARY ROSE
TARQUIN'S SHIP
THE MOSQUITO LOG
A HERITAGE OF SHIPS
A WORLD TOO VAST: THE FOUR VOYAGES OF COLUMBUS

AGAINST THE ODDS

Battles at Sea: 1591–1949

ALEXANDER McKEE

NAVAL INSTITUTE PRESS
Annapolis, Maryland

Copyright © 1991 by Alexander McKee

First published 1991 in Great Britain by Souvenir Press Ltd,
43 Great Russell Street, London WC1B 3PA
Published and distributed in the United States of
America and Canada by the Naval Institute Press,
Annapolis, Maryland 21402.

Library of Congress Catalog Card No. 91-60985

This edition is authorized for sale only in
the United States, its territories and possessions,
and Canada.

All Rights Reserved. No part of this publication
may be reproduced, stored in a retrieval system,
or transmitted, in any form or by any means, electronic,
mechanical, photocopying, recording or otherwise without
the prior permission of the Copyright owner

ISBN 1-55750-025-8

Printed in Great Britain

ACKNOWLEDGEMENTS

Although every effort has been made to locate all owners of copyright, this has not been possible in all cases. However, our thanks are due to the following for their kind permission to use or quote from various books, articles or documents:

Harper Collins Publishers for the quoted works of Blake, Stayner and Lurting from *Robert Blake, General-at-Sea* by J. R. Powell (1972); *History Today* magazine for a quote from John Paul Jones on command in war, published in the September 1965 issue in an article, 'Paul Jones in Battle' by Oliver Warner; Constable Publishers for quotations from *Captain Marryat: A Re-Discovery* by Oliver Warner; Time-Life Books Inc. for quotes from David Porter's writings published in *The Frigates* by Henry E. Gruppe and Time-Life (1979); B. T. Batsford Ltd for contemporary speeches and writings published in *Coronel and the Falklands* by Geoffrey Bennett (1962); the Putnam Berkley Group Inc., New York, for extracts from *The Log of a U-Boat Commander* by Captain Ernst Hashagen. *The News*, Portsmouth, for extracts from an article, 'Night Attack in the Channel' by Commander Peppe RN (20 April, 1967); Gus Britton, Assistant Curator, and the Royal Navy Submarine Museum, Gosport, for much helpful advice and the sight of contemporary documents concerning the exploits of C3 and her crew at Zeebrugge, 1918; the Royal Naval Museum, Portsmouth, and the Portsmouth Central Library for information and sight of books concerning Kronstadt, 1919; personal correspondence with Peter Cornish, leader of the expeditions to find the sunken X-Craft in Altenfjord; the Ships' Histories Branch of the Department of the Navy, Washington Navy Yard, for much information regarding the USS *Franklyn* and the USS *Bunker Hill*, 1945.

A more complete bibliography will be found at the end of the book.

CONTENTS

LIST OF ILLUSTRATIONS

PREFACE

In choosing the subjects for this book I was given a fairly free hand. Consequently, they were chosen largely because I personally happened to like them, and with the bias—or limitation—implicit in that. In no sense are they graded according to degree of difficulty or courage; or even of success, for that would have been to imply that God is on the side of the small battalions when, clearly, He is not. Nor is it implied that in every case the man responsible was justified in the decision he took—on the contrary, I leave that verdict to the reader.

The selection prevents this book from falling into the well-worn category of 'Deeds That Won the Empire'. As my subjects include (in alphabetical order) Americans, British, French, Germans, Italians, Japanese and Russians, a reader expecting any such approach would soon begin to wonder what empire was being referred to.

I very soon dropped any idea of necessarily picking only 'new' subjects, when I discovered that to most of today's public 'the Falklands' means a late-colonial conflict of the 1980s and 'Zeebrugge' a recent car ferry disaster.

I have resolutely avoided using almost any excessively nautical term—some to the general public must seem distinctly absurd, such as admirals 'wearing' their flags, as if covering up sudden nudity. I have, however, been at some pains to explain where these events took place; and to set them in their contemporary background as far as possible.

I can claim some personal knowledge of the construction of most of the ships I write about, which are the homes of our heroes. As a child from a naval family, I knew many of the ships which fought in World War I as places visited for Christmas parties, and am well aware of the difference between a paper-thin hull and armour. My experience of much earlier ships came later in life, when I took up underwater exploration and the excavation of historic battleships, such as a French two-decker of 1698 and a Tudor carrack of the early sixteenth century.

Indeed, in World War II I knew so much of what was likely to happen to warship crews that, failing to become a fighter pilot, I joined the infantry rather than risk dying like a trapped rat as did so many men whose stories are told here.

Alexander McKee,
Hayling Island,
March 1990.

Chapter One

SIR RICHARD GRENVILLE OF THE *REVENGE*

The Azores, September 1591

Few major warships were lost during the reigns of the Tudor monarchs. There was the *Regent*, 1,000 tons, burned with the French carrack she had boarded in the battle off Brest in 1512; the *Mary Rose*, 700 tons, lost at Spithead off Portsmouth in 1545 by reason of 'rashness and great negligence'; and the *Revenge*, 500 tons, taken by the Spaniards in the Azores in 1591 'by the unadvised negligence and wilful obstinacy of her captain, Sir Richard Greynvile'.

The captain of the *Mary Rose* was also named Grenville. His Christian name was Roger and he was the father of Richard, who had been born in June 1542, three years before his father's drowning at Spithead with more than 400 men, a great tragedy witnessed by King Henry VIII himself. The 'rashness and negligence' in that case had not necessarily been Grenville's, although a captain must take formal responsibility. However, he was not there in July 1545 to answer charges; and nor was his son, Sir Richard, in September 1591.

The defeat of the Armada in 1588 had gone to people's heads. English prestige had reached a peak, in England and abroad, even in Spain. But looked at coldly, the Armada had not really been defeated: it had been frustrated and driven off. Partly because of a bad Spanish plan, partly because England's strength at sea had proved so formidable, an invasion had not even been launched. The only Spaniards who had landed in England had been prisoners.

In 1589, a year after the Spanish Armada had been sent home without achieving anything, the English Armada sailed for northern Spain and Portugal, with orders first to mop up the damaged ships returned from the failed 'Enterprise of England', where they lay being repaired, then to capture Lisbon and after that to take the Azores as a base from which to harass and perhaps cut Spain's communications with the Americas. They were to be assisted by a mass uprising of the Portuguese 'Resistance', supposedly eagerly awaiting them.

The English Armada was organised on the usual near-fatal lines, the command divided between Sir Francis Drake for the sea forces and Sir John ('Black') Norris, veteran of the wars in the Low Countries, as land forces commander—both highly competent men, but no one man in overall command of both planning and operations. The English discovered to their cost that defending against invasion was so very much easier than actually carrying out an invasion yourself.

As usual, it was the side which had been worsted previously which had taken the lessons to heart. To ensure the safety of the less bulky but most valuable cargoes—the silver and gold whose flow from the New World kept the Spanish war machine going, just as oil now subsidises modern armed forces—Alonso de Bazan, brother of Santa Cruz who had planned the Armada, proposed building gallizabras, small, very fast but well-armed ships which could run from any ordinary warship or defeat a smaller swift one.

Most ominous of all, for the impudent English, was King Philip of Spain's decision to build a war fleet capable of escorting the convoys of merchant ships across the Atlantic from the Caribbean. In this same year, 1589, he ordered a dozen galleons built in the Biscayan ports, nine more at Lisbon in Portugal, and contracted for a dozen Ragusan galleons.

Unaware of these developments, the English conceived a simple plan of sending out small squadrons in relays to cruise on the treasure fleet routes, and it was just such a squadron with which Sir Richard Grenville now served in the *Revenge*, Drake's old flagship in 1588, under the overall command of an inexperienced nobleman. As a contemporary letter put it:

> My Lord Thomas Howard hath kissed her Majesty's hand, and is gone down to his ships, Sir Richard Grenville being his Vice-admiral, and they and their partners I assure your Lordship make a very goodly fleet. God send them good speed, and a safe return: My Lord of Cumberland is not yet ready.

The Azores are on the latitude of southern Spain, and in July it was very pleasant being at sea among the islands. In the *Revenge* a young gentleman volunteer named Philip Gawdy wrote home by the pinnace which had brought out letters from the Council in England, that they all prayed heartily every day for the coming of the Spanish treasure fleet—the 'Silver Galleons',—bringing the cargoes from the New World. He thanked God that they had good ships with the *Revenge*, both Her Majesty's and those owned by private venturers. They had watered at Flores, one of the islands of the Azores group, and had had some adventures:

> I saw the dolphin course the flying fish, whereof I saw one fly as far as your young partridges will do at the first flight. I never had my health better in my life, thanks be to God . . . I like the sea and the sea life, and the company at sea, as well as any that ever I lived withal. The place is good and healthful to a willing mind . . . I am now so in love with the sea as I had rather be married to a mermaid . . .

The next letter Gawdy sent home was written from the prison in the castle of Lisbon. In the meantime, appalling things had happened.

By the end of July that sickness which was the scourge of wooden sailing ships, and of land forces too, had crippled the English fleet. Fifty per cent of the men were out of action and the ship worst affected, the *Nonpareil*, had to be sent home. In the *Revenge*, when her time came, 90 out of her 250 man crew were below, incapacitated. That was the result of four months' cruising in hot weather in enemy waters.

Enemy waters or not, something drastic had to be done. An anchorage had to be found, the sick put ashore until they recovered (or died), the ballast stones removed, the hull interiors thoroughly cleaned and fresh ballast brought on board. This took time, and while it was being done the ships were very vulnerable. A fast pinnace was stationed on patrol out to the west, to give warning of the approach of the *flota* from New Spain. Doubtless it was reckoned that only a few of those vessels would be sizeable warships.

But the Council back in England had miscalculated—badly. And in the new circumstances that could be fatal.

The situation at the end of August 1591 was that the English squadron in the Azores consisted of four galleons of medium size

—*Defiance* (Howard), *Revenge* (Grenville), *Bonaventure* and *Golden Lion* (replacing *Nonpareil*), all of about 500 tons; plus the smaller *Foresight* of 300 tons and *Crane* of 250 tons; also the pinnace *Charles* of 60 tons. The 70-ton *Moon* had been sent back for victuals.

A strong reinforcement of six well-armed merchant ships of between 200 and 300 tons had been delayed at Plymouth by bad weather but by this time was only a few days' sail away from their rendezvous near Fayal.

A powerful squadron under the Earl of Cumberland was keeping watch on the Spanish coast. And it was part of this force, watching the port of Ferrol, which reported the emergence of Don Alonso de Bazan's formidable fleet bound for the Azores. Cumberland sent a fast pinnace, the *Moonshine*, under Captain Middleton, to warn Howard and Grenville of this new, unexpected danger. Middleton came close enough to Bazan's ships to count them, and then ran on ahead for the Azores.

There were now four groups of ships converging on the Azores: the *flota* of 70 or more vessels from the Indies on the final stage of its journey across the Atlantic; the English cruising squadron under Howard and Grenville eagerly waiting for them; the six well-armed merchantmen sent out from Plymouth under Captain Robert Flick to reinforce the English squadron; and the unknown joker in the pack—the 55 ships under Alonso de Bazan approaching from Spain, 20 of them warships and carrying in all 7,000 men.

By 20 August (by the English calendar, the Spaniards would reckon ten days later) Bazan's fleet had reached the island of Terceira, the Spanish stronghold in the group of newly conquered Portuguese possessions. There they learned from a friar and a pilot who had been taken by the English and then released, that the English had no more than 22 ships, of which only half-a-dozen were sizeable galleons of the Queen. Of the remainder they counted, some must have been victuallers arrived from England recently. Bazan's fleet alone outnumbered their enemies by more than two to one, without counting at all the seventy or so ships of the *flota* approaching the Azores from the west. Several of these had already been snapped up by English privateers. A despatch-boat arrived with the news that the English were at the most westerly isles of the Azores, Flores and Corvo, and Bazan sailed to intercept them. For a week, stormy and unfavourable winds kept him beating about in an attempt to get forward.

But by what on Spanish reckoning was 7 September, they got a good

wind from astern, and the following day were so far advanced that
fifteen leagues (less than 50 miles) from Flores they met their reconnaissance craft with the latest information. The English were still at
Flores, and Bazan decided to hoist as much sail as possible in order to
be on their enemy at first light next day, with all the advantage of
surprise.

However, he had second thoughts when it was reported to him that
one of his galleons had broken her bowsprit and therefore could not put
on much sail. Rather than leave her behind in enemy-patrolled waters,
he gave up his advantage; so that at dawn the next day he was still eight
leagues distant. This conservative decision very probably cost him a
great victory, because it meant abandoning his original plan, which
was to divide his force—one part to go direct to the north channel
between Corvo and Flores, the other to circle round to the west of the
island so that the English would be caught not merely by surprise at
dawn but in both front and rear simultaneously.

Captain Middleton's *Moonshine* had already warned Howard and
Grenville of the approach of this unexpected and formidable enemy,
but the ships were in such disorder that rapid flight was impossible.
They were mostly without fresh ballast or with insufficient, they had
not completed topping up their water, and there were still a great many
sick men convalescent on shore.

Two men from the *Revenge*, who were soon afterwards brought home
by a ship of Lyme, gave official testimony, as did four others who on
arrival in Cornwall were examined by Sir Francis Godolphin. Sir
Walter Ralegh had this virtually first-hand evidence on which to base
his pamphlet, *A Report of the Truth of the Fight about the Isles of Açores*,
which he wrote shortly afterwards.

> And that which was most to our disadvantage, the one half part of
> the men of every ship sick, and utterly unserviceable. For in the
> *Revenge* there were ninety diseased; in the *Bonaventure*, not as many
> in health as could handle her main sail.

All the more cause to wonder why Sir Richard reacted to the crisis in the
way he did.

The wind was still blowing from the east towards Flores when a
pinnace brought Alonso de Bazan the news that the English cruising
fleet had been alerted and were about to depart: they had hoisted and

lowered the topsails on their mainmasts four times and fired two guns, obviously signalling to men still ashore. Almost at once the squadron of Marcos de Aramburu, ordered by Bazan to reconnoitre the channel between Corvo and the northern end of Flores, also fired two signal guns to warn that the enemy was in sight and was coming out. All the Spanish squardons therefore altered course for the Flores-Corvo channel. Fifty-five ships against 22, and the incoming *flota* from the Indies not far away to the west.

No one will draw a track chart of the ensuing manoeuvres. To start with, the exact site of the English anchorage is not given anywhere, not in the English accounts nor in the official Spanish 'Relation'. All we know is that the wind was from the east, behind the Spaniards, that the English ships were showing their right sides to the Spaniards and that Bazan's objective was to close and board them, using his superiority in soldiers. Howard was leading in the fleet flagship *Defiance* and Grenville in the vice-flagship *Revenge* was last, having stayed to 'recover the men that were upon the Island, which otherwise had been lost', according to Ralegh. When Bazan saw them coming out, they were under fighting sail only—main-topsails and foresails—the great sails being furled.

The English ships were generally faster and handier than the miscellaneous collection of European shipping employed by Spain, but it was a near thing. Ralegh says so, and the Spanish 'Relation' confirms that Howard's ships only just managed to escape upwind of their enemy. With the exception of the *Revenge*. According to Ralegh, the sailing master of the *Revenge*, seeing that even Drake's old flagship could not escape the oncoming Spanish squadrons, advised Sir Richard not to risk it but, trusting in her abilities to outsail any other great ship afloat, to cast about and run west before the wind. And Sir Richard would not have it.

He would not run from the Spaniards. He would sail straight at them and force the squadrons of Seville to give way.

Meanwhile, Bazan and Howard were in action.

At five o'clock in the afternoon the firing began, the dull thudding of the cannon overlaying the lighter sound of arquebus and musket, for the ranges were close. The Castilian galleons of Aramburu, a veteran of the Armada campaign, were first engaged. They were followed by the great ships under the direct command of Alonso de Bazan. Two of his galleons, the *San Felipe* and the *San Barnabe*, steered to board Howard's *Defiance*, failed, and delivered broadsides instead. Howard was known to the Spaniards as inexperienced and no sailor; but still he evaded the Spanish onslaught; the rest of his ships likewise. All except one: Grenville's *Revenge*.

Sir Richard was well known to the Spanish as a famous corsair with a formidable reputation. Now, according to their official account, he came 'swaggering up' (*gallardeano*) in the very ship which under Drake had given them such a hard time the previous year. In Armada year the Spanish guns had proved remarkably ineffective even at fairly close ranges. Possibly Sir Richard was gambling on that to preserve his masts and rigging from crippling damage and, using the speed and agility of the *Revenge*, to burst through the pack of avenging galleons.

The leading Spanish ship was the *San Felipe* of 1,500 tons (as against the 500 tons of the lower-built *Revenge*). The towering hull and castles of the Spaniard quite overtopped the sleek *Revenge* and this, combined with the spread of her canvas, completely stole the wind from the English galleon. At once, the *Revenge* lost way and soon would not answer her helm, the rudder moving fruitlessly in still water. Sir Richard's dash for open sea had ended almost before it had begun.

The great *San Felipe* crashed alongside with a rumbling and straining of timbers, and nine or ten Spaniards leaped down onto the deck of the *Revenge*. A rope was thrown after them and they secured it, but while the English galleon had lost way the huge Spanish hull was still moving. The rope came taut and began to make ominous noises as it quivered with strain; then it parted and the English ship was free.

Close behind the *San Felipe* now was the *San Barnabe*, and in her was Martin de Bertendona, another veteran of the defeated Armada of '88, with scores to settle. She closed the *Revenge* on the other side, and this time proper grappling irons came hurtling across the water; and they held.

The *Revenge* fired her lower tier of guns—the heaviest battery she had—into the *San Felipe*, which sheered off and abandoned her boarders. Seven of these brave attackers were slaughtered by the English, but the two or three still alive escaped onto Bertendona's ship which remained firmly locked with the English galleon.

It was now growing dark and Howard's ships, having tacked clear of the Spaniards, hoisted their mainsails and sped away for England, closely pursued by Alonso de Bazan and his best ships. They nearly caught the *Defiance*, Howard's command being the worst sailer of them all. The Spanish commander had lost his chance of a famous victory.

At this time the *Revenge* was not quite abandoned to Spain. One of the small, lightly-armed victualling ships, the *George Noble* of London, having suffered some shot damage to her light hull, came under the lee of the *Revenge*, and her master 'asked Sir Richard what he would command him, being but one of the victuallers and of small force: Sir Richard bade him save himself, and leave him to his fortune.'

Somewhere out there in the growing darkness, doubtless hoping to be mistaken for just another Spanish sail among so many, was the *Pilgrim* of Plymouth under Jacob Whidden, loath to see a fellow West Country-man (the Grenvilles were from the borderland between Cornwall and Devon) abandoned to an enemy. The Spanish vessels had hundreds of soldiers on board each ship; the English had none, apart from a few gentleman volunteers and servants.

The castles at bow and stern, although lower in English warships than they had been during the reign of Elizabeth's father, Henry VIII, really were castles. When boarding could not be prevented, the men shut themselves up there and continued to resist. The planking of these upperworks was necessarily much lighter than that of the main hull, but they were arranged for defence; could carry guns firing down into the waist of the ship and, almost certainly, the ladders by which they entered could be drawn up after them.*

The boarders, penned in the waist without cover, and shot at from both front and rear even if they escaped being hit by enfilade fire as they made the dangerously uncertain jump over the water from the one hull to the other, would be in an unenviable position. This would be especially so if the masts of the assaulted ship had been shot away and the vantage point of the fighting tops been denied them. To reduce their casualties it would be necessary to blow to splinters the light planking of the castles, and so deprive of cover any of the enemy who were not killed by the bombardment. This it seems is what the Spanish were trying to do that night.

A least fifteen Spanish ships took turns to lie alongside the *Revenge* in the darkness. After the *San Felipe*'s hot reception, Bertendona had closed on the port side and saved the remnants of the *San Felipe*'s

---

*Just such a ladder by the stern castle of the *Mary Rose*, recovered in 1982, has puzzled the experts because its positioning suggested that the nearest heavy gun was not allowed to recoil, which seems absurd. But if it was simply drawn up before close action, the mystery is solved.

boarders. Then Aramburu had come up, nudging his bow castle against the poop of the English galleon. Spanish soldiers had leapt on the upper deck, captured the *Revenge*'s ensign and, killing some of her men, had fought their way as far as her mainmast.

In the encounter Aramburu's ship sustained severe structural damage and had to sheer off and light flares for assistance.

Next Don Antonio Manrique in the galleon *Ascensión* boarded by the prow of the *Revenge* and also across Bertendona's decks. The decks of the ships were widest near the waterline and became progressively narrower the higher up they were, so that even when the hulls were touching near the waves the upper decks were still some distance apart. Consequently, when the ship of Don Luis Cuitino came up, she simply came alongside Manrique. Using each other's ships as bridges, all night long the Spaniards tried to pour assault troops into Sir Richard's battered galleon, boarding mainly by the prow where the beakhead projected out over the sea past the stem. But they were repeatedly beaten back again into their ships or into the waves.

One hour before midnight on 31 August, Sir Richard Grenville, standing on the poop, was shot down by a musket ball in the body. As the surgeon began to dress his wound he was hit again, this time in the head, and the surgeon killed beside him.

At no time during the night were there less than two galleons alongside the *Revenge*, pouring shot into her and sending away boarding parties. Ralegh gives a telling picture of her helplessness, saying that she was 'not able to move one way or the other, but as the sea was moved with the waves and billow of the sea'. Her enemies could retire and be replaced with fresh ships, fresh soldiers could be sent to board her. Her masts were gone but her lower deck guns continued to fire. As the range was point blank, the shot did some hurt. The galleon *Ascensión* sank that night; the vessel of Don Luis Cuitino, flagship of the hulks, did not go down until next day, her crew being saved by Bertendona's ship.

One could wish that the gifted young letter writer Philip Gawdy, so fresh with descriptions of dolphins and flying fish, had spared time to describe the appalling horror which at daybreak was the *Revenge*. If he wrote such a letter it did not survive, although he himself did.

Lying below the waterline were the sick, 90 of them, too ill to move. Only a hundred men were fully fit when the battle began; by morning 40 of these were dead, and most of the remainder were wounded in some degree. Most of her powder was spent and all her pikes were broken.

Ralegh described her from the evidence of the seamen: her 'masts all beaten overboard, all her tackle cut asunder, her upper works altogether razed, and in effect evened she was with the water, but the very foundation or bottom of a ship, nothing being left overhead either for flight or defence.'

According to Spanish testimony, Sir Richard's headwound had been made by a ball from an arquebus, and it was serious. One would expect a marked shock effect to the nervous system, and loss of will. On the contrary, Grenville seemed to be enraged. He was above all determined not to lose the *Revenge* to Spanish captors. The last thing he intended to do was surrender. He ordered the master gunner to blow a hole in the ship's bottom and sink her. Nothing very dramatic—the fight had used up virtually all the powder in the stores—just a scuttling charge. But its result must be that all the badly wounded and sick—including himself —would die.

It is not really so strange, considering what sort of man he was and the very similar character of some of the men he led. While still in his teens, he had gone off to fight on the continent as part of an aristocrat's plain duty in the face of invasion by the Sultan and the Moslem threat to Vienna. A contemporary historian, Camden, wrote of these English volunteers 'who, according to their innate fortitude thought themselves born to arms, not to idleness, when gentlemen out of all parts of Europe were excited upon the fame of the Turks, went into Hungary', naming Grenville as one of them.

He was, of course, a violent man. While still under age, he took part with friends in an affray during which he ran an opponent through with his sword, the blade penetrating six inches. The victim lived only an hour after that. For this murder he was pardoned and later became a member of Parliament, which laid further responsibility upon him. And he was now, although badly wounded, still the Vice-Admiral aboard a flagship of the Royal fleet.

The dying man's arguments convinced the master gunner and many others that they should all perish rather than surrender; but others, notably the captain and the master, took another view. There were, they said, many men aboard with less than mortal wounds, who if saved might thereafter render the country and the Crown acceptable service. They were prepared to ask the enemy for terms and were sure that the Spaniards would give them. Grenville, in spiritual as well as physical agony, declared that he would not have the Spanish glory in the capture

of even one ship of Her Majesty. To this, those of other opinion replied
that the *Revenge* had six feet of water in her hold, three shot holes below
the waterline which were but weakly stopped, and must sink at the first
rough sea encountered.

The master of the *Revenge*, who had received ten or twelve wounds on
head and body, according to a Dutch merchant called Linschoten who
saw him as a prisoner shortly before he died of them, was taken on
board Alonso de Bazan's flagship, the *San Pablo*, and did indeed secure
favourable terms of surrender: the ship's company to be repatriated,
the officers (the 'better sort') to pay reasonable ransom and meanwhile
be free from the galleys or the prisons. When this news was brought to
the *Revenge*, it was gladly received by almost everyone except Grenville
and the master gunner, who tried to kill himself with a sword.

This scene took place in the brutal aftermath of battle, 'the ship being
marvellous unsavoury, filled with blood and bodies of dead, and
wounded men like a slaughter-house'. Grenville fainted for a few
moments while he was being carried away to the Spanish flagship, then,
reviving, asked his ship's company to pray for him. The Spaniards
treated him with respect, even admiration, until a day or two later
Richard Grenville died.

His last words were reported by Linschoten who was then at Terceira
and conversed with the Spaniards and some of the English prisoners.

> Here die I Richard Grenville, with a joyful and quiet mind, for that
> I have ended my life as a true soldier ought to do, that hath fought
> for his country, Queen, religion and honour . . . but the others of
> my company have done as traitors and dogs, for which they shall
> be reproached all their lives and leave a shameful name for ever.

He died enraged that his ship's company had thwarted his last
wishes. Certainly he was not referring to Howard or any others in the
fleet. Apart from the *George Noble* of London, the *Pilgrim* of Plymouth
had waited through the night near the *Revenge* but at dawn had been
recognised by the Spaniards and 'was hunted like a hare among many
ravenous hounds, but escaped'.

Bazan's fleet finally made their junction with the *flota* from the Indies,
the combined Spanish force now amounting to some 140 ships in
addition to the *Revenge*. Almost at once they were struck and dispersed
by the worst storm in living memory, which moreover lasted for more

than a week. For three weeks after the storm the bodies of drowned men came driving ashore among the islands of the Azores. From some ships, there were no survivors. The captured *Revenge* 'was cast away upon a cliff near to the Island of Terceira, where it brake into a hundred pieces and sunk to the ground', according to Linschoten who reported the outspoken comments of the Portuguese upon the Spaniards:

> The taking of the *Revenge* was justly revenged upon them, and not by the might or force of man, but by the power of God . . . so soon as they had thrown the dead body of the Viceadmiral Sir Richard Grenville overboard, they verily thought that as he had a devilish faith and religion, and therefore the devils loved him, so he instantly sunk into the bottom of the sea, and down into Hell, where he raised up all the devils to the revenge of his death.

The Elizabethan Admiral Sir William Monson accused a temporal power, the King of Spain, who 'being sensible how much the safety of that fleet concerned him, caused them to disembogue so late in the year that it endangered the shipwreck of them all.'

His verdict on the conduct of Sir Richard Grenville at the Azores was equally critical:

> The marvel I speak of is, that notwithstanding the apparent dangers and casualties of the sea aforesaid, yet not one of her Majesty's ships ever miscarried but only the *Revenge*, which I said, in her voyage of 1591, was taken by the Spaniards by the un-advised negligence and wilful obstinacy of her captain, Sir Richard Greynvile.

Ralegh's pamphlet is uncritical, naturally. As author of *The Truth of the Fight about the Isles of Açores*, he had to perform a balancing act. Grenville was his cousin; he could hardly condemn him. Howard was an important member of the ruling 'Establishment'; it would not do to criticise him for timidity. It was necessary also to glorify England; the loss of the *Revenge* and the scattering of Howard's ships was a plain defeat; but somehow it had to be turned into a victory. In achieving this, Ralegh used a formula which has been copied into the present century. At the same time he conceded that his cousin might have been wrong in trying to break through the Spanish fleet and that those who

suggested that he cast about and use the *Revenge*'s speed to get away
might have had the better case.

The verdict of a French general upon the charge of the Light Brigade
at Balaclava suggests itself: 'It is magnificent but it is not war.'
Certainly, Monson approved of Howard's decision to avoid battle as
'wary and discreet'.

There were two Spanish reactions. The official 'Relation', probably
written in the flagship, is unemotional and more or less a straight-
forward war diary, but carefully avoiding criticism of the management
on the Spanish side, as one would expect. The formidable nature of the
captured ship is given without ornament or exaggeration.

> The Admiral-galleon was one of the best there were in England;
> they called her the *Revenge*. She was the flagship that carried Drake
> to Corunna . . . She carried 42 pieces of ordnance of bronze less
> three which were given to another ship a few days before, the 20 on
> her lower deck of 40 to 60 quintals, and the remaining 22 of 20 to 30
> quintals, all good.

The 'Relation' admits the loss of two ships and some 100 men of
whom two were captains, Luis de San Juan and Don Jorge Broano. Of
Howard's fleet it is stated that they

> took to flight in disorder, some bearing west and others towards
> the Isles [i.e., east] taking advantage of the obscurity of the night,
> and others by different ways; of whom up to now we do not know
> that they have collected together, nor seen them, except for one
> very far off plying to windward . . .

The only gentleman captured in the *Revenge* was Philip Gawdy
of Lincolnshire. He was soon to join William Monson (the future
Admiral) in the prison castle of Lisbon, from the walls of which Monson
had already watched the triumphant return of the galleon *San Andreas*
from the Azores.

> On being upon the walls at our usual hour, we beheld a great
> galleon of the King's turning up the river in her fighting sails,
> being sumptuously decked with ensigns, streamers and pendants,
> with all other ornaments to show her bravery. She let fly all her

ordnance in a triumphant manner for the taking Sir Richard Grenville in the *Revenge* at the island of Flores, she being one of that fleet and the first voyage she ever made.

The *San Andreas* was one of King Philip's 'Twelve Apostles', laid down the year after the Armada as Spain's answer to the English galleons. The sight of her coming up to Lisbon bragging of victory over England irritated Monson so much that he wagered another prisoner that he would live to see her taken. And she was. In the 1596 attack on Cadiz, Ralegh himself attacked both the *San Andreas* and the *San Felipe* and avenged his cousin: the former was taken, the latter burnt.

But whether in 1591 Grenville did well or ill is still debated.

Chapter Two

ROBERT BLAKE, GENERAL-AT-SEA

Santa Cruz de Tenerife, April 1657

In the parish church of the Conception, in the seaport town of Santa Cruz on Tenerife, hang stained and torn battle flags, not often seen by modern tourists because neither the Spaniards nor the English wish to popularise the defeat of England's greatest naval hero, Horatio Nelson. They are British ensigns captured from his fleet which in 1795 assaulted the fortified port with heavy loss but no success at all. Nelson himself was wounded and eventually lost an arm to one of the brass cannon mounted in a fort, which can still be seen. The weapon supposed to have done the damage is still mounted there, together with its massed companions. One cannot now imagine the British boats coming in through the surf from the line-of-battle ships standing off in deeper water, because of the modern docks and breakwaters and the artificial rock reef protecting the beach, of imported Sahara sand, which has been built for the tourists. Many British visitors died here that day in a badly planned, chaotic operation which proved ultimately futile.

The island has known many seafarers. Columbus sailed past in 1492, on his way to what he thought was Japan or China; Drake and Hawkins came here to trade illegally with the locals in 1567. Tenerife makes a good rendezvous for seamen, with the volcanic cone called Teide rearing to over 12,000 feet—the highest mountain in Spain, it can be seen many miles away and is distinctive.

But 90 years after Drake and Hawkins, in 1657, the harbour of Santa Cruz and its guardian forts were attacked by a former foot soldier in the Puritan army at the head of a Commonwealth fleet, and achieved total success without serious loss. The foot soldier who, early in the Civil War, helped in the defence of Bristol against the Royalists, was Robert

Blake. By holding on when the Parliamentary governor of the town had
retired, he nearly got himself hanged.

Robert Blake was born in 1599 at Bridgwater in Somerset, a West
Countryman like the Grenvilles. But whereas Richard Grenville was
the arrogant young heir to a rich estate, Blake was of quiet and
intellectual disposition; he studied at the University of Oxford for ten
years until, when he was only 24, his father died and he had to return
home to take over the family business and the care of his ten younger
brothers and sisters. Like Grenville, he too became a member of
Parliament; but at a critical time for that institution. War was not his
chosen profession; he came from a family of merchants, not aristocrats.
At Taunton, commanding the defenders against the Royalist besiegers,
he answered a call to surrender by saying that, as he had four pairs of
good boots, he would eat three of them before giving in, a quiet joke
which went down well with the West Countrymen.

The English Civil War had the not unexpected result of building up
experienced fighting forces well tried in battle, particularly Oliver
Cromwell's New Model Army, the best-paid professional force in
Europe. But as many of the ships had gone over to the King during the
war, the Navy needed rebuilding and re-organising and, reasoning that
a warship was primarily a mobile gun battery defended by foot soldiers,
Cromwell turned some of his successful generals into admirals—where
they proved equally successful. This in spite of the fact that, early on,
their main enemy was Holland. The Dutch had a large and efficient
fleet led by brilliant seamen, crewed by men very similar to the English.
There were often defeats and no easy victories. Blake took part in both,
but at the battle of Plymouth, when he led the English fleet, he defeated
Van Tromp, although he himself was badly wounded in the thigh by a
bar shot. The savagery of the fighting and the actual nature of war was
not concealed by the Puritan press. A newspaper man wrote that

> all the men-of-war who are taken are much dyed with blood, their
> masts and tacks being moiled with brains, hair, pieces of skull . . .
> dreadful sights though glorious, as being a signal token of the
> Lord's goodness to this Nation.

Many Englishmen, particularly in Cromwell's army, did not
approve of fighting the Dutch, who were Protestants like themselves.
But the Dutch wars were deemed to be in the national interest, as a

matter of trade. Nevertheless Cromwell, now military dictator of England, intended to go further and sway the balance of power between the two most powerful nations, France and Spain at that time, and to keep secret for as long as possible just which one he was going to attack.

Blake was given command of the largest fleet and sent to the Mediterranean with sealed orders. So strict was security that Blake showed the outsides of the letters, with their seals, to his captains, but would not let them read the contents—an extreme case of not 'needing to know'. In other respects, too, the Lord Protector (as the dictator called himself) was a good commander-in-chief. He wrote to Blake that he 'must handle the reins as you shall find your opportunity, and the ability of the fleet to be', a refreshing latitude when compared to the itchy fingers of many later Whitehall war lords.

At this time, 1655, Blake was suffering from dropsy, scurvy and the effects of the wounds he had had off Portland in 1653. A Venetian envoy wrote that 'he seems to be a very touchy and particular old man, who treats his Captains with extreme severity.' And an envoy representing Florence elaborated by writing that

> Blake is a deep sombre man of few words; owing to his advanced age he never shows himself, even on his own ship, except when the sun shines, and although invited, he would never go ashore [at Naples] to see the place and gratify his countrymen.

The Venetian envoy gave an unwilling tribute to Blake's security measures by writing that the Spanish ministers had begun 'to feel doubtful about the proceedings of General Blake whose plans it is not easy to find out'.

His captains were given the time and place of the next rendezvous, but that was all; not even in wine or in someone else's bed could anyone give away the fleet's ultimate objective: France or Spain? Or neither of them?

In January 1655 Blake sailed with his ships for Tunis, in North Africa. The Dey of Tunis, for what seems sufficiently good reason, had imprisoned some Englishmen, and Cromwell wanted something done about it. The harbour for Tunis was Porto Farina, north of the city. Nine of the Dey's ships lay there under the protection of the castle. Extra batteries were being emplaced and thousands of Berber horse and foot were gathering. Fort and ships flew blood-red flags, and the

Admiral a green and white flag. Both the foot soldiers and the Berber horsemen flourished scimitars which flashed in the sunlight, to demonstrate defiance of the Europeans.

Short of food and water, Blake made a reconnaissance to test the place, its depths and the effectiveness of its artillery fire, and then he sailed away to get provisions. He also wrote home to clarify a point in his orders. Had he, or had he not, authority to attack Porto Farina?

On 18 March he was once again off Tunis, where he found the Berbers as intractable as before:

These barbarous provocations did so far work upon our spirits, that we judged it necessary for the honour of the fleet, our nation, and religion, seeing that they would not deal with us as friends, to make them feel us as enemies.

To lull the enemies into a sense of security, Blake once again sailed away, staying for a week at Trapani. On 3 April he returned to Porto Farina. The nine warships were lying a pistol shot away from the Berber gun batteries. They counted sixty guns emplaced and forces of musketeers in readiness to greet them. Blake thought he had now solved the problem of how to take out those war galleys in spite of the powerful gun defences covering them. Cannon emplaced behind strong walls were considered far more effective than similar guns mounted on the decks of ships moving on and moved by, the sea. Wood against stone. A steady platform against an unsteady one.

Blake ordered the ships to go in by squadrons at dawn the next day. The first squadron, led by Cobham in the *Newcastle*, anchored near the galleys; the remaining squadrons of Badiley, Stayner and Blake anchored within musket shot of the Berber castle and its 60-odd guns. There was water enough, as Blake knew, and the enemy's guns were short-ranged and ill-served. Furthermore (a critical factor), there was an onshore wind carrying the rolling clouds of white smoke down onto the castle—seen by Blake as a mark of divine approval: 'the Lord being pleased to favour us with a gentle gale from off the sea, which cast all the smoke upon them, and made our work the more easy.'

While the castle was being overwhelmed by the masked fire of three squadrons, the first squadron sent away its boats towards the moored war galleys which were dismantled and had only skeleton crews on board. Those crews jumped overboard and swam to the shore and the safety of the castle, when they saw the 'boats of execution' under Captain Jeffery Pierce approaching. By 8 a.m. that morning all nine galleys were ablaze, the guns of this squadron discouraging any attempts at fire fighting by the Berbers.

By 11 o'clock it was all over and the ships began to warp out of the harbour. In the ships there had been few losses, but in the assault boats 25 men had been killed and some 40 wounded. The galleys burned all that day and far into the night. Contrary to all the lessons of war, for the first time ships had prevailed against land fortifications.

Blake then took his fleet to Tunis, to renew a treaty with the Dey concerning repatriation of British sailors; and while there some Dutch sailors escaped and swam out to the English ships. However, a ransom was still payable and the crews of the English ships agreed to contribute a dollar each to set their former enemies free. As sailors' pay—and that of Admirals, too—was sometimes many months and occasionally years in arrears, this contribution was more than a charitable gesture.

On 2 May Blake received orders from home regarding 'a former instruction touching the Plate Fleet coming from America'. Blake's Mediterranean cruises had seemed to threaten the ports of southern France more than they did those of Spain, but that was just Cromwell's double game. The Treasure Fleets, and the galleons sent out to convoy them home, were truly the lifeblood of Spain. Further, any of the treasure ships captured would alleviate the financial crisis in England. Everyone was short of ready cash. The days when governments could simply print money and then raise interest rates were far in the future.

In September 1656 the squadron under Stayner intercepted a part of the Plate Fleet returning without escort and almost home. Stayner took two, sank or burned three; two escaped. The Spanish Rear-Admiral's cargo included 45 tons of silver ('plate'), 700 chests of indigo, 700 chests of sugar, plus drugs and other goods. The main body of the Plate Fleet was not expected until December. The English received certain news of it from a pitiful prisoner, the sixteen-year-old Marquis of Baydex. His father, the Governor of Peru, and his mother and sister, had burned to death in one of the treasure ships set on fire by the English; he and his younger brother were now orphans and penniless. He was also without guile and talked freely of life in Peru, mentioning that ten galleons of the *flota*, with millions in plate aboard, were due to arrive in Spain, via the Canaries, in December.

That winter saw more tiresome blockade duty, in ships foul with weed, their hulls and rigging strained to danger point, sheathing defective rations bad and short, conditions aboard cold, damp and monotonous, relieved only at intervals by the arrival of a merchant ship from England carrying thousands of letters for the crews of the blockading ships, or a Dutch prize carrying a cargo of tobacco.

On 19 February Blake was still blockading the Spanish fleet in Cadiz—the potential escorts for the *flota* if it came—when an English ship closed him to report that he had met twelve galleons steering for the Canary Islands. Some of the captains were all for sending a force of frigates after them, but Blake refused to divide his fleet and so expose it to defeat in detail. In the last week of March victualling ships arrived from England, with food and beer. From now on reports poured in, becoming more and more detailed. The *flota* had reached the Canaries and had unloaded the treasure. Then a confirmation that the *flota* lay in the harbour of Santa Cruz on the east coast of Tenerife and that the port was strongly fortified. Further, it seemed that the Spanish force in Cadiz was unlikely to stir. Blake decided to sail for Tenerife with his whole force.

On 18 March the north-eastern tip of Tenerife, the Punta de Anaga, was sighted in hazy weather, with little wind, so that had the fleet held on for Santa Cruz the defenders would have had plenty of warning. Blake led southward out of sight of land. On 20 March they were four leagues out to sea, awaiting the reports of two scouting ships. They reported that the *flota* was in the harbour of Santa Cruz. There was tension between Blake and his captains, who supported Stayner's plan of sending in frigates to destroy the Spanish ships. Blake agreed, but said he would come in with the rest of the fleet to smother the land defences, much stronger here than the Berbers had been at Porto Farina.

The flota was anchored in a shallow roadstead rather than the port itself which was small, but the whole roadstead was backed by a line of fortifications which overlapped both ends of it, so that any attacker would meet with fire from three directions. The southern extremity was anchored on St Philip, a stone fort holding 40 guns. Then from the town of Santa Cruz northwards stretched seven more stone forts, linked by breastworks for musketeers.

The defenders were confident of repelling any assault. To a Fleming who asked permission to leave before the battle the Spanish Admiral said contemptuously, 'Begone if you will and let Blake come in if he dares.' A prisoner from Hispaniola afterwards said that the Spaniards laughed at the English 'and were, for Spaniards, very jolly'.

Stayner's orders were brief. The frigates to follow him in in line and to lay themselves alongside the galleons at several hundred yards from shore, leaving room enough to veer their ships during the fight and afterwards. Not a gun was to be fired until they had anchored.

At eight o'clock Stayner in the *Speaker* led his squadron of a dozen ships into the roadstead. The Spanish defences, the 16 galleons of the *flota* moored in front, stretched for five miles. The wind, as at Porto Farina, was blowing onshore. Blake, with 11 ships, waited as floating reserve until after 11 o'clock, when the situation had become clear.

Stayner stated that he anchored within pistol-shot of the two flagships of the *flota*, using their great hulls as cover from the cannon emplaced ashore. Much later, after the Restoration, when he was serving the Crown and not the Commonwealth, he claimed to have blown them up. But this is contradicted by the evidence of Thomas Lurting, boatswain of the *Bristol*, who later became a Quaker. 'The wind blew very right upon the shore,' he began . . .

> . . . and the smoke being somewhat abated, we found ourselves to be within half a cable's length of the [Spanish] Vice-Admiral . . . and not a cable's length of the [Spanish] Admiral . . . and within musket-shot of some forts and breastworks: when we had brought up our ship, we were about half a cable's length from the Vice-Admiral.

The distances, then, were between 100 and 200 yards, with the tricky business of dropping anchor and then finding out by experience of wind and tide at that time just how their ship would lie in relation to the flagships of the *flota*, which were of course armed and in action, although the British gunsmoke rolled down upon them. The Spanish vice-flagship veered on her cable until she was only a musket-shot from shore. The *Bristol*'s captain put a spring on his own cable, so that the English ship lay across the enemy's hawse, presenting a 28-gun broadside to the enemy's ill-armed bow. With her second broadside, the *Bristol* put a shot into the enemy's powder room and the vice-flagship blew up.

Not a man escaped, said Lurting, but they all now expected the Spanish Admiral 'to serve us as we had served his Vice-Admiral'.

However, at their third broadside, they saw the crew of the Spaniard jumping overboard, and a minute later she too blew up.

With both the masking galleons gone, they were in the field of fire of a small castle, but shot back in such manner that 'in a short time we made them weary of it'.

By now Stayner's squadron had suffered severely and, furthermore, he had lost control. Some of the galleons had sunk, but his captains were trying to secure as prizes five which still remained afloat. Three ships, the *Plymouth*, *Worcester* and *Maidstone*, were each in process of towing off a prize; as was Bourne in the *Swiftsure*. The *Bridgwater* also had a Spanish ship in tow. How they were to get out against the wind and under heavy fire was the problem, but their captains were determined. Although the bars of silver and gold had been sent ashore, the bulk of the valuable cargoes remained on board the Spanish ships, representing a considerable fortune for the captains and crews who could carry them home. A contemporary Army view of the sailors was that they were unfit for land service, 'unless it be for sudden plunder, and then they are valiant much'. It is understandable. Unlike the Army, the Navy was illpaid, if it was paid at all; and a laden Spanish galleon as prize was like winning the Pools today.

Blake three times ordered the captains to burn the Spanish ships where they were, and they would not obey. Then, reluctantly, they began the work of destruction. To complete it, Blake sent in his boats to make sure of them all, their advance being covered by the rolling smoke of his guns billowing shorewards.

Lurting was sent in a longboat with seven or eight men to burn a galleon lying inshore, apparently deserted. But as they rowed nearer, the crew jumped up and manned their guns, the shot however only going over their heads. They reached her and burned her. Then the smoke drifted away to reveal three galleons a musket shot from the *Bristol* and fifty yards from the shore. One really was abandoned, and he fired her without trouble; and cutting her cable, saw her drift down on the other two, setting them on fire also. In all this excitement, the *Bristol* forgot to give him covering fire. In the absence of gunsmoke, he became exposed to a breastwork nearby. A volley of fifty or sixty balls whined into and around the boat. Two of the English sailors were killed at once and the man next to Lurting was shot in the back.

By four o'clock that afternoon, most of the Spanish ships were fired beyond saving; of those not on fire, only their masts rearing out of the water remained. Blake ordered all his ships to withdraw. The *Bristol*, working her way out past St Philip's castle, came under fire from the fort. They were so close that the Spaniards could not depress their cannon sufficiently to hit the hull, and their shot, wrote Lurting,

> did us little harm, only in our rigging: and I was on the clue of the main-tack, getting the main-tack on board, and a shot cut the bolt-rope a little above my head . . . The fourth deliverance in six hours time.

Stayner's flagship the *Speaker* had come off worst. She had holes three feet wide and four feet long blown in her side between wind and water; and eight feet of water in the hold, so that pumping and bailing barely kept it in check. Her main yard had been shot away and her main topmast above that. Her rigging was so cut to pieces that the masts were tottering. The only sails she could set were on the bowsprit. Hides had been nailed over the holes in her hull as a temporary repair, but they were not watertight nor would they last long. The Spaniards put fresh men into their batteries and the faltering fire became a lively cannonade. Blake sent the *Swiftsure* to tow out the *Speaker*, which was still at anchor to keep her from drifting onshore with the wind. Stayner reported:

> They paid us extremely and so we rid till the sun went down: then the wind came offshore, and we set those pieces of sail we had, and cut away the anchor. Just as we passed by the great Castle, either by our shot or some accident among themselves, there was a great quantity of powder blown up. After that they never fired one gun more at us.

Hardly had Stayner got clear than all the masts of his ship thundered down. The *Plymouth* took the battered, mastless hulk in tow and the other ships sent over carpenters and seamen to repair her.

Many of the other ships, maimed and penned in the bay until after sunset, when the wind changed and they could work clear, were in little better case. It had been a chaotic day's battle in the gunsmoke, which cost the Spaniards all sixteen galleons of the *flota*. The English had no loss in ships, although some were little better than wrecks. Blake reported to Cromwell, 'We had only fifty slain and 120 wounded . . . to God be all the glory.'

It was an extraordinary result, achieved by a sick man. On 7 August, 1657, as his ship was entering Plymouth Sound, the Commonwealth Admiral died. He had intended to go ashore there to settle up his estate, but was already blind by the time they had sighted the Lizard. He charged his secretary to remind the government of 'the sad condition of the fleet we left behind'.

To the sound of trumpets and musket volleys fired by his old regiment, Robert Blake was buried in Henry VII's chapel at Westminster Abbey. In 1661, four years later almost to the day, his remains, together with those of Cromwell, Deane, Pym and other Commonwealth leaders, were disinterred and thrown into a pit nearby.

This morose, elderly batchelor must rank near to Nelson as a leader of fleets in decisive battles. Nelson always intended to fight battles of annihilation, but never quite managed it. At Santa Cruz, Blake did. Moreover, by preventing the delivery of gold and silver to Spain in that year, his victory brought the Spanish offensive against Portugal to a halt; without pay, or even hope of it, the Spanish forces simply melted away. Further, Blake's main opponents during his long career were the Dutch—very efficient fighting fleets led by excellent admirals. Nelson and the other English leaders at sea during the wars with revolutionary France and her satellites confronted naval forces which had been sacrificed to the needs of the French armies. Their victories were rather easier to achieve and consequently read better on the printed page, besides perpetuating the myth that Britain is invincible at sea.

The fault, if fault it be, is due largely to official Naval propaganda in Nelson's day. This was long before the image of the 'Silent Service' was being modestly cultivated; on the contrary, the Admiralty paid popular song writers to compose stirring ballads about British successes at sea. It is of course a good idea, when dealing with new intakes of recruits for a large-scale real war, to instil confidence. But one should beware of overdoing it.

So Nelson's pre-eminence is easy to explain in terms of past—and present—Royal Navy propaganda. Or largely so, for he had a fair measure of genius. But also because his story was a huge publicity bonanza at the time. England's most brilliant young admiral elopes at the height of a campaign with the lovely young wife of an elderly aristocratic ambassador. Sex, snobbery, scandal! The wronged wife!

The cuckolded husband! What a meal the media would make of it today. Especially when the young admiral goes on to a crowning glory which rids England of the spectre of Bonaparte's invasion, and expires almost at the moment of vital victory. The story largely writes itself.

Second only to Nelson in public esteem comes Francis Drake. There the essential ingredients are that the hero is a man of the people who pulls himself up into the aristocracy by bravery, bravado and an unerring nose for treasure ships (until his final, pathetic years). Not sex but gold: local boy gets rich and makes good. And also of course the Armada: seadog of the people bashes overbearing invading Spaniards. It is great stuff, but rather obscures the real qualities of the man.

The cognoscenti would naturally include Cook among the foremost sea heroes of England, although among the general public today his pupil 'Breadfruit' Bligh would probably rank higher, largely because of the parodies of a performance by Charles Laughton in a Hollywood epic.

But as for Robert Blake, he lies dismembered in an unknown grave, and deserved better.

Chapter Three

THE COMTE DE TOURVILLE AT BARFLEUR

Cherbourg Peninsula, May 1692

Anne Hilarion de Cotentin, Comte de Tourville, was born in 1642, the youngest of three sons, at the castle of Tourville in Normandy. The Normans are not French but the descendants of Vikings who conquered that part of France and later invaded England. But this third-born did not look like a Viking; he was a pale and sickly child. Yet he was to serve France at sea in many wars for forty-five years.

Both his parents being high-born, the future Comte was admitted to the Order of the Knights of Malta at the age of fourteen; when he reached eighteen he became a full-fledged Knight and served in the galleys of the Knights against the Barbary Corsairs. The galleys of Malta were the scourge of the Moslems in the Mediterranean. It was an excellent apprenticeship. His services were particularly appreciated by the Venetian Republic and eventually his fame reached France. In 1667 he was called to the French Court and granted a commission as captain in the Royal Navy of France.

This was exactly the right time for an ambitious and talented officer to join the French sea forces. Jean-Baptiste Colbert, Louis XIV's great minister, had during 1660–1670 rebuilt the French Navy on the basis of 50 line-of-battleships. France had had a large and efficient fleet during the reign in England of Henry VIII. This was allowed to decline until the arrival in power in 1624 of Cardinal Richelieu, when at the outset the French Navy did not possess a single battleship capable of compare with those of the British and Dutch. Richelieu ordered five large ships and other smaller ones from Dutch yards, including the famous *St Louis* of 60 guns. Shortly afterwards the French had trained sufficient shipwrights of their own to build vessels as good as or in many cases better than those of the English. Yet once again, the great French fleet was allowed to decline until Colbert restored it, followed by his son Seignelay.

This policy of intermittently supporting a great navy has been lamented by French historians, and was to be again after Tourville's most famous fight; but it is reasonable. The greatest landpower on the Continent usually builds up a mighty army to subdue its neighbours and make itself supreme in Europe. All it needs then for complete conquest and control is a navy strong enough to defeat that of the British. So far, no one nation—whether France in her time or Germany in hers—has had both the manpower and resources to be totally supreme both on land and at sea. The British have always interfered. It was in one final effort by France to put paid to this outside irritation that Tourville was launched upon his impossible odyssey.

But before that moment arrived he had to climb in rank to Commodore, and then Admiral, and then Commander-in-Chief. On the way up he again fought in the Mediterranean against the Turks in a failed offensive in Crete; then he fought in the English Channel against the Dutch, with the Royalist English as allies; then he went back to the Mediterranean, where this time he fought the Spaniards off Sicily and against the Dutch led by the great De Ruyter, who was fatally wounded in one of these battles. And then came peace, which the French used to build up their fighting navy to 120 ships-of-the-line, plus another hundred smaller vessels.

The fleet was used for general pacification purposes which served as good training: first Algiers was bombarded, then Genoa (guilty of helping Spain, then thought to be on the verge of war with France), and then another Barbary Corsair target, Tripoli. Eventually, when again war came with Britain as enemy, Tourville was Commander-in-Chief of a force at sea which was numerically equal to the combined fleets of both Britain and Holland, much smaller powers then.

The Dutch leader, William of Orange, in 1688 had secured the British throne for himself as well. Louis XIV, already at war with Spain, Sweden and Germany, now added Britain and Holland to his enemies; but believed that he had a reliable ally in the ex-King of Great Britain, James II. So his first move was to put an invading force into Ireland, landing King James and 5,000 men at Kinsale. Except for Ulster, the Irish welcomed the invaders. A British fleet which attempted to interfere with the invasion was defeated.

By 1690 the French had brought their Mediterranean fleet round to

Brest and formed a formidable concentration of naval force in the English Channel. Seventy-five ships-of-the-line, plus five frigates, 18 fireships and 25 galleys. The British under Torrington had 56 battleships, one frigate and 20 fireships in all, the Dutch and the British combined. But as the land conflict in Ireland had reached a critical stage and it seemed as if the British must lose, Torrington had to give battle.

The Dutch took the brunt of the French attack (William was their monarch, after all), fighting back desperately against overwhelming odds, one Dutch against two or more French. The *Vriesland*, with 230 men killed or wounded, refused to strike while a gun could still fire. The French officer who took a prize crew into her reported that 'there was not a foot of space above the waterline that had not been hit, and the deck was strewn with dead and dying'.

As night fell one of the Dutch flagships was burning, and continued to burn all night; another, the *Noord Quartier*, sank in the darkness. In his despatch Tourville wrote:

> The enemy has fled, having ordered out his pinnaces to tow his ships away, leaving ten disabled vessels which we would take if there was a breath of wind. We have captured one ship, dismasted eleven, sunk two, and three fireships, and sunk a fourth fireship that was bearing down on us.

The British and Dutch retired to the shelter of the Thames Estuary, with seventeen of their ships missing. The French claimed the sinking, burning or capture of 15 ships, the British admitted the loss of more than ten. It was a victory but, considering the numbers of the French, not an annihilating one. The day after the Battle of Beachy Head, King William defeated ex-King James at the Battle of the Boyne outside Londonderry, a victory which nowadays causes twentieth-century British governments great embarrassment.

French historians like to put it about that the British, by anchoring when the wind fell dead calm, obtained an unfair advantage; but the winds and the tides were neutral. In Paris they judged that Tourville had been too cautious, unwilling to risk his greatly superior fleet for a much greater victory. The French Minister of Marine called their great admiral 'brave of heart, coward of the head'. In short, he lacked not physical courage but moral, to risk his country's fortunes on his own decisions, win or lose. True or not, the jibe must have rankled; and explains what he was to do when next confronted by a combined Dutch and British fleet, this time in greatly superior numbers to his own French forces.

This conflict took place in the spring of the campaigning season of 1692. The wretched ex-King James, who had fled from the Boyne to France, had with the help of Louis XIV gathered an army of French and Irish troops at St Vaast-la-Hougue on the Cherbourg peninsula, for what they were heralding as the 'second Norman Conquest'. The French Navy was to be concentrated and at all costs set this force ashore in Britain, where the political climate was thought to be favourable for the return of the Catholic monarch, James.

The new War Minister who had succeeded the efficient Colbert and his son wrote briskly to Tourville:

> His Majesty definitely desires him to leave Brest on the said day, April 25th, even should he have information that the enemy is at sea with a force superior to that in readiness to sail with him . . . Should he meet with enemy ships he is to chase them back to their ports, whatever number they may be . . .

This smells of army thinking. The pace of marching troops can be reasonably well calculated; but the speed over the ground of wind-driven vessels is something else again. The French concentration of naval force was not achieved, the Anglo-Dutch was. The squadron of twelve Toulon-based ships from the Mediterranean reached Brest late and were then further delayed by adverse winds. Of the reinforcements sent from Rochefort on the Atlantic coast of France only five reached Tourville in time. More than a dozen further ships were left in French harbours for want of crews to man them. Furthermore, a message sent on by despatch vessels, instructing Tourville not to engage after all because it was now known that the Dutch fleet had joined the British, failed to get through.

So Tourville, with 44 ships-of-the-line supported by 13 frigates and fireships, sailed out to meet the allied fleets spurred by his original instructions which, while inflexible on the need to accept losses while convoying the army, were allowed to avoid any battle on the return journey where they were heavily outnumbered; but this was to be ascertained without doubt by Tourville, for 'His Majesty desires him to approach close enough to discover for himself when that should oblige him to fight.' That final civil servant's instruction may have been the last straw which sent Tourville into battle regardless.

To the French 44 battleships and 13 smaller vessels the enemy could this time oppose 63 British battleships and 36 Dutch, plus 38 frigates and fireships. That is in total, 99 battleships against 44, 38 smaller vessels against 13; 6,756 guns against Tourville's 3,240; 53,463 men against Tourville's 20,900. At dawn on 29 May Tourville saw an absolute forest of masts and sails rise out of the sea 'all aglow with sunrise', seven leagues north-west of Barfleur Point. Now he knew for sure that he had all his enemies in front of him and not just a single fleet.

Tourville fought with skill as well as courage. Russell, the English admiral, wrote afterwards to Tourville, congratulating him 'on the great valour he had shown by attacking in such a dauntless manner, and by fighting so valiantly although having an unequal force.' The Frenchman had the wind and could have avoided the battle, but having decided to engage at odds of two to one, he was in danger of being enveloped on both flanks and taken in the rear. Tourville's initial answer was to order his ships to spread out so as to try to match the enemy's front. But eventually he was largely enveloped, while trying to break through the British centre ahead of him, when a mist crept over the sea; and the thunder of the cannonading died away.

When a north-east wind got up, sweeping away the mists and giving the windward advantage to the British now, Admiral Russell decided to launch his fireships down on the French. No less than five—like a salvo of modern torpedoes—were aimed at Tourville's flagship, the 98-gun *Soleil Royal*. One was dodged by putting over the helm, another by cutting an anchor cable, another diverted by the ship's boats. None struck the riddled flagship.

By the time darkness fell none of the French battleships had been burnt, sunk or captured; all were still capable of manoeuvre, although the *Soleil Royal* was to be so badly damaged as to become a liability. The French losses were given as 1,700 killed and wounded, and they estimated their enemies' losses as some 5,000, including two admirals killed. This was the result of fifteen hours of almost continuous action.

At daybreak, the French had retired out of contact and the bulk of their fleet managed to escape past the Channel Islands, twenty of them passing through the dangerous Alderney Race and getting into St Malo with the aid of the tide. One group under Nesmond got away into the North Sea and so home round Scotland. Tourville himself held on too long to the now slow and leaking *Soleil Royal*, unwilling to give her up. But it was now too late, She went aground at Cherbourg, together with the *Triomphant* and the *Admirable*.

The British under Sir Ralph Delavel came in almost at once to destroy them where they lay in the shallows, but the guns of the *Soleil Royal* beat him off. Next day he came back again, sending in his fireships escorted by launches. The French guns blew up one fireship, another hit an obstruction. But two reached their target. Although the French flagship's guns were still thundering, Captain Heath of the fireship *Blaze* grappled the *Soleil Royal* at the stern. Great wooden warships with their gunports open created a tremendous draught and the flagship was a roaring volcano of flame in moments, outdone only by the explosion as her main magazine went off. Then the fireship *Wolf* ignited the *Triomphant* and some of the British boats' crews set fire to the *Admirable*. All three were roaring pillars of flame at the base of billowing smoke clouds.

Cherbourg was not the fortified harbour that it later became; and St Vaast-la-Hougue was just a small fishing port, suitable for embarking troops in boats but not of affording shelter to ships-of-the-line. But they were the only shelter the French then had on that coast. At least the French and Irish army of invasion lay there under Marshal de Belle-fonds and King James, and their guns. It was for this reason that Nesmond, before fleeing for the North Sea, had left his two most severely damaged battleships here in the shelter of a long narrow sandbank that pointed out to sea from the peninsula of La Hougue.

Unfortunately for Tourville and the French Navy, his orders now placed him under the command of the Army. They discussed what to do, and did nothing for a day, ending in a decision to beach six of Tourville's ships behind La Hougue and the remaining six in the protection of a little islet called Tatihou, first removing their contents and providing 150 boatloads of soldiers for their protection, plus a garrison on the islet of Tatihou to cover them.

On 2 June the British assault force of boats' crews and fireships attacked the islet and set fire to all six ships there, without resistance from the French Army. Indeed, they looked on so calmly, 'as if they were at a firework display', that one suspects the usual inter-service jealousies. A notable French Army strategist had declared that sea battles were 'just piff-poff, piff-poff and afterwards the sea looks just as it was before.'

The French naval officers improvised a sketchy defence of the remaining six French ships beached at St Vaast itself before the British could fire those, too. But when the British came in at high tide the next day, although some of the newly mounted guns caused damage to their boats, the assault was irresistible. The last six of Tourville's stranded fleet went up in roaring flames and belching smoke. Then the British went on to burn some of the invading force's troop transports, until the falling tide put an end to their depredations.

By no means was this the end of the French Navy. Fifteen battleships lost was only the same total as the Dutch and British had lost at Beachy Head two years before. And great French fleets were to sail again and—more devastating to British and Dutch commerce—the work of the corsairs such as Jean Bart and Duguay-Trouin was to ravage the Channel. But what this battle signified was a loss of will, of confidence in France of her destiny at sea. Henceforth she was to place greater emphasis on her Army. This also was illusion, for France had been trying to fight the world in order to control Europe, and it was not possible; just as it was to prove impossible when the balance of populations was to make it Germany's turn. Only the United States of America, in modern times, has managed it.

For Tourville himself, however, there is a galaxy of praise, particularly from the British and the Americans, for his conduct of a fleet fighting without hope of victory—'The strongest proof of military spirit and valour ever given by any navy,' wrote the American Admiral A. T. Mahan.

But it was perhaps praise from the enemy's admiral, who after all was there as well and knew exactly what he was writing about, that might most have satisfied Tourville when his own compatriots had doubted him. The words 'great valour', 'dauntless' and 'fighting so valiantly although having such an unequal force'.

Chapter Four

THE TURTLE v. THE EAGLE

New York, September 1776

David Bushnell was a student at Yale, majoring in science, who had begun experimenting with gunpowder. He was the son of a farmer living at Saybrook in Connecticut. Bushnell wanted to put his brains to work for the Colonies in their unequal fight against England and, above all, against the British navy whose power extended to the very harbours of the colonists. His idea was to build a submersible vehicle which could convey a substantial charge of gunpowder to be exploded underwater against the hulls of battleships. In 1941 this was a daring experiment in modern warfare carried out by Italian 'frogmen' riding strange underwater vehicles.

Yet David Bushnell's idea of dealing with battleships was conceived and worked out in 1776, some thirty years even before the battle of Trafalgar. And it almost worked. It probably would have worked but for one tiny physiological fact the inventor did not appreciate because it was outside his field of study. Everything else was as well thought out as it could possibly be, given the technological limitations of eighteenth-century science and engineering.

Such limitations as he knew about he was only too well aware of, principally the undersea vehicle's lack of speed—hence the name he gave his invention: the *Turtle*. The shape looks wrong to us. We are accustomed to what seem to be long, narrow, slim submersibles (for so they appear on the surface which is where we normally see them, or photographs of them). Such pencil-shaped hulls proved to be highly unstable and dangerous, as numerous early theorists found out, if they survived. Bushnell's hull was like an egg placed upright, the fattest end at the top, with the detachable explosive charge slung onto it, like a backpack. Not the perfect under water shape but convenient for the seated human body, strong and easy to construct out of two half-shells.

The submariner sat on a bench, his head inside a little dome with glass ports topped by two snorkel tubes with ball valves attached which shut off the outside if a wave broke over this tiny conning tower or if it submerged to just under the surface (it was not designed to go deeper than a few feet).

Forward propulsion was by one of two means: hand-operated or foot-operated mechanisms driving a screw propeller (which could also be driven in reverse if necessary). No great speed could be had from a one-manpower screw such as this; the craft would need to be towed by a boat to within launching distance of its target and then loosed so as to drift down with the tidal current. Its own propulsive mechanism would be used for making final adjustments of the machine against the hull of the ship chosen as victim.

There were two means of submerging. One was a vertically mounted, hand-operated screw which, when the machine was ballasted so as to be neutrally buoyant, could force it down a few feet or raise it again to the surface. A certain amount of water could be let in as ballast, or pumped out if required by a small hand-operated pump. There was also a rudder bar controlling a rudder, of possible use for fine adjustments. There was a compass for steering, when trimmed right down or running just submerged. And most important, a depth gauge as a check that the submariner did not let his craft sink too deep, or rise to the surface at an awkward moment.

The 'armament' of this projected submersible consisted of a detachable screw mounted by the pilot's face, which he was to insert into the wooden hull of a warship. This detachable screw was connected by line to a watertight charge of gunpowder (with its own quick-release) slung behind the operator's head. So when the screw was firmly embedded in the planking of the target ship, the slightly buoyant explosive cask, made out of two pieces of oak, would stay in contact with the victim's hull. This is basically the same idea as the Italians used against British battleships in 1941, but with updated materials and explosives. The timing device inside Bushnell's American bomb was probably clockwork, firing a flintlock into the powder.

Under the heading of safety precautions, perhaps, one could count 200 lbs of lead ballast which could be released on a 50-foot long line and then recovered if necessary; and, quite vital, a ventilation pump for forcing out used air and forcing fresh in. How effective this was, one doesn't know. Presumably some sort of weapon, a pistol or a dagger, must have been carried in case of boarding; certainly, Bushnell seems to have thought of everything else.

Indeed, the pilot of the submarine, originally the inventor's brother who had carried out all the tests on the completed device, must have had quite an extensive checklist to make sure he had all the operating procedures clear in his mind. George Washington seems to have had no doubts. He ordered: 'Bring the water machine to New York to attack the British fleet.'

The redcoats were on Long Island and the fleet of Admiral Richard Howe lay off the coast. In these circumstances, it was near disaster when the inventor's brother became ill. One asks what the illness was. There was only a very small air space inside the machine, and although the air was supposed to last for half-an-hour, the trouble may really have been CO_2 poisoning—the build-up of bad air which used to affect the old-style helmet divers into modern times. Hard physical work can bring this on, and certainly the pilot of the *Turtle* had plenty to do, propelling and controlling the machine.

General Parsons asked for volunteers to man the *Turtle* and received three applications; the man chosen was Ezra Lee, a sergeant in the Colonial army. The risk of being eased into this egg-shaped container with no rapid means of escape in emergency seems dire; the difficulties enormous, for this was to be a night attack and the craft had to be steered, once the tow had been released, by a man whose eyes were only a few inches above the surface of the water. Even short distances would appear immense, the task of steering a straight course in tidal waters for a distant object tricky indeed; speed perhaps two knots and response to rudder minimal. Yet the target, lying off Staten Island, seemed worth all risks: it was Lord Howe's flagship, the 64-gun battleship *Eagle*.

Luckily the night was calm and the water still, although flowing, when on 6 September, 1776, Ezra Lee entered his machine at Whitehall Stairs and was towed out into the main stream by two American whaleboats. His target was one vessel among a squadron of British warships anchored off Staten Island.

Lee carried out the plan of attack, staying on the surface with his head out of the hatch so as to navigate better, relying on the low silhouette and odd and unexpected appearance of his craft for protection. Indeed, it is said that he was seen by a sailor on deck, but taken for a barrel which indeed the submersible resembled. But the pull of the tide, although it must have been slackening, had been miscalculated; the *Turtle* was swept past the English flagship and Sergeant Lee had to try to fight his way back, which seems to have taken him about two hours. The current would then of course fall slack for a period before beginning to run inwards, back towards the *Eagle*, back towards his start point. And it was slack water which was needed for Lee to nuzzle the unwieldy submersible in under the curve of the ship's hull, while he began the work of drilling into a plank to fasten the explosive charge. The sergeant must have been fatigued by this time, perhaps perilously so.

Anyway it was at this final stage, when everything had been dared and triumph seemed so close, that problems appeared. Lee nuzzled his craft against the enemy's hull, only just submerged, and began to work the screw which was to secure itself in the hull below the *Eagle*'s waterline; and when that was done, Lee would take the submersible down a few feet further, thus freeing both the screw and the gunpowder charge attached to it. But, inexplicably, he could not do it. Something was stopping the screw. Thinking perhaps that he had struck metal bracing near the keel, Lee tried two other places; but still the screw would not penetrate into the timber for a secure hold.

First light was near, when Lee would be caught in daylight in the British fleet anchorage in a craft that could not outrun any of the guardboats and could not submerge to any worthwhile depth. He abandoned his task and made off for home, aided by the now incoming tidal current. The running tide would in any case probably have prevented him from remaining nuzzled in to his victim. A guardboat did spot the strange object in the water and gave chase. Lee promptly ditched his explosive charge, which must certainly have puzzled the boat's crew and made them wary. In due course it blew up, proving that the plan was practicable—in theory. But when the Americans recovered the *Turtle*, they found Sergeant Lee unconscious inside. He was got safely ashore but his boat swamped and sank; to be salvaged later.

George Washington's verdict on the effort was: 'I then thought and still think that it was an effort of genius, but that many things were necessary to be combined to expect much from the issue against an enemy who are always on guard.'

A number of different explanations have been advanced for the final failure of a brilliant scheme, far in advance of its time. The most usual one is that the cunning British had sheathed their fleet in copper and that it was this sheathing which baffled the screw. The British fleet was indeed in process of having the underwater bodies of their hulls covered by thin sheets of copper as protection against wood-hungry organisms which infest most seas, such as the tiny gribble and the foot-long teredo. Up to this time a thin layer of removable wooden sheathing was the normal anti-fouling measure. But the copper sheathing was paper-thin, and is an inadequate explanation, to my mind. Another explanation is that there was a metal bracing on the keel which Lee unfortunately struck. This too I doubt (from much experience of wooden warship wrecks from the sixteenth to the nineteenth centuries). Yet another theory is that Lee was near the stern, where the rudder is hung on heavy bronze gudgeons and pintles. That is possible.

But on balance I tend to favour the physical effects on the pilot of working in a close, contaminated atmosphere, using very great exertion literally to screw himself back uptide towards the *Eagle* and, when at last he had reached her, being both too exhausted and too poisoned by CO_2 to know properly what he was or was not doing.

Very early in my diving career, in 1952, using a helmet suit while under instruction by telephone, I suffered just this effect—a kind of drunkenness, when the senses are disorientated (similar to but not to be confused with nitrogen narcosis). I was brought up sharply by the instructor's sharp command: 'Stop moving, Diver!' I did. And the irrational, confused behaviour ceased after a minute or two as I began to breathe at a slower rate and no longer consumed part of my own poisonous exhalations.

Lee had no such friendly voice to command him. He was on his own, not only in enemy waters but in physiologically foreboding circumstances which neither he nor the inventor of the *Turtle* understood. As I see it, he was a very lucky man, as well as a very brave one.

Chapter Five

JOHN PAUL 'JONES' OFF FLAMBOROUGH HEAD

North Sea, September 1779

John Paul was not a Welshman named Jones; he was a Lowland Scot named John Paul. Born in 1747 in Kirkcudbrightshire, he went to sea as a young boy in ships out of Whitehaven on the north-west coast of England. His father was a gardener but that station in life, in Scotland though not in England, did not mean 'uneducated'. The lad is said to have been interested in sailing, poetry and naval history. Poetry, in Scotland though not in England, did not imply 'precious', 'weak' or namby-pamby—for that John Paul certainly was not. Quite the reverse.

Some of the English were to call him a rascal. He did some quiet smuggling, served in a slaver and, at the age of 21, was made master of a brigantine. In command of a ship he earned a reputation as what a Scotsman would call a 'black bastard'. The first time he is supposed to have killed a man was when, barely out of his teens, he ordered the flogging for a minor offence of an elderly seaman, who died soon after.

Five years later his command was challenged outright by an unpaid crew whose spokesman gave John Paul to understand that he was not on the holystoned decks of a battleship with King's Regulations behind him; he was just a merchant seaman like the rest. There was an altercation. John Paul later said he had slipped while trying to defend himself. Unfortunately his sword had entered the body of the man. Witnesses said they saw nothing like that. The victim had done nothing except get himself murdered.

This, according to one account, is the real reason why John Paul became J. P. Jones and left the West Indies very rapidly. English accounts are vaguer. An elder brother who had emigrated to the

American colonies had died, leaving an estate; J. P. Jones went to the Colony to look after it.

Within two years the War of Independence began and to start with the rebels had virtually no navy. The first list of its officers contained sixteen names; only two were Southerners, the rest were Yankees. Of the two 'Southerners', J. P. Jones was one. The American naval ensign they hoisted was a yellow silk banner embroidered with a rattlesnake and the legend 'Don't Tread On Me'.

Jones distinguished himself in the war against British commerce —the Colony could not possibly fight a fleet action yet—and Jones was given a captain's commission in August 1776; technically the first. But whatever he did at sea, his name steadily slipped down the Navy List as new officers were listed ahead of him. In January 1777 he was superseded by an officer eight numbers junior to him; and in October he was listed as being only eighteenth in seniority. Southerners suspected that this was because he was not a Yankee. But might it not have been something more?

However, in 1778 J. P. Jones was given command of a warship called the *Ranger* and set off to break out across the Atlantic to refit at Brest and then cruise his old haunts in the Irish Sea. His most spectacular feat was to land in England and capture briefly the fort at Whitehaven, where he had begun his sailing career long ago. This was first-rate public relations stuff. More solid from the military point of view was his successful battle with a British warship, the sloop *Drake*, which he captured after killing 42 out of her crew of 160. Jones lost only two killed and seven wounded, and brought the prize triumphantly into Brest. Perhaps not so triumphantly after all, for the officer he put in charge of the captured sloop sailed off on his own and she had to be chased and retaken by Jones before she could be brought in.

While in France, 68 members of Jones' crew signed a petition asking for him to be relieved of his command; they included both his servants, freed slaves who had been with him a long time. So, having nearly lost his prize to a mutinous officer, he lost his own ship, the *Ranger*, too, for she was sent back to America with badly needed supplies for America's Continental Army, and Jones was given the story that he was for diplomatic reasons required at the French Court, although His Majesty never spoke to anyone lower than an Admiral (the corsair Jean Bart being an exception).

The story might even have had some truth in it, for the rebel government was gaining recognition as a possible force for the future —quite apart from the interest many nations had in getting the better of the British when they were tied up overseas in what amounted to civil war. The American ambassador, Dr Benjamin Franklin, introduced Jones to ladies at Court, including the Duchesse de Chartres. Often, in Paris, the ladies had more influence than many of the men, and in this case it proved decisive. Louis XVI was prevailed upon to grant an audience to the captain who had invaded England and defeated the *Drake*. The King could not give him command of a French battleship because Royal ships had to be commanded by a member of the nobility, but the American would be given a 40-gun East Indiaman, an armed merchantman suitable for carrying soldiers, and a force of marines. The audience took place on 17 December, and on 4 February, 1779, Jones had his ship.

France had come into the war in June, 1778, partly as a result of the Colonists' success at Saratoga the previous autumn. From the European point of view, the main conflict now was just another round between the two heavyweights, Britain and France, for the dominant position. Viewed in this light, the results of the Royal audience can be seen in perspective, not as a haphazard good-hearted gesture to a noble cause. The East Indiaman—she was twelve years old, almost a lifetime for a wooden ship in those days—was an expendable asset for a junior ally. Private money was available to pay the remaining 27 members of Jones' crew who remained loyal to the Scotsman; it was supplied by the Duchesse de Chartres, presumably out of patriotism.

In a short time a formidable (on paper) raiding force was assembled around John Paul and his Indiaman. In April, the American colonists contributed a brand-new frigate under the command of Pierre Landais, a disgraced French ex-officer. Her name was the *Alliance* and as passenger she carried another French adventurer, Marie Joseph Paul Yves Roch Gilbert du Motier, Marquis de Lafayette, who was interested in organising an invasion of Britain. He was soon deep in plans with Jones.

The French Royal Navy matched the American contribution by detaching the frigate *Pallas* and the brig *Vengeance*. Frigates were fast well-gunned warships ideal for commerce raiding, and able to sail away from a battleship which could defeat them.

A group of Court Ladies from the circle of Marie Antoinette found it fashionable to support the dashing Americans who intended to strike at the heart of the enemy. They contributed the cutter *Cerf* and two privateers, the *Monsieur* and the *Grandville*.

So in addition to the 40-gun East Indiaman, whose original name was the *Duc de Duras*, the raiding squadron comprised two proper warships, the frigates *Alliance* flying the Stars and Stripes and the *Pallas* under the Lily banner of the Royal French Navy, plus the Royal brig *Vengeance*, the cutter *Cerf*, and the licensed pirateships *Monsieur* and *Grandville*. The measures which Jones took to arm and crew the ex-*Duc de Duras* lent to the entire force a tone reminiscent of one of those fictional units of the Second World War so beloved of unusual-combat authors—that is to say, they were recruited from criminals. These plots are basically unlikely, because criminals may well fight for profit but are unlikely to sacrifice themselves for such abstractions as country.

The first thing Jones did with his old Indiaman was to rename her in honour of his patron, Dr Benjamin Franklin, who was the author of a work famous at the time called *Poor Richard's Almanac*. She was now to be called the *Bon Homme Richard*.

Her armament was something else again. As an ex-merchant ship she was pierced for light guns—six-pounders. But Jones intended to fight, as he was to say later, 'to go in harm's way', and so he re-armed her with 42 guns of heavier metal, 18-pounders presumably on the lower deck and 12-pounders for the upper. These guns he obtained from a scrap metal dump in the dockyard at L'Orient.

The crew he manned her with were a bunch as mixed as her new armament. Many were prisoners taken from British Royal Navy ships, most of them in fact Irishmen; stranded American seamen and ex-changed prisoners; Portuguese and Maltese seamen; and a contingent of French Marines. A hard nucleus of experienced American officers and seamen gave the backbone necessary to the organisation of the *Bon Homme Richard*, which was a very indifferent sailer. Besides, at least four languages would be spoken by the various contingents on board. French, Portuguese, Maltese (Malta was not then under the protection of the British Crown), English, and Colonial American. Add to that Irish dialects and the captain's Scottish accent, and the first few days must have been bedlam.

Presumably in order to get most of them to agree to go in the first place, the captains of all these vessels, American and French, signed a concordat which gave each and every one of them the freedom to cruise as he thought fit, and not as a united raiding squadron. A less viciously determined man than Jones might have despaired. The squadron sailed from L'Orient on 19 June, 1779, and was back on 21 June: Landais' *Alliance* had fouled Jones' *Bon Homme Richard*. It was 14 August before repairs were completed and the squadron could sail once more.

The plan worked out by Jones and Lafayette was to land the French Marines from the *Bon Homme Richard* at Liverpool, the great port on the Mersey on the north-west coast of England, and later at Leith, a port on the Scottish east coast near Edinburgh. These were to be commando-style raids designed to extract ransom from the inhabitants and incidentally strike a very public and shaming blow at Britain and the Royal Navy.

However, on 23 August, only a week or so out of port, when the squadron was cruising off the coast of Ireland on the run up towards Liverpool, one officer and twenty men succeeded in deserting from Jones' own ship, the *Bon Homme Richard*. Then the *Cerf*, detached to search for a small boat lost in fog, took the opportunity to desert. And she was followed by the privateer *Grandville* which captured a prize and took it home. Captain Philippe G. de Roberdeau of the other privateer, the *Monsieur*, quarrelled with Landais of the frigate *Alliance* and, having stripped a prize, headed back for France. On 26 August Landais refused to obey an order by Jones to hover off the Irish coast to pick up merchantmen returning laden from the Indies, and sailed off on an independent course.

But Landais and the *Alliance* were back on 31 August with a captured privateer, so Jones called a council on board his ship. Landais refused to come on board, on the grounds that if he and Jones met on shore 'we must kill one another'. Then he sailed away again. The two remaining captains, Cottineau of the French frigate *Pallas* and Ricot of the brig *Vengeance*, spoke in discouraging terms of the chances now of a descent on Liverpool with the three ships left. So Jones decided to attempt the second objective—the landing at Leith near Edinburgh.

The much reduced squadron sailed north-about round Scotland and the Orkney Isles and so into the North Sea. But they were seen entering the Firth of Forth—the hills near Edinburgh are a good vantage point—and warning fires blazed all along the shore. There was alarm in the Scottish capital, but a strong west wind blew Jones and his little squadron out to sea. There would be no point in returning now to that thoroughly alarmed coast; but why not try farther south—in England? By chance he encountered Landais in the frigate *Alliance* on 23 September and arranged to keep a rendezvous with him off Flamborough Head, a distinctive promontory on the coast of Yorkshire near Bridlington which points a long finger into the North Sea.

That afternoon another group of ships sighted Flamborough Head, more than 40 British merchantmen escorted by two warships—the powerful new 44-gun frigate *Seraphis* commanded by Captain Richard Pearson and a hired sloop, the *Countess of Scarborough*, armed only with 20 6-pounder guns, under Captain Piercy. The British warships had the wind of the raiders and correctly steered towards them to protect the convoy in case they turned out to be foes.

The American force was the stronger—two frigates, the American *Alliance* (under the former Frenchman Landais) and the French *Pallas*, and the 42-gun *Bon Homme Richard* which would be hard to classify, considering her age and what Jones had added to her designed armament, and of course the brig *Vengeance*.

It would be interesting to know what Captain Pearson of the *Seraphis* made of this odd-looking ex-Indiaman, as rearmed by Jones and packed with 150 French soldiers under Colonel Chamillard. His ship of course was large, new and had trained gun crews; we know he was superior in a gun battle, ship to ship, to the *Bon Homme Richard*. He might not have realised his adversary's superiority in trained soldiers; and he must have been well aware that he was up against odds, three biggish ships and a brig against his single frigate and a sloop. What he could not have anticipated was the action of the two strange frigates, which quite failed to combine against him with the ex-Indiaman. Jones had ordered them to form battle line and attack together, but their captains had their own ideas, some of them difficult to discern.

The British tacked ahead of the Americans, covering the mass of merchant ships. It was now about six o'clock in the evening and the rumour of an impending sea fight had brought a great many spectators to the vantage point of Flamborough Head. According to an American account Captain Pearson stuck to protocol and challenged Jones with 'What ship is that?' and Jones is supposed to have replied, 'I can't hear what you say,' in an effort to entice the British frigate closer. This was certainly not the case in modern wars when British warships became notably trigger-happy in the presence of aircraft or submarines—but of course these could do you vital damage in the twinkling of an eye and self-preservation ruled.

Certainly both ships went to quarters—their battle stations—by about seven o'clock. The sea was calm and even after sunset there was plenty of light from a harvest moon. The East coast had tended to see little action since the Vikings gave up raiding in favour of farming, and after this encounter nothing much was to happen until the German battle-cruisers bombarded Scarborough, a town just to the north of Flamborough, in 1916, followed in 1940 by dive-bomber visitations at Bridlington and Driffield. This encounter was less spectacular than the more modern ones; but it lasted longer, much longer, and inflicted more grief and agony.

When Captain Pearson threatened to fire if the *Bon Homme Richard* did not declare herself, Jones replied with a broadside. It was devastating—for Jones. Two of his salvaged eighteen pounders blew up on their gun's crews. Lieutenant Mayrant, in charge of this lower deck battery, was blown through the deckhead above, bloody and burnt, clothing charred, temporarily blinded. Other wounded were carried below to the cockpit, where the surgeons were ready with their cutting and sawing instruments, but without anaesthetics in the modern sense. It was now about 7.15.

The lower deck eighteen pounders of the *Seraphis* continued the carnage which Jones' own guns had begun. When he had delivered each broadside, Captain Pearson pulled ahead with his faster, better ship to reload in safety; and then came in for another strike at the wallowing ex-Indiaman.

Landais in the *Alliance* was too far away to help, and the other frigate, the *Pallas*, had picked an easier enemy—the armed sloop *Duchess of Scarborough*. Captain Piercy put up a creditable defiance against his much more powerful opponent, but was forced to strike. But at least he kept the *Pallas* from helping Jones, because the French frigate spent the rest of the night making her prize secure.

Meanwhile, Pearson was firing both solid shot and cannister into the *Bon Homme Richard*. The solid balls tore open the sides of her battery deck while the cannister—masses of musket balls encased—spewed out death and hurt among the French infantry stationed on the poop and upper deck; the French colonel fell wounded. Against that fire, French muskets seemed useless and Jones judged that his French allies were wavering. He seized a musket himself and loosed a shot at looming British frigate as example, and when handed another, fired that also. He is said to have fired half-a-dozen musket shots, in order to put heart into the French. He had a point. Small arms do seem peculiarly useless when you are firing them against bulwarks rather than men, but it is not so.

However, he soon had sterner things to do. When the *Seraphis* came in to deliver her next trained, co-ordinated broadside at close range, Jones saw his number two gun on the starboard side dismounted and 19 men killed or wounded, and with still other guns blown from their wooden carriages.

Half an hour after he had given his order to open fire on the British frigate, the *Bon Homme Richard* had only three guns left firing, and one of those was being pointed by Jones himself.

Although her main armament had been largely overwhelmed by the British cannonade, the ranges were short; men abandoned the ruined gundeck where the iron shot came whistling in, and took to the rigging. From there they maintained small arms fire down on to the British deck. Man after man at the wheel of the British frigate was shot down; man after man picked off in the rigging.

That made her harder to handle, and may have been responsible for what happened soon after. Jones' ship, however, was in a bad way. Holed in places, the water sloshing about deep in her hull; on fire above in places, the flames eating away at the bodies of the dead and wounded, the stench of scorched flesh; the howling whine of shot passing overhead and the shattering thump as the iron balls struck timber. A nightmare of noise and confusion. In all this Jones could still think and plan accurately. He went to where Lieutenant Richard Dale was re-organising the decimated guns crews and told him to issue small arms for boarding. And he tried to steer his crippled ship nearer to the enemy. How he managed it, no one knows.

Then it seemed that victory was almost theirs. Landais' US Frigate *Alliance* at last seemed to be about to join her battered consort. Up to now, her manoeuvres could have been interpreted as an attempt to get in among the fat merchantmen of the convoy rather than take on a British warship, which offered the chance of death rather than wealth. The US frigate passed astern of the *Bon Homme Richard* and, as she did so, she opened fire—not at the *Seraphis* but at Jones. Vertical water-spouts all around the *Bon Homme Richard* marked the indiscipline of that ill-aimed broadside; but a few shots hit, killing two men and disabling the tiller.

Meanwhile the *Pallas* was occupied with securing the *Duchess of*

Scarborough and in the darkness Landais in the *Alliance* joined in this fight, firing at both ships, the French frigate and her prize.

The *Seraphis* continued to pound the ex-Indiaman, and the thunderous shock of this bombardment, almost all of it incoming fire, caused a panic among the British captives held below in the *Bon Homme Richard*; they had been taken from ships sunk by the raider during the cruise. Their American guard released them and at once there was a momentary opportunity for them to take the ship; but there was no one with initiative to lead them and one man—John Paul Jones—to realise the danger and, with help from an officer, drive them below with an order to man the pumps. That apparently sensible order achieved what a gun muzzle or two might by themselves have not.

One crisis was no sooner settled than there came another. One of the wounded American gunners, recovering consciousness, saw the Stars and Stripes shot into the water by the British fire and a deck strewn with bodies and parts of men, and shouted that the ship was sinking (which it was). His cries were heard from the *Seraphis* and Captain Pearson, gazing across the water at this ruin of a ship and crew, shouted: 'Have you struck? Do I understand that you have surrendered?'

'Struck, sir!' roared Jones. 'I've just begun to fight!'

The ships had now drifted so close that an English boarding party leaped on board the *Bon Homme Richard*; Jones was in the rush which repelled the British, losing his hat to a musket ball in the process, and now Americans were leaping onto the *Seraphis*.

It was at this moment that the battle was decided.

Two officers, Midshipman Fanning and Lieutenant Gardner, climbed up to the starboard yardarm which overhung the deck of the British frigate. Gardner handed up the grenades; Fanning dropped them. His difficult target was a small hatch in the deck which led to the midships powder magazine and had to be kept open for ammunition supply. The first grenade missed, bouncing off harmlessly. He cut a shorter fuse and dropped the second grenade. That missed also. The third was a bull's-eye—directly down the hatch into the ready-to-use cartridges. The explosions virtually destroyed the *Seraphis*'s main armament and killed or wounded most of the gun crews. Those who weren't dead were stunned.

The situation in the *Bon Homme Richard* was certainly no better, but what may have tipped the balance for Captain Pearson of the *Seraphis* was the report he now had that the *Duchess of Scarborough* had surrendered to the French frigate, combined with the sight of the US frigate under Landais apparently taking part in that battle. Facing, he must have thought, two undamaged ships as well as his mortally wounded opponent, Pearson gave in. One feels that Jones's determination NOT to give in also played a part, and that Jones, in that same position, would not have given up hope. Certainly it couldn't have been done without him. Even to taking advantage of Pearson's inexplicably allowing the *Seraphis* to close the *Bon Homme Richard*, it seems it was Jones who, with his own hands, tied the locked ships together. At each crisis, he was there, leading from up front.

The explosion on the *Seraphis*'s gundeck led Pearson to strike his colours but that did not stop the battle. Men on both sides, oblivious to anything but the few feet of space around them, continued to load and fire. An American called out to Jones: 'He has struck!' A British lieutenant, commanding the upper tier of guns in the *Seraphis*, heard the shout and misunderstood. He ordered, 'Cease fire!' and rushed up to his captain for confirmation. 'Has he struck, sir?'

'No, I have,' was the answer.

It was now about 10.30. The battle had lasted three hours. Everyone was exhausted, not merely physically but by the nervous outpouring of battle which buoys you up, then leaves you grey and drained. There was a sad scene as the British officers offered the Americans their swords. Jones told Pearson that he had fought heroically. The butcher's bill is not surely known. The crew of the *Bon Homme Richard* numbered 304 in one American account, 380 in a British account. An American version gives her loss as 49 dead and 106 wounded; and that of the British frigate as 62 killed. Certainly both crews had fought each other to a standstill.

The French frigate *Pallas* played some part in the late stages, the American frigate *Alliance* was said by Jones to have peppered everyone indiscriminately but the Americans rather more than the British. Her French captain's curious behaviour speaks clearly of what the British in modern times called 'vertical breeze-up', so blinded by fright that they didn't care who they fired at. The brig *Vengeance* remained a spectator of the action.

About ten o'clock next morning, before even her littered dead could be buried, the *Bon Homme Richard*, her sails still set but down by the head, sank into the North Sea.

As captain of the *Seraphis*, John Paul Jones struggled slowly towards a

Dutch port, preceded by *Alliance*, *Pallas* and *Vengeance*. The captured British frigate was so damaged that she was ordered to be broken up at L'Orient.

Naturally, both the British captains, Pearson and Piercy, were court-martialled, as was and is the custom. Piercy of the *Duchess of Scarborough* was honorably acquitted but Pearson in addition, was knighted. He had of course taken on three ships his own size to protect the convoy and the convoy had indeed been saved; that was the purpose of an escort.

When Jones learned this, he said, 'Should I have the good fortune to fall in with him again, I'll make him a Lord!'

After the War of Independence was over, Jones took service with Catherine the Great of Russia as a Rear-Admiral, to the great indignation of her British naval advisers, none of whom ranked above Captain. He had had great success with the ladies in Paris and owed his command to them, but in Russia he was unwise enough to seduce one of the ladies of the Russian Imperial Court, which Catherine, then 59 and into her twelfth affair, considered scandalous. His Russian colleagues produced unproven charges that he had raped a 14-year-old girl, and Jones left Russia for Paris where he died in 1792.

The American Ambassador declined to pay for the funeral and did not attend; the new, revolutionary government of France paid instead and sent pall-bearers. The site of the grave, in the St Louis cemetery for Protestants, became lost for a century until, after a six-year investigation, the remains were found and identified in 1905.

President Theodore Roosevelt was expanding American naval power and in search of invincible heroes. Jones, it was thought, would do very well. So he sent four battleships to France to escort the neglected hero home after 113 years. At Annapolis a patriotic ceremony was held, but the actual coffin was dumped behind a staircase and remained there for a further seven years.

It really does rather look as if, throughout his career and even after his death, in certain circles it was thought that Jones was not quite acceptable. Useful in war, of course, as such people often are; but as an example for naïve and worshipping youth? Well, hardly.

However, eventually they got around to giving him a noble sarcophagus proclaiming: HE GAVE OUR NAVY ITS EARLIEST TRADITIONS OF HEROISM AND VICTORY. Which was true enough, so far as it went.

In a letter to a Frenchman on the lessons of the war, Jones, after calling his own successes 'few and feeble', went on:

> True, this has been on a small scale; but that was no fault of mine. I did my best with the weapons given to me. The rules of conduct, the maxims of action, and the tactical instincts that serve to gain small victories may always be expanded into the winning of great ones; because in human affairs the sources of success are ever to be found in the fountains of quick resolve and swift stroke; and it seems to be a law inflexible and inexorable that he who will not risk cannot win.

That would be a better epitaph for the Scottish gardener's son who beat professional naval officers at war and rose in life to mix with the highest.

Various attempts have been made to find the wreck of Jones' flagship; American, British and French interests supported a search by Sydney Wignall in 1976, to coincide with an anniversary of the war; and recently, in 1989, a consortium of tourist-orientated people from Hull launched another effort. But the North Sea is grave to so many thousands of wrecks that finding and then identifying the right one is a huge job.

Chapter Six

BATTLE OF THE WINTER STORM

Bay of Audierne, Brittany, January 1797

After the Revolution in France, the aggressive policy of the Directorate (as the government was then known) had been astoundingly successful in Europe. The policy of *l'attaque, l'attaque, et toujours l'attaque*, aided by much superior manpower, had increased the influence of France. As one result, first Holland and then Spain declared war on Britain; their fleets, combined with that of France, completely outnumbered the British Royal Navy and made the landing of troops on British soil a practical proposition. The French planned accordingly.

In 1796 the French General Hoche met the Irish representatives, Arthur O'Connor and Lord Edward Fitzgerald, in Switzerland. A major landing in Ireland was contemplated, using 25,000 French soldiers. The Irish told the French that 15,000 would be sufficient, for the moment they landed a quarter of a million armed Irishmen would join them in the struggle against the English. The French, who had not engaged in Irish diplomacy before, were carried away by the prospect put before them and expanded their invasion plan to include India, although further thought convinced them that only the conquest of Ireland was practical in a single campaign.

The final plan was technically good, unlike, say, the Spanish Armada of 1588 or the not-too-serious German operation 'Sealion' of 1940. Three different landing places inside Bantry Bay on the west coast of Ireland were chosen, to fit different wind conditions; and even if conditions were impossible there, the mouth of the River Shannon offered an alternative.

The extreme south-west coast of Ireland was also the right place for a French beachhead, politically and militarily. It was assumed that there would be little opposition from the British Navy. A more questionable assumption was that December and January were favourable months for launching a seaborne campaign, particularly on south-west facing bays and estuaries when south-westerly gales could be expected; although tactical surprise might be gained thereby. Armies are exposed to weather, but not half so much as fleets.

The base for the invasion fleet was Brest, the French naval base in Brittany in the north-west corner of the Cherbourg peninsula, south of Devon and Cornwall and offering a convenient passage to the south-west coast of Ireland. But by 15 December of the invasion year, 1796, only two of the three French warship squadrons had assembled at Brest. The third squadron under Villeneuve (the future loser at Trafalgar) still had not arrived.

Even so, the French fleet numbered 17 battleships, 13 frigates, 6 corvettes, 7 transports and an ammunition frigate. They carried 18,000 soldiers of the land army, together with their guns, horses, and stores. The British fleet had gone into Portsmouth for the winter, leaving a squadron of 13 battleships and few frigates to lie off Brest. The battleships remained safely (in view of onshore gales) some 40 miles out to sea, but the British frigates kept station so close in to Brest that the French were deceived into thinking that the battleships were only just over the horizon, in sight from their tops.

Fearing that their fleet could be destroyed in detail if it emerged in line through the main channels, the French decided to come out by a dangerous and little-used channel. Then the weather blew up and made that route impossibly risky, and they changed their minds.

To signal the alteration of plan a corvette was stationed to fire guns, rockets and blue lights along the correct course. However, a British frigate charged right in among the main body of the French and began to fire guns, rockets and blue lights. This confused the French so much that their battleship *Seduisant* went aground and, as a distress signal, also fired guns, rockets and blue lights.

The battleship was lost with more than half the 1,300 men on board, and the emerging French fleet was scattered into small squadrons, each inferior in force to the united British squadron waiting over the horizon. The French Navy and Army commanders, who had embarked together in a fast frigate, were not in contact with any part of their force, which was technically leaderless.

The British squadron did sight a French force, but it was Villeneuve arriving late; and he escaped. In a storm-weather pursuit the British suffered gale damage and were scattered; at the end of December the British admiral had only six of his ships in company when he returned to Portsmouth, the main British base on the south coast.

Notwithstanding these misadventures, the main body of the French invasion fleet made their emergency rendezvous off Ireland with only one battleship and three frigates missing, apart from the wrecked *Seduisant*, lost at Brest. But in one of the missing frigates were the Navy and Army commanders of the force. The officers next to them in seniority took over. They were Admiral Bouvet and General Grouchy (he who later helped Napoleon to lose Waterloo). They decided to carry out the landings as planned.

That winter was the coldest in living memory and the weather at sea was wild. On Christmas Day, while the British were trying to get their main battlefleet out of Spithead, its anchorage off Portsmouth, the French were trying to disembark their soldiers, guns and stores in Bantry Bay, the weather their only opponent. It was impossible. After days of trying to invade, all that they achieved was the loss of some ships and damage to others, from running aground or colliding with each other.

Eventually they gave up trying and the force returned to France, in small groups or individually. One of the last to leave, on 7 January, 1797, was the new 74-gun ship-of-the-line *Droits de l'Homme*, commanded by an experienced and senior officer, Commodore Jean-Baptiste la Crosse and with General Jean-Joseph Humbert commanding the 549 soldiers aboard; in addition there were 639 French crew and 105 prisoners from captured British ships, including two women and six children.

On 13 January the battleship was overtaken by foul weather blowing out of the Atlantic, while heading for Belle Isle on the coast of Brittany where there were a number of secure bases. Through the rain driving over a sullen sea la Crosse sighted two large ships. He did not know that they were French and was glad to lose sight of them, in case they were part of the British blockading squadron. Two hours later, with the rising note of the coming storm beginning to howl through the rigging and set the blocks rattling, backing south-west as indication of worse to come, two more ships were sighted—this time ahead, between the lone battleship and the land la Crosse was making for.

The larger of these looming ships was the *Indefatigable*, a former 64-gun ship-of-the-line cut down to 44 guns on a single main deck to

turn her into a powerful frigate, and commanded by Sir Edward Pellew.
It was Pellow in this frigate which had caused the mayhew at Brest in
December, which had resulted in the wreck of the *Seduisant*. He was now
back on his blockade station. Some eight miles astern of him was the
36-gun frigate *Amazon* under Captain Robert Reynolds.

Almost at once, the situation changed. Frigates were too lightly built
to take on a battleship; indeed, were forbidden to engage them. If any
captain did so—and lost, as he was virtually bound to do—the verdict
at his inevitable court martial would ruin him. War is a business, like
any other.

But now, with the gale making all the ships plunge heavily, and
squalls gusting aloft, the top masts of both the fore and main masts of
the *Droits de l'Homme* were carried away, leaving a chaos of canvas,
cordage and broken spars on deck and hanging over the side. The main
sails were still drawing; what was affected chiefly was the manoeuvring
power of the anyway clumsy battleship. This was decisive for la Crosse.
Once he had the wreckage cleared away, he steered east, before the
wind, for the safety of the Brittany bases.

Pellew, the best frigate captain of the age, weighed the chances. The
battleship had three times his fire-power—and her heaviest guns were
the big 32-pounders mounted on her lower deck. In addition, for every
seaman aboard there must be at least one soldier; in men he must be
outnumbered five to one. On the other hand, battleships carried their
main armament lower down than a frigate. In this sea, the working of
the battleship's heaviest guns would be hampered; she would have to
keep her ports closed until it was time to fire, and then be very careful to
choose the right moment—or risk having her whole lower gun deck
swamped. The gunpowder cartridges would be soaked, the flints
useless. For a gun battle at a distance, her complement of soldiers
would be a disadvantage; her decks must be uncomfortably crowded.
His own crew were battle-experienced, used to working and fighting
together; a superb team.

By the time Pellew had come within range of the battleship it was
about 5.30 p.m.—almost completely dark on a winter's afternoon
heavy with rain and a bitingly cold wind. The seas were surging and
vicious. Under topsails only, for better control, Pellew took the *Indefatigable* across the almost defenceless stern of the *Droits de l'Homme* and
fired his guns into her as they bore. Then he drew ahead in an attempt
to repeat this raking manoeuvre on the battleship's equally ill-armed

bow. But la Crosse foiled him and got off a dangerous broadside, backed up by the 'pepperpot' fire of the French soldiers' muskets. The French commodore then tried to run alongside the frigate and board, but Pellew evaded that manoeuvre.

The *Amazon*, under Reynolds, came into action at about 6.45 p.m., when it was fully dark. She had been eight miles astern when Pellew opened fire and since then, with much sail set, had been steering on the gun flashes. Reynolds closed astern of the French battleship, fired a broadside into her quarter, and attempted to turn and rake the Frenchman's stern with the loaded battery on her other side. La Crosse tricked both his enemies, manoeuvring the frigates to his weather side, the highest side of the heeling battleship. Now he could open his lower deck ports and run out the heavy 32-pounders. No frigate could stand much of this, and Pellew drew ahead out of the arc of fire to repair rigging and bring up more ready-to-use ammunition from the hold. Reynolds could not have remained even if he had wanted to; he had a lot of sail on in order to come up and could not take in canvas while his crew were busy at the guns.

In the battleship there had been a bad accident. A 24-pounder gun had burst. Possibly a wave had stopped up its muzzle at the moment of firing. Apart from casualties due to explosion and flying fragments on the gun deck, all the other guns' crews would become wary in case the same happened with their own pieces.

At 8.30 p.m. the two British frigates came in again to the attack. They had to keep clear of the battleship's broadsides, or as much as they could. The batteries of 32-pounders on the lower gun deck and 24-pounders on the upper gun deck could smash them, particularly the lighter 36-gun *Amazon*. So they tried to keep on either side of the bluff bows of the *Droits de l'Homme*. For his part, the French commander, by yawing from side to side, endeavoured to bring at least some of his guns to bear and, with luck be able to close and board. But the British captains were alert to that, and did not give him the chance he wanted.

The ships were heeled over away from the direction of the rising storm, steadier than a modern powered vessel would be; but the lower parts of their heeled decks were awash, the gun crews sometimes wading waist-deep in water. How they kept the ammunition and ignition dry is a wonder, or how they served their guns at all; normally in a gale, one wants at least one hand (sometimes two) for one self, and another (if there is one left over) for the job one has to do. Otherwise one can be hurled the length or breadth of the deck, with subsequent damage. It is possible to be wedged into a corner and holding on with both hands, and still be hurled loose down the deck.

The weight of the guns was between two and three tons. They were placed on carriages with four small wheels (which served to slow recoil); were controlled by a system of ropes and pulleys attached to ring-bolts let into heavy frames in the side of the ship; and finally braked at the end of their recoil by a breeching rope also fixed to ring-bolts in the ship's side.

The gun was fired when as close to the port as it would go, the recoil taking the piece inboard where the bore could be cleaned of any burning fragments of the charge by ramming a sponge down the muzzle and turning it several times; at every third shot it had to be additionally cleaned by the use of a kind of screw known as a 'worm'. To insert a fresh charge of gunpowder into smouldering fragments of the last cartridge was not wise. After the new cartridge had been inserted and rammed down the barrel to the far end, so that it lay under the vent hole, the shot was then rammed down on top of it and secured with a wad of old rope. Using the tackle, the gun was then rolled back to the port and aimed by crude means—a wedge to alter elevation, a spike to train it round.

This neat description must now be translated onto a heeled, heaving deck, swept by water, rising and falling with the waves. If the guns being fired were on the low side of the ship, then they would have to be hauled uphill after firing, by use of the ropes and pulleys and plenty of muscle; if on the high side, then they would have to be hauled uphill into firing position but their recoil could be augmented by the heel and the impact of the waves. In the *Indefatigable* sometimes the controlling ropes broke, and had to be renewed, and in several cases the recoil was so violent that the ring-bolts were pulled bodily out of the side of the ship.

Conditions in all three vessels engaged did not differ; it was the same for all, except that the battleship's guns were heavier. When the Frenchman's lower deck ports were briefly opened to fire the 32-pounders, the main deck became a river which the scuppers could not immediately dispose of, and water poured down onto the unfortunate British prisoners, men, women and children alike, where they were penned below the waterline in the cable tier, unaware of how the battle went. Amid the flat thunder of the guns ran the rippling musket fire of the French soldiers, who had similar tasks of sponging out their pieces and equally tricky techniques of loading, and as a musket is a two-handed weapon they had in addition the problems of how to wedge themselves in place in order to get off a shot.

In these conditions, the battle went on hour after hour, in numbing cold and mind-dazing noise and continual uneven motion. At about 10.30 the effect of the frigates' fire was seen to take effect. The mizzen-mast of the *Droits de l'Homme* was visibly tottering. La Crosse did not wait for it to fall but limited the damage it would have caused by ordering it cut away so that it would fall clear. But in addition to square sails the main fore-and-aft sail of the battleship was rigged on this mast; its loss made the 74-gun ship hard to handle.

The British frigates now took station on her quarters—close to her vulnerable stern and the command post on the poop; one on each side.

At about midnight there was a sign that the battleship was in trouble. Instead of firing round shot, she began to fire shell—that is, hollow cannon balls containing an explosive charge detonated by a burning fuse. Literally, 'shells'. She had exhausted her supply of solid shot, which is the best projectile for penetrating hulls. She had lost 103 men killed and 150 wounded.

The *Amazon* had lost most of her mizzen-mast—only a stump was standing—so her manoeuvrability also was impaired. Besides that, her main and fore masts and their yards had been badly damaged and her rigging had been repaired so often that there was no spare cordage left. There was three feet of water in her hold, but her casualties were only three killed and fifteen wounded.

The *Indefatigable* had all her masts standing, although damaged, and four feet of water in the hold; her casualties totalled nineteen wounded. No one had been killed.

But the Frenchmen, despite their fearful casualties, were still working their guns and the British were replying. The flash of gunfire still rent the blackness of the night under the racing clouds which hid the moon.

At 4.30 on the morning of the next day, 14 January, the storm stripped the clouds away and the moon shone out over the tumultuous sea, stained with foam. Lieutenant George Bell, stationed on the forecastle of the *Indefatigable*, ran aft to report. Land to the north-east, closer than two miles, and a rage of breakers in front of that unknown coast. Before he could make his report, the officers on the poop had seen it too. This was a danger more deadly than the *Droits de l'Homme* and threatened all three ships; but not equally.

Pellow gave three orders in succession: signal to *Amazon* (crippled by loss of her mizzen mast), you are standing into danger; to the gunnery lieutenants: cease fire; and to the sailing master: turn away to seaward across the wind.

The last order was the tricky one. For a sailing ship to turn across the wind is difficult; if too much canvas is carried, she may be dismasted and must then drive ashore; if too little, then she will not turn all the way, but will stall and broach-to among the waves. Difficult in normal circumstances, but with torn canvas, cut rigging, damaged masts and yards? How much would the frigate take?

The *Indefatigable* swung round, and at the moment of the stall hung for a moment, and then followed through until her sails filled on the other tack, and she could steer off from the peril of the coast. Pellew had judged it precisely.

The *Amazon*, lacking the steering sail which had been on the shot-away mizzen-mast, could not repeat Pellew's manoeuvre and there was not room enough for her to wear round with the storm. Before 5 a.m. she was ashore. Six men who stole a small boat for their escape were drowned. The rest, including all the wounded, were got to land on rafts made up on the spot. The rafts, much safer than a boat in breaking seas, were simply drifted onto the beach by the wind and the waves.

The *Droits de l'Homme* was less fortunate. She had already lost her mizzen-mast. When La Crosse tried to turn her up into the wind, both her fore-mast and her bowsprit carried away; only her main-mast with the main-sail was left. La Crosse ordered the anchors dropped, but they simply bounced across the sandy seabed without holding. She struck on an inshore sandbank, was carried farther in by the breakers, and struck again, losing her main-mast. Still the storm and the raging sea had not finished with her. She was forced farther inshore, struck another bank, swung broadside to the combers racing in, then fell over on her beam ends, with the sea bursting right over her great hull.

At this point, discipline seemed to break down. The officers and men who had fought so valiantly for so many hours now looked only to themselves. Or so it is said. I doubt that the critics fully realised their situation. The ship was not upright, with a deck to stand on; she was right over on her side and half full of water. True, the shore was only a few hundred yards away; but struggling through pounding surf and giant waves is not easy for comparatively puny creatures like men. A sea like that in the shallows has awe-inspiring power. Swimming is of little use—you would be underwater most of the time. All that could be done would be to cling to some fitting inside the hull, or stand on top—if you weren't swept away by the rearing combers—and wait for low tide.

It is extremely difficult for the average author—and the average reader—to think themselves inside a battleship of nearly 200 years ago which is heeled nearly 90 degrees from the vertical. The only existing examples are wrecks. I am thinking especially of another French battleship, the 54-gun *Hazardieux* built in 1688 (the *Droits de l'Homme* was a 74 built in 1794), which was wrecked in a gale on the coast of Sussex in 1706 (having been captured in 1703); she struck in shallow water, going over on her beam ends, in very similar circumstances and on an almost identical coast. Her guns, some of them still on their gun carriages, are there today, lying against the frames on her port side. Excavating those decks and those guns makes plain the predicament faced by the crew of La Crosse's command. All honour to them that they got up their prisoners from below, even when overwhelmed by disaster.

At this moment, no one knew where they were. Possibly an island off the coast of Brittany, perhaps even Brittany itself. The crew of the *Indefatigable*, having clawed off a lee shore, found themselves again facing breakers ahead, and having made another emergency turn, discovered that yet more breakers lay in their path. They were trapped in darkness inside some vast bay.

About 6.30, with the coming of first light, they could see breakers hurling themselves masthead-high into the air. Their course to clear them, and to avoid the perils of the shore they had left behind them, meant wearisome beating up against the gale, four more terrible hours of sea-soaked toll for the exhausted men. By now the wrecks already ashore were visible—the *Amazon*, and two miles to the south of her, the huge, whale-bulk of the French battleship lying on her side, swept by the breakers. They were caught in the great bay of Audierne, and the foam-spouting rocks ahead of them were the Penmarcks, a reef of dire repute.

To the watchers on the shore, it seemed that the British frigate was doomed to perish on the Penmarcks but Pellow had fought his way clear to open sea by eleven that morning. Reynolds, as we have seen, rafted all his men ashore—bar the six men who without orders had unwisely stolen a boat and drowned themselves. In the *Droits de l'Homme* two-thirds of the seamen and soldiers were supposed to have perished; but modern research in France scales down this tragedy. The best figures (few such figures can be wholly accurate, even in modern times), give the total in her as 1,293 including the British prisoners and more than 600 as the number of the dead.

The French general on board, Jean-Joseph Humbert, was one of the survivors. He was to return to Ireland the following year, 1798, with another invasion fleet, this time in command of the whole force. As this amounted to just over 1,000 men its main significance was as a prop to the rising of the United Irishmen in County Mayo. Humbert, who had started in life as a dealer in goat and rabbit skins at Lyons, had risen through the Revolution, winning fame under General Hoche in the Vendée, where the rebels were French. In Ireland, commanding French troops and Irish rebels, he inflicted on British soil at Castlebar a resounding defeat on a British army.

But it was only a diversion, intended to embarrass the English. On his return from Italy in December 1797 the new French 'star', General Bonaparte, had been appointed Commander-in-Chief of the grandly named 'Army of England'. With 35,000 fighting men in 130 transports, escorted by 13 battleships and 42 smaller warships, in the early summer of 1798 the 'Army of England' set sail—for Egypt. The man of destiny had decided that England was not an attractive or possible target.

The remains of the *Droits de l'Homme* and the British *Amazon* lie buried still in the sand of Audierne Bay. Some interesting recoveries, including the ship's bell, have been made from the *Droits de l'Homme* as tokens of that appalling tragedy.

Chapter Seven

THE BATTLE OF THE BASQUE ROADS

Lord Cochrane off Rochefort, April 1809

The fireship was the sailing navies' equivalent of the torpedo, although rather more chancy because aiming was difficult. It was best used, not in a fleet engagement in the open sea, but against anchored ships which could not quickly move out of the way. Drake's use of improvised fire vessels to dislodge the Spanish Armada from its French anchorage in 1588 is the best known instance, but by no means the first; it was a standard gambit at the time. But probably its last use was in April 1809 against a fleet of Napoleonic France lying in a protected anchorage off the mouth of the River Charante leading to the inland port of Rochefort.

General Bonaparte had replaced the Directory by his own personal Imperial rule, with vaster ambitions and even greater bloodshed, but he had failed to rid Europe of the irritatingly interfering British. After the defeat by Nelson of the combined battlefleets of France and Spain at Trafalgar in 1805, it was not possible even to threaten Britain with invasion. But he still possessed warships and they, unless contained, could as raiders do much damage to his enemy's seaborne commerce. His problem was that they were bottled up in small numbers in various ports and could easily be defeated by the blockading British.

Then, in February 1809, it happened that Lord Gambier's fleet blockading the great French port of Brest, on the Cherbourg peninsula, was blown off station. The French Rear-Admiral Willaumez seized his chance and escaped with eight ships-of-the-line and some frigates. Although his intended destination was the French base of Martinique in the West Indies, Willaumez lured away from the French port of Lorient, farther south in Brittany, the British squadron on blockade duty there; and three more French ships-of-the-line with accompanying frigates got out. Then, in a final move to gather as large a force as possible, Willaumez headed farther south in the Bay of Biscay to collect reinforcements from Rochefort. And here the British pursuers closed in and blockaded the French.

Now the British problem was how to actually get at the enemy fleet in its defended anchorage and, by totally destroying it, reduce the strain of blockade on their own navy.

The estuary of the Charente leads into a wide bay shielded to the north by the Îsle de Re and to the south-west by the even larger Île d'Oleron. The latter island gave its name to the early maritime agreement known as the Laws of Oleron. The anchorage lay some nine miles inside this almost enclosed bay, near to the mouth of the Charente where a long peninsula crowned by an artillery fort looked across to another artillery fort on the tiny Île d'Aix. These two forts, Enez and Liedot, covered the actual anchorage of the French ships, but another fort guarded the final approach to the anchorage past the Boyart Shoal on the Île d'Oleron. Any attacker would have to pass within gun range of at least three forts.

The Admiralty decided to use fireships, and the most suitable officer to command such a venture was felt to be Lord Cochrane of the frigate *Imperieuse*, who had acquired a reputation in the Mediterranean for balanced daring. No doubt many brave blockheads were available, but the requirement was for success in a most difficult enterprise. The future naval novelist Frederick Marryat was one of his midshipmen. His thrillers of naval life were based on the adventures he took part in under Cochrane's command, although later, as a Captain, he engaged in a good many of his own devising. Of Cochrane he wrote: 'I never knew anyone so careful of the lives of his ship's company, or anyone who calculated so closely the risks attending any expedition.'

The most obvious risk attending fireship attack was that the crews, if captured, would receive no quarter; swift execution was certain. At the same time, that risk had to be accepted; for the fireship's crew to take to their boat too early so as to ensure their own survival would almost certainly mean that the blazing vessel would either miss its target or be grappled and pulled clear by the guard boats which any prudent enemy would station around the anchored fleet.

Lord Gambier, in charge of the battleship squadron which should follow up the fireship offensive, was in overall charge of the operation. Captain Lord Cochrane had to plan and execute the attack of the fireships. But he was also the junior Captain present and many other officers coveted the job. Admiral Sir Eliab Harvey was so eager to run the show that he used intemperate language to Lord Gambier and was sent home for court martial. This was about the only decisive move that Lord Gambier was to make.

On the French side, Admiral Willaumez, who had achieved the concentration of force, was replaced in command by Vice-Admiral Allemand. Recognising that the greatest danger to his fleet would come from fireships he took firm measures to meet it. He protected the anchored ships by a strong floating boom which should stop any vessel from coming close; he covered the boom with the fire of frigates anchored near; and he had armed guardboats to lie by the boom throughout the hours of darkness.

The British fleet, from which the fireships would issue forth, was nine miles away, but for the last two miles of their passage to the attack the fireships would have to sail under fire past the Boyart Shoal on their starboard hand and the batteries of the Île d'Aix to port. Beyond that lay the floating boom and beyond, protected by it, lay the French battleships anchored in two main lines.

The fireships were late in arriving so Cochrane took some of the transports already with the fleet; but it was Gambier who fitted them out and had them manned; Cochrane had other work to do. If the boom was not broken, the fireships would be useless, so he prepared three 'explosion vessels' designed to blow holes in it. Into each of these craft went 1,500 barrels of gunpowder plus a ten-inch explosive shell. Around this mass of explosive were packed 3,000 grenades. The hulls were strengthened to contain the effect of the gunpowder, which is a low explosive and in open air merely burns. Cochrane himself took charge of one 'explosion vessel', while Mr Midshipman Marryat captained the other. The third was kept at the stern of the frigate *Imperieuse* as a reserve in case either of the first two should fail or their effect be insufficiently disruptive.

Apart from the 'explosion vessels' there were three other groups of ships. Cochrane's frigate and four other vessels were to station themselves at the seaward end of the Boyart Shoal to pick up the fireship crews escaping in their boats. Two ships with lights screened from the land were anchored as guide vessels to show the fireships the channel between the shoal and Île d'Aix. And a group of ships fitted with rocket launchers and heavy mortars firing explosive bombshells were positioned to drench the enemy batteries with high-angle fire, falling from above. Neither of these weapons was as reliable or accurate as their modern equivalents, but they would certainly tend to discourage the enemy gunners.

Naturally, the operation was timed to coincide with the flood tide which would take the attackers in towards the anchorage. At 8.30 in the evening they sailed, in darkness.

When Cochrane's 'explosion vessel' hit the boom, he lit the fuse and then he and his four men got into the dinghy they had been towing and set off for a hard pull back against the incoming tide. In the excitement, their dog got left behind in the 'explosion vessel' with the fuse sputtering away; so they turned back to pick him up. The result was that they were very close when the vast explosion occurred—and that saved them from death or injury, for the trajectory of the debris hurled skyward took it all clean over them to fall harmlessly into the sea beyond. As they pulled hard past the shoal, some of the fireships passed them on their way in to the attack.

In the second 'explosion vessel' was Frederick Marryat. He lit his fuse and with his four rowers escaped in a four-oared gig.

If ever I felt the sensation of fear, it was after I had lighted this fire. We were not two hundred yards off when she exploded. A more terrific and beautiful sight cannot be conceived; but we were not quite enough at our ease to enjoy it! The shells flew up into the air to a prodigious height, some bursting as they rose, and others as they descended. The shower fell about us, but we escaped without injury and we had the pleasure to run the gauntlet among the fireships, which bore down on us in flames fore and aft.

There was no need for the third 'explosion vessel'. Cochrane's had begun the work, and Marryat's finished it. The fireships could sail straight on to the anchored French battleships. But only four did so, out of 20. They were badly handled. Some crews lit their fuses and abandoned their ships a mile or more before they even reached the channel. One prematurely abandoned vessel, fires roaring away, nearly collided with the *Imperieuse*, which had the reserve 'explosion vessel' secured alongside. That was the nearest Cochrane came to disaster, not from the defences of the enemy.

Not unnaturally, the sight of the exploding vessels breaking the boom had an intimidating effect on the French. They were not to know that the fireships were only ordinary incendiary vessels and not floating bombs. To get clear, they cut their cables; but as their topmasts had been stowed they were not under full control in the strong tide.

With dawn the British success was apparent. Just before 6 a.m. Cochrane sent the first of a series of success signals to Gambier's flagship:

Half fleet can destroy enemy. Seven ashore.

Gambier acknowledged receipt of the signal but took no action. At 6.40 a.m. Cochrane signalled:

Eleven on shore.

Again an acknowledgement but no sign of anything happening. Cochrane, a red-haired giant, heir to the Scottish Earldom of Dundonald, was seething; but he had no authority even to attack with his own ship let alone the other frigates with him. Gambier was in overall command. The French fleet was aground and helpless for the moment, but the morning's flood tide would float them off. At 7.40 a.m. he made the signal:

Only two afloat.

This was acknowledged, but there were still no signs of action by the battle fleet. Cochrane signalled:

Frigates alone can destroy the enemy.

There was no movement of the fleet; this signal was not even acknowledged. At 9.25, with the tide high, Cochrane signalled:

Enemy preparing to haul off.

Once afloat, the French ships could retire with the flood tide up the River Charente towards Rochefort, where they would be safe. It was hit now in force, or not at all. At 9.35 a.m. the British fleet got under way, only to anchor again a mile away from Cochrane's frigate, to seaward of it. The last two French battleships still afloat went aground almost at the same time. Every battleship they had was on shore, a mass of helpless targets.

In a fighting Service direct disobedience of orders is unwise, to say the least; but a certain amount of subterfuge is sometimes possible without punishment. Spurred by the sight of the nearest French ship, a great three-decker of around 100 guns, just about to float off and become mobile, Cochrane ordered the frigate's anchor to be raised but no sail set. The *Imperieuse* began to drift shoreward down the channel with the incoming stream, almost imperceptibly; if questioned, then naturally her anchor had dragged. Who could disprove it?

For half-an-hour she drifted towards the stranded French, past the batteries on the Île d'Aix which proved far less formidable than first thought. At 1.30 p.m., when it was too late for Gambier to recall Cochrane, he signalled to the battle fleet:

Enemy superior to chasing ship, but inferior to fleet.

And when even that produced no action he made to Gambier:

In want of assistance.

That did produce a reaction. Gamber sent in two ships-of-the-line and five frigates in half-hearted support. Meanwhile Cochrane was broadsiding one French ship, the *Calcutta*, and engaging two others with his bow and stern chasers. They were stuck while he was mobile and could choose his firing position for best effect and the least exposure of his own vessel. To be bombarded without being able to retaliate is depressing; when Cochrane sent his boats away to board the *Calcutta*, her crew escaped onto a sandbank and ran away. The two other ships, *Aquilon* and *Ville de Varsovie*, struck their colours later on and were taken as prizes; but the *Calcutta* was set on fire and blown up. The *Tonnerre* was fired by her crew and abandoned, and she also blew up.

Cochrane wanted to tackle the French flagship *Ocean* but was unable to do so alone; and Gambier would not send in a battleship to support him. Before making the withdrawal signal to the reluctant Cochrane, Gambier ordered the two captured French ships to be set on fire rather than take them back to England as prizes. To their captors, they represented a lot of money, more to the captain and officers than the men but a substantial windfall nevertheless.

Of course, it was not Cochrane who reported to the Admiralty and the Government, it was Gambier; and in his report the Commander-in-Chief gave Cochrane a good deal less than his due. It was not the first time this has happened, and it will not be the last; nor is it confined to the Navy. But in this case, there were two abnormal factors. Firstly, Lord Cochrane was Member of Parliament for Westminster, and secondly, he was not an Englishman, he was a Scot.

When the normal vote of thanks was put to the vote in Parliament to give thanks to the gallant Lord Gambier for his great victory in the Basque Roads, Lord Cochrane got up to oppose the motion, on the grounds that the noble lord had not earned any thanks, having neglected to do his duty and destroy the French fleet.

One would like to have been there, as a fly on the House of Commons wall. This sort of thing simply is not done in England. Lord Cochrane was asked to withdraw, and he refused. He was offered a bribe, in the shape of the command of a squadron of frigates; and refused. He was threatened with hints of what might happen to his career in the Navy if he did not obey; and he refused. He probably got a good deal of innocent fun out of baiting the English. And they got their revenge, of course; his career, in the British Navy at least, was at an end. But he forced Lord Gambier to request a court martial upon himself, so as to defend his conduct as Commander-in-Chief at the Basque Roads.

The Naval trial took place in July aboard HMS *Gladiator*, and lasted nine days. The President of the Court was a close personal friend of Lord Gambier; the members of the Court were in his favour. The verdict completely exonerated Cochrane's opponent. Any other verdict would have been utterly surprising, indeed thoroughly unEnglish. But the public grumbled and historians have by no means accepted that verdict as gospel.

Cochrane went on to commit other offences against the 'Establishment'. He attacked the Admiralty for withholding the pay and pensions of poor seamen, who had no great estates to fall back on. He was a Radical, a subversive, an embarrassment. They ganged up on him.

In 1814 a most curious trial took place. It was alleged that Lord Cochrane had through prior knowledge benefited from dealings on the London Stock Exchange. There was a story of a mysterious Frenchman posing as a member of the Rifle Brigade, who told Lord Cochrane that he needed civilian clothes in order to escape his creditors, and that Cochrane had lent him those clothes. Then it transpired that this strange Frenchman had appeared in Dover the previous night dressed in the red uniform of a British staff officer with the splendid news that the Emperor was dead; Bonaparte had been killed in battle. And this was really all a hoax so that a gang of cheats could sell their shares at inflated prices. There were doubtful witnesses and lurid outbursts from the judge, Lord Ellenborough, who was a political opponent. One would love to have been a fly on many walls, to learn the inside story behind this trial in which Lord Cochrane was found guilty.

The judgement was spectacularly severe. Lord Cochrane was fined immensely—£1,000, a vast sum in those days—and also sent to prison for a year. He was expelled from the House of Commons. He was expelled from the Navy. His banner as Knight of the Bath, granted for his raid in the Basque Roads, was removed from where it hung in the Henry VII Chapel in Westminster Abbey. His disgrace was absolute —if you believed in the verdict of the court. Not everyone did. His constituents voted him back to Parliament. And public subscription paid his fine.

But the British public could not restore him to the Navy. So he served abroad with other navies, in other nations' wars, and behaved brilliantly. He commanded the Chilean navy in a war, then that of Brazil, and that of Greece against Turkey. In the end, there was a new King in England and a new regime. Cochrane was granted a pardon (less than he wanted, for it implied he had been guilty), and restored to the Navy List. He became an admiral and a Commander-in-Chief of the North American and West Indies stations. When he died in 1860, aged 85, Queen Victoria commanded that his banner as Knight of the Bath be restored to its place in the Henry VII Chapel of Westminster Abbey.

Lord Cochrane's wife and his descendants through generations always maintained that his trial at the Guildhall under Lord Ellenborough had been unfair. But Lord Ellenborough had relatives too, and eventually one of these became so incensed at what he regarded as the slurs on his family name that he started to write a book to prove his case. Lacking the necessary legal skills he handed part of his task over to a Mr Attlay of Lincoln's Inn, who found that there had been substance behind Lord Ellenborough's judgement.

But only the flies on the walls could really tell.

Chapter Eight

DAVID PORTER v. JAMES HILLYAR

Duel off Valparaiso, March 1814

In a sense, America's War of Independence was the continent's first Civil War. Patriotic publicists then and now depicted the conflict as a crusade against a hated foe, while in the British Isles traditionalists deplored the attitude of those rebels against the Throne. The second war between Britain and her old colonies is usually known as the War of 1812, but it did result in one duel between small ships with rival captains who had known each other in the Mediterranean while they were both on the same side and the Barbary pirates on the other. Indeed, another American officer had given passage home to the wife and family of the British captain, so the latter was in the debt of the Navy which he was now ordered to fight.

The British Navy was of course immensely more powerful than the new American Service, but for much of this period it had France as its main enemy. Being an island rather than a continent, and dependent on seaborne trade, its sea power numbered around 800 ships manned by some 130,000 men from a population of about eight million, as against some 30 million of the French. It was the problem of manning this Navy which had helped bring about the war, for the British counted as British anyone who had been a British subject at the time of the War of Independence; American seamen and British seamen claiming to be Americans were therefore 'pressed' for the Royal service. There was no conscription—or 'draft'—such as we have in our own times. The bureaucracy did not exist to implement it and the documentation was lacking. People were 'free' in a sense in which they are not now—the Government did not even know you existed, they just grabbed you when and where they could. Only the orderly and logical French had conscription, so their Emperor Bonaparte, when he lost one army, simply raised another by calling up the younger generation and the elderly.

Waging war with America was difficult. With France it was a matter of buying sufficient allies and their armies until one's combined land forces outnumbered those of the enemy, because it is the big battalions which are most likely to win. But fighting a largely uninhabited continent, with a mostly agricultural economy on its fringe, offers no key targets—as the Americans were to discover later in Vietnam.

The weapon used by both sides was blockade and commerce raiding; a rather ineffectual sort of war: the ability to hurt but not to kill. The commerce raider we are concerned with here was David Porter of the light frigate *Essex*, whose naval heroes were all British seamen who had preyed on Spanish commerce in the Pacific as long ago as the sixteenth century—Drake, Cavendish and later, Anson. They had all captured Spanish treasure ships and in so doing struck heavy blows at the Spanish economy and war effort. But Porter was an American and this was the nineteenth century; the trade he mightily disturbed was British whaling. In the end, however, his desire to fight real warships and not whalers got the better of him.

He did not like the frigate he had been given and doubted her warlike value. For America's frigates this was unusual. The new nation had not attempted to match Britain in ships-of-the-line, but sensibly concentrated on turning out as commerce raiders super-frigates designed to beat any British equivalent, which they did. They were heavily-gunned —24-pounders—and heavily-built, with almost continuous framing. Nowadays one might call them pocket battleships. Initially, they were aided to victory by Britain's complacency resulting from a long string of victories at sea—the natural, arrogant assumption that British was best and that you didn't have to try or, in one notorious case of a spit-and-polish captain, the famous slogan 'Bullshit Baffles Brains'. The ominous string of American victories over British frigates also exploded a myth: that the supposed ease of handling of the British 18-pounder gun would enable it to match the fire of the more cumbersome 24-pounders. It did not.

There was now an innovation from Scotland, a product of the Carron iron works—a very short, light gun firing a very heavy shot, and called a carronade. The drawback to this formidable piece was its short range. And it was this factor, as it now existed in the frigate *Essex*, which worried Porter.

When originally fitted out, the *Essex* had been a superb light frigate rated at 32 guns. Her armament had consisted of 26 12-pounder cannons carried on the main deck plus 16 24-pounder carronades on the spar deck above—a nice balance of fire-power, for which the ship was designed. But in 1810, under a previous captain, she had lost 20 12-pounder cannons which had been replaced by 40 32-pounder carronades; this had also adversely affected her sailing qualities. She was left with only six long guns, the rest being short-ranged 'smashers', fine if you could close, because they increased the weight of shot to be fired from 348 to 612 pounds. When Porter got her he protested to the Secretary of the Navy.

> Was this ship to be disabled in her rigging in the early part of an engagement, a ship armed with long guns could take a position beyond the reach of our carronades and cut us to pieces.

The bureaucratic reply was, understandably, that the Navy could not afford to replace the armament of the ship every time she changed captains, but that Porter could, if he wished, swap a few of the 12-pounder long guns for 18-pounders of the same design. Porter did not accept this none too generous offer.

He had had an adventurous career at sea, in his youth fighting Barbary pirates (and being captured by them), and later saving his ship from Haitian pirates; he had stabbed and killed a drunken mugger who attempted to molest him, and when he was 27 had fallen in love with and married Evalina Anderson who was only 15. In this respect he rivalled even Lord Cochrane, who eloped with Kitty Barnes, a pretty 16-year old orphan schoolgirl twenty years his junior.

On his first war cruise of the 1812 affair Porter took a number of prizes near Bermuda and captured the British 20-gun sloop *Alert* by pretending to be a sleepy merchantman until he was well within range. He did not give her a chance to stand off. The *Alert* was the first British warship to be taken by the Americans in the war. However, when he returned to an American port, he asked Washington to give him another ship, even a smaller one, because of his 'insuperable dislike to Carronades, that render the Essex the worst frigate in the service'.

Still in the *Essex*, Porter was ordered in October 1812 to join the big frigates *Constitution* and *Hornet* off Brazil, to form a formidable raiding squadron in the South Atlantic. Of course, in the context of world events this was only a tiny part of the picture—for this was the fatal year for Napoleon. The Emperor of the French had invaded Imperial Russia with a vast army of 600,000 men—the so-called Grand Army, formed not only from the French army but recruited also from all the subjugated satellite states of Europe. The fate of that vast force would affect the naval war off America, allowing Britain to blockade her Atlantic coast with battleships as well as frigates.

However, in the meantime the *Constitution* and *Hornet* had won a victory and returned home. Porter correctly judged that this must be the reason they had not kept the rendezvous, and decided on a bold move: to enter the Pacific, like Drake and Cavendish and Anson, and prey on the enemy's undefended commerce there. Porter explained this in an open letter to his crew, sweetening the hazards and discomforts by pointing out that the prizes they could expect:

> will give you an abundant supply of wealth; and the girls of the Sandwich Islands shall reward you for your sufferings during the passage around Cape Horn.

In fact the passage of the Horn was made with favourable winds; only after entering the Pacific was the *Essex* nearly swamped and sunk during five days of horror. After putting in to Valparaiso to refit, Porter spent most of the summer of 1813 mopping up the British whaling ships in the Pacific. A strong believer in telling his men what a good job they were doing, he wrote:

> Fortune has at length smiled on us, because we deserved her smiles. The first time she enabled us to display *free trade and sailors' rights*, she put in our possession near half a million of the enemy's property. We will yet render the name of the Essex as terrible to the enemy as that of any other vessel.

It is unlikely that Porter actually believed this, but certainly his psychology was correct. His hero model was Anson, who took the Spanish treasure ship *Cavadongo*; but her gold cargo was so heavy that it took 32 oxcarts to convey the bullion to the Tower of London. Nevertheless, the lone American raider had carried on a long campaign, replenishing her stores and supplies from the enemy, and causing alarm and despondency among British bankers.

In September 1813 he learned that a British squadron had been sent out in pursuit of the *Essex*. In order to make the frigate not merely seaworthy but battleworthy, and her crew also, Porter sought a safely distant sanctuary, where the ship could be scraped free of marine organisms, the rigging repaired, and the men given a healthy spell on shore. So he headed for the Marquesas Islands, 2,500 miles south-east of Hawaii, where they spent an idyllic seven weeks repairing and recuperating. In 1813 the islands were an unspoiled paradise the like of which can be found nowhere on earth today. White, unsullied beaches, lush vegetation, sparkling waterfalls pouring down from the hills. The natives were anxious to offer food—delightful after shipboard fare—in exchange for items their culture lacked, fishhooks, iron hoops, glass bottles. Porter was much impressed by one particular teenager:

> . . . of fair complexion and neatly attired, her skin and glossy black hair annointed with cocoa nut oil, her carriage majestic; and her whole appearance striking in the extreme.

Work lasted until four in the afternoon, scraping, fumigating and repairing. Charcoal fires suffocated the 1,500 rats found in the hull, but these were replaced, alas, with swarms of the local cockroaches. After 4 p.m. one quarter of the crew were allowed liberty with the villagers —and the village women. All, that is, except for the younger midshipmen who were put in the charge of the chaplin; it seems a cruel alternative.

There was a price to pay for all this co-operation. The local chief wanted the help of Porter's men in a small war he was engaged in; even in paradise, there was little peace. Porter was soon in the business of sending Marines off to fire volleys at other natives and burn their villages. He himself wrote their epitaph: 'The valley, which on the morning we had viewed in all its beauty, was now a long line of smoking ruins from one end to the other.'

He then graduated by stages to distinctly British-style imperialism. He built a fort and named it 'Madison' after the President, and then assembled everyone in sight—natives, his own crew, the British prisoners—and declared that he had annexed the island to the United States. It was now to be called Madison's Island, likewise the bay was to become Massachusetts Bay. He told his listeners (those who could understand him, that is) that the Marquesans had asked 'to be admitted into the great American family, whose pure republican policy approaches so near their own . . . Our chief shall be their chief.'

In just this haphazard way, at the whim of this adventurer or that, did the British acquire several empires, one of which they had just lost and were apparently trying to regain. When President Madison, nine months later, received the news that he was now chief also of the Tomavheenahs, Attesapwyunahs, Tickeymahues and Attakakahaneuahs, he was engaged in dealing with a British invasion of Chesapeake Bay and neglected to put the matter to Congress.

On 13 December, 1813, to a chorus of weeping native women and the mutterings of a semi-mutinous crew, the *Essex* left the island of Nuku Hiva accompanied by a converted whaler, the *Essex Junior*, bound for Mocha Island on the west coast of South America, which Sir Francis Drake in his time (as Porter well knew) had used as a base for obtaining water and provisions, as indeed he had himself on the outward passage. Porter was a talented artist and his sketches of the Marquesans and their islands remain a valuable archive of the Pacific and its inhabitants at that period; we can well understand why he admired them.

In a cruise which lasted 17 months Porter had taken 22 British ships as prizes, but he was not satisfied. In his own reckoning, he had not matched his British heroes, Drake and Anson, nor his American compatriots, Hull, Decatur and Bainbridge.

He had fought weakly armed merchantmen, not warships. In global terms his contribution could not stand alongside the march of events in Europe: Napoleon's invasion of Russia, whose result could not yet be known to him. He wrote to the Secretary of the Navy;

> I had done all the injury that could be done to the British commerce in the Pacific, and still hoped to signalize my cruise by something more splendid before leaving that sea. Believing the British would seek me at Valparaiso, I determined to cruise about that place.

It was not then thought crazy, but honourable, to seek 'glory'; and five days after reaching Valparaiso on the coast of Chile, Porter saw it come up over the horizon—the 36-gun frigate *Phoebe* and the 28-gun sloop *Cherub*, both commanded by Captain James Hillyar.

The 50-year old Hillyar did not believe in personal glory as the aim of a commander but in success, achieved with the least casualties for his own side. All this, however, with the background of chivalry common to both sides and indeed to the century.

Valparaiso was a neutral port, so Hillyar sailed straight in and headed directly for the *Essex*. Porter cleared for action, had his guns and boarders ready. As the British frigate was closing him bows on, he later claimed that had he fired his broadside into her, she would have been destroyed within fifteen minutes. Hillyar certainly was taking a risk, but justified in the event; he came close enough to the American to hail that he did not intend to engage inside the harbour.

Porter snapped back: 'You have no business where you are. If you touch a rope yard of this ship I shall board instantly.'

The British ships sailed on to anchor half a mile astern of the two American ships; ordered to be enemies but forbidden to fight because of the neutrality of the port. With, in those days, a common language, the rivals broke out rude banners revealing the influence of propaganda even then. The crew of the *Essex* put out a huge banner reading:

FREE TRADE AND SAILORS' RIGHTS

which was their side's given reason for making war.

The crew of the *Phoebe* within hours hung out an even clumsier reply (doubtless prompted by propaganda and edited by their officers):

GOD AND COUNTRY: BRITISH SAILORS' BEST RIGHTS:
TRAITORS OFFEND BOTH

The assault, from being visual, soon became audible. The Americans attacked with renderings of 'Yankee Doodle', which the *Cherub*'s crew countered with what must have been their own special ship song, entitled apparently 'The Sweet Little Cherub that Sits Up Aloft'. Porter judged that while the Cherubs sang better (there must have been Welshmen in the crew), 'those of the Essex were more witty and to the point'.

One is reminded of an incident of the Spanish Civil War of the 1930s, when soldiers were dug in close enough to shout at each other. To the query, 'What are you fighting for?' the Nationalists replied, '*Espana* (Spain)'. The Government men boiled down their war aims to: 'The Bread of Our Brothers'.

While the fighting was confined to slogans the two commanders, Porter and Hillyar, met on shore at the house of the American envoy to Chile, Joel Poinsett, to resolve the impasse. They would not violate the neutrality of the harbour, that much was agreed. But when Porter argued that the *Essex Junior*, being a converted whaler and not a real warship, could not be reckoned equal to the *Cherub* and that therefore only the two frigates, *Essex* and *Phoebe*, should fight, Hillyar refused. He saw no good reason why he should throw away his advantage.

Surprisingly to modern eyes, so accustomed are we to being diet-fed on hate propaganda, these meetings were cordial. Porter was to write: 'No one would have supposed us to have been at war. Our conduct bore so much the appearance of a friendly alliance.'

But of course it wasn't. It was to be life or death for many. It was Porter's duty to trick Hillyar and Hillyar's duty not to be lured; and they understood each other perfectly well. Porter's gambits failed, he could not lure the British into a rash action.

A gale ended the manoeuvring. Strong winds cost the *Essex* an anchor, and she began to drag the remaining one. Rather than get up another anchor and go through all the hassle of repositioning and re-anchoring, Porter took a quick decision: shake out the sails, and away! *Phoebe* and *Cherub* were not caught napping; they raced out of Valparaiso on the heels of the American. But while still inside Chilean waters a squall struck the *Essex*. Normally, sail could have been reduced, but the running-rigging jammed; and, on the fail-safe principle, it was the topmast on the main-mast which went overboard, taking four or five seamen with it.

Porter had no option but to fight, at several disadvantages. The *Essex Junior* had not been able to follow him, so it would be one ship against two. Further, his ship was semi-disabled; the enemies would be faster and handier. And, finally, there was that fatal flaw in the armament: the *Essex* was armed only for a close fight. At long range, she could be battered to pieces without being able to reply effectively. Porter took his winged ship into a bay, anchored inshore and raised his battle ensigns.

About 4 p.m. the first shots were fired. The 36-gun *Phoebe* positioned herself off the stern of the *Essex*—the ends of any ship being the weak points structurally and necessarily mounting the least number of guns—while the 20-gun *Cherub* lay off the American's starboard bow. Porter played a sadly deficient hand as well as possible. He moved three of his six long-range 12-pounders aft to fire from the stern ports, and by using springs on his anchor cables tried to swing the ship round to bring his broadside to bear. But the spring lines were shot away and although he managed to cause damage and casualties to the British, this was as nothing to the results of the fire being poured into him.

The British drew off a little and then repositioned themselves carefully out of range of the bulk of the *Essex*'s armament, just as Porter had feared would one day happen, and continued to pound her. Porter's last card was to cut his cables and try to sail closer to his opponents; but most of the rigging controlling the sails had been shot away. It was easy for the British to open the range again. On board the American frigate one of the few 12-pounders had gone through three gun crews; most of them, or bits of them, were lying around the gun. A Scotsman, whose leg had been torn away, dragged himself to the rail and went overboard. Porter's final bid, to drive the frigate ashore, also failed, as wind and sea kept pushing her hull away. By 5.45 p.m. she was unmanageable.

Then a magazine blew up, flames erupting from the hatches. Porter told his surviving crew that they could swim to shore if they cared; and around six that evening the American flag came down. One of the first British officers to board, when he saw at close hand the heaped, dismembered corpses and the convulsions of the moaning wounded, fainted. This was 'the something splendid' that Porter had hoped to achieve; the sight of actual 'glory'.

Out of her 255 men, *Essex* had lost almost half—58 killed and 65 wounded. No crew could have done more. Hillyar's careful tactics had cost the British force five men killed and ten wounded.

The British captain's report to his superiors gave full credit to the conduct of David Porter and his crew:

> Her colours were not struck until the loss in killed and wounded
> was so awfully great, and her shattered condition so seriously bad,
> as to render further resistance unavailing.

Hillyar released Porter and the other survivors. Porter's final arrival through the British blockade to Long Island in a small boat had an inauspicious sequel. He was arrested as a British spy! However, when his identity was proved he was gratified to find himself a hero. It was his cruise as a raider in the Pacific which was remembered, not the loss of his ship and so many men.

The irony of the whole situation was that, a month after the loss of the *Essex* off far away Valparaiso, the defeated Emperor of France abdicated, the peace treaty being signed in May, 1814; peace with America soon followed.

A tradition of victory is a useful thing for any fighting force to have, particularly for a new one; consequently the US Navy added the *Essex* to its roll of frigate honours. A certain cynicism is in order. On the British side there is always the official emphasis on Nelson, whose victories were scored against French and Spanish fleets of poor quality, rather than on admirals fighting in less auspicious periods. But if it was actually possible to choose your own commander, under whom would you prefer to serve—David Porter or James Hillyar?

Chapter Nine

CONFEDERATE KAMIKAZE

Charleston, February 1864

The most severe conflict in North American history was the Civil War between the industrialised North (the Union) and the largely agricultural and cotton-growing South (the Confederates). The basic issue was for power—as in Europe through the centuries, a struggle for who was to be boss. The North American issue was decided by only a single war—although a most bloody and bitterly fought struggle.

To begin with, the Confederate armies proved much superior to those of the North; although numbers and industrial muscle eventually wore them down. To those factors must be added blockade by sea. By the end of the war the Union Navy possessed 600 warships, nearly as many as the British Navy had numbered during the revolt of the Colonies; and 60 of them were armoured. Some were steam-powered. In all they took, 1,500 prizes.

To combat this menacing stranglehold the Confederates replied in kind by commerce raiding, sometimes using ships built in England beyond the range of the Yankees, and sometimes by reverting to underwater weapons first pioneered by the rebel colonists of the North against the British.

The South's underwater weapons were given the general title of 'Davids'—for obvious reasons. There was a giant which needed killing, and these tiny weapons were intended to do it. The first type were, by the standards of the time, almost mass-produced. The victorious Union captured a number of them. They were not true submersibles at all, but a combination of new ideas with desperate expedients adopted because twentieth century technology had not yet arrived to provide the right weapons.

Basically, they were small whale-shaped vessels powered by a steam engine driving a propeller. They ploughed along, almost but not quite submerged, offering only a low profile which might be mistaken for a log, except for the open hatchway and funnel. The low profile, combined with an open hatch, was a good recipe for suicide: a few small waves, even the wash of a passing vessel, might easily swamp the 'submersible'. Then for a weapon it had only an explosive charge on a 20 ft wooden boom, known as a 'spar torpedo'; the wave effect of the explosion alone was almost certain to sink the 'David'. Yet they were built in numbers and volunteers came forward to man them. One of them even scored a hit.

This particular vessel had sunk previously when caught by the wake of a passing steamer, but had been raised, repaired and manned. On 5 October, 1863, she made a night attack on the armoured Union warship aptly named the *Ironsides* which was part of the blockade force opposite Charleston. The David was seen and reported as an object like a log approaching—the low superstructure some ten feet long could be so mistaken. The explosion of the 134-lb cannister of gunpowder fitted to the 'spar' in her nose rocked the anchorage but only slightly damaged the ironclad. The David appears to have been partially swamped causing Lt Glassell and two crew members to get out and swim. It seems that Glassell was captured but the two other men found the submersible still afloat but with fires out; they relit the boiler and escaped.

The Confederates developed a new type of undersea weapon; this really was a submersible, in some respects like a scaled-up, lengthened version of David Bushnell's *Turtle*. In this regard it perhaps owed something to various foreign experimenters in Germany, Russia and France. The spar torpedo was retained as a weapon but the propulsion was like Bushnell's, except that in a 60-ft long, narrow cylindrical hull eight crewmen helped work a propeller shaft by hand. Such a long, thin hull had to be markedly unstable, which in a submarine makes for dangerous living.

The inventor of this craft was Horace L. Hunley, who died testing the design. On trials the submarine, called a Hunley after its brave inventor, sank five times and was five times raised and repaired. On two of these occasions there were no survivors—all eight crew and their commander who controlled the boat from a tiny, portholed turret, perished; on the other occasions some men survived.

The prototype was called the *Pioneer*, the inventors being Hunley, another Confederate naval officer named James R. McLintock and Baxter Watson, a civilian engineer; the place was New Orleans and the year 1862. She was lost in Lake Pontchartrain, either by accident or by deliberate scuttling because the Union fleet under Captain Farragut was menacing the city.

The inventors escaped capture by the Union forces and began to build the second prototype at Mobile in the works of Parks & Lyons. This boat, some 25 feet long, sank in a storm while being towed away to Fort Morgan for an attack against the blockading fleet of the North; but no lives were lost.

As the Confederate authorities would not pay for a third prototype, Hunley offered to design a new boat and pay for it himself. His team were joined by W. A. Alexander and the third prototype was built, which after much loss and effort was to become the first submarine to score an absolute success in war, and became known thereafter as the *Hunley*.

Construction utilised existing methods developed by the industrial revolution. The basis was a 25-foot long boiler with a four-foot diameter. This was to be the hull. It was made higher by cutting it in half along its length and then inserting a one-foot wide iron strip between the two halves, thus making its height five feet, which gave a little more room to the men inside who would manually work the machinery which turned a helical propeller. The completed hull was given slightly pointed ends, so that the overall length now was 30 feet. Access was through two small hatchways, one at each end of the hull, sealed by rubber gaskets on iron covers and topped by tiny conning towers fitted with glass observation ports. These were for the two officers who still had insufficient room to stand upright; they also blocked the way out, in the event of emergency, to the men slaving away at the cranking machine which drove the propeller. Between the two towers was a hinged one-inch diameter pipe four feet long, which could draw air into the boat while she was just under the surface—the forerunner of the snorkel tube used by German U-boats in the Second World War and by swimmers from about the same time.

The trim of the boat could be altered by ballast tanks fore and aft, operated by the officers in the towers; the officer at the stern tower also had to help crank the propeller, so was not idle. The captain, in the forward tower, controlled the hydroplanes, had a mercury depth gauge to help him and a small magnetic compass. Illumination, after sub-mergence, was by the light of candles.

In this way, nine men were to be sent to war and break the Union blockade.

Lieutenant John Payne of the Confederate Navy was appointed her first captain in 1863, when she was moved to Charleston as the base for her first operation. A trial run was to be made there first of all, and as the submarine with hatches open was slowly cranked away by the slave gang below, the wash of a passing paddle-steamer swept over her low hull and water poured down the open hatches into the interior. With virtually no freeboard, the vessel had little reserve buoyancy; just a small weight of water was enough to tip the balance and send her and eight men to the bottom. Only John Payne, standing in the forward tower, was able to get out.

The hull with its gruesome cargo was raised and again prepared for sea trials; and was again swamped while on the surface with hatches open, this time by a sudden squall. Payne got out, followed by two other men; but the remaining six drowned. The reluctance to close hatches early, which was the cause of both disasters, may have been due partly to fouling of the air which must have soon become apparent after closing down, and perhaps also to an assumption that it would be easier to escape if they were open than if they were closed. No doubt there was a symbolical finality in the closing of the hatches above them, which in fact made them safer, even if only marginally.

Once more the *Hunley* was raised and its cargo of white, drowned corpses removed, while notices were posted in town calling for further volunteers to man the untried attack submarine.

When again manned for a trial the *Hunley* was secured alongside a ship in the port, the crew inside and the hatches open for ventilation. Some combination possibly of wind and tide, or wind against tide, made the other ship swing at its moorings and slam violently against the submarine, forcing it over so that once again water poured through the open hatches into the interior.

For the third time, unsurprisingly, John Payne escaped; but also three other men. In the first accident the *Hunley* had taken eight lives, in the second disaster six, in the third and latest, five. The odds on survival were becoming better, probably because each new crew had worked out a drill for this emergency. Even so, three accidents had cost nineteen men their lives.

The Charleston garrison's commander, General Beauregard, forbade any attempt to salvage the boat, but James McLintock, Hunley's fellow officer and inventor, successfully argued: 'If I can bring my own men down from Mobile, the men who built her, we'll prove that she can fight.'

When the men from Parks & Lyons arrived from Mobile, a series of successful diving trials were carried out, with Hunley himself as captain and Thomas Parks as Second Officer. The official report on the final trial dive on 15 October, 1863, said that the submarine

> left the wharf at 9.25 a.m. and disappeared at 9.35. As soon as she sank air bubbles were seen to rise and from this fact it is supposed that the hole in the top by which men entered was not properly closed.

This time there were no survivors. Some men had apparently drowned almost immediately; others, including Hunley and Parks, might have lasted an hour before becoming unconscious from breathing foul air; certainly they had tried to escape, for both these bodies were found with arms raised as if to open the hatch.

General Beauregard, who had authorised the attempt, was present at the salvage:

> The spectacle was indescribably ghastly. The unfortunate men were contorted into all sorts of horrible attitudes, some clutching candles . . . others lying on the bottom tightly grappled together. And the blackened faces of all presented the expression of their despair and agony.

Nevertheless, there was a war on, the most bloody in the history of North America; with more dead and wounded than in either of the two World Wars or the colonial Vietnam affair. Beauregard authorised further trials of the underwater weapon; as usual, by volunteers only and each man warned of the *Hunley*'s record.

It had now been established that the cause of this last accident was 'pilot error'—and that it had been made by Hunley himself, the man who best of all should have known the technical details of the vessel. The bulkheads fore and aft, which also acted as ballast tanks, did not, like the watertight compartments of the liner *Titanic* of 1912, reach the top of the hull. Hunley had opened the seacock so as to submerge the boat, apparently intending a steep dive, and had forgotten to close the seacock again; consequently, water must have slopped over the top of the bulkhead, flooding the craft beyond recovery.

A new crew came forward, all inexperienced submariners now as the inventors and manufacturers were dead, and as a trial run in safe conditions were told to carry out a dummy attack on their depot ship, the *Indian Chief*. The *Hunley* was seen to dive but did not come up again. A Confederate officer wrote:

> After a week's efforts she was brought to the surface and the crew of seven were found in a bunch near the manhole. Lieutenant Dixon said they had failed to close the after valve (to the stern ballast tank).

Other reports, however, pointed to a different cause—a cable hanging down from the *Indian Chief* which had fouled the controls. Unarguably, seven more men had died, bringing the *Hunley*'s toll to thirty-five.

A new captain was chosen, Lieutenant George E. Dixon, and a new crew of volunteers shipped. On the evening of 17 February, 1864, the salvaged *Hunley* crept out of Charlestown harbour. This was no trial. This was an operation.

Carried down on the blockading Union fleet by the ebb tide, the *Hunley* was last seen on the surface just before she dived. Dixon had no periscope and would have been forced to rely on a small compass for direction, a pocket watch for distance run and a guttering candle for illumination.

Among the blacked-out warships riding at anchor off the Confederate port was the *Housatonic*, a new 1,240-ton Union corvette. It was 8.45 p.m. when her acting master, J. R. Crosby, spotted an unidentified object approaching and, with the promptitude that only real war brings, ordered the anchor raised and the engine to go astern. Even so, he was too late.

A vast explosion reverberated around Charleston Bay as the Hunley's spar torpedo set off the magazine of the *Housatonic*. The Union ship heeled over and then sank by the stern until she arrived at the bottom with parts of her masts and rigging sticking out of the water as a handy refuge for her crew, of whom only five lost their lives.

The attacker was not seen again and it was assumed that she had escaped. But a few weeks later, while divers were exploring the hull of the sunken Union warship, they found the Hunley's narrow hull lying by the hole her spar torpedo had blown in the side of her opponent, possibly dragged down by the inrush of water. Inside the little submarine were seven bodies.

The *Hunley* had cost the Confederacy forty-two lives; it had cost the Union five men and a sizeable warship, the first ship ever to be sunk by a submarine. The memory of the men who volunteered to be her crew, as time after time she sank on trials and was salvaged full of contorted corpses, must surely rank as among the bravest of the brave.

A third type of 'David' was designed, which lacked underwater capability but because of that had more reserve buoyancy. This was simply a picket-boat, steam-propelled, fitted with ballast tanks and capped by an armoured turtle-back deck. The attack had to be carried out entirely on the surface, the low silhouette being hard to see at night and the upper part proof against small arms fire. In April 1864 the Union vessel *Minnesota* was sunk off Newport News by such a vessel which—unusually—escaped after her attack.

So, although the 'Davids' did not slay Goliath, they did score some historic successes. But the submarine as a workable warship had to wait a while longer; for more efficient motive power—petrol engines, diesel engines, electric engines; and a 'torpedo' which was really a small, very high-speed submarine capable of striking and killing from a great distance.

Sir Richard Grenville of the *Revenge*, fatally wounded in his struggle with the Spaniards off the Azores in 1591.
Photo: National Maritime Museum, Greenwich

Robert Blake, hero of Santa Cruz de Tenerife in 1657.
Photo: National Maritime Museum, Greenwich

The Battle of Barfleur, 1692. *Photo: National Maritime Museum, Greenwich*

Replica of the *Turtle*, the amazing embryo submarine used by the Americans against HMS *Eagle* in 1776.
Photo: Royal Navy Submarine Museum, Gosport

John Paul 'Jones', whose chequered career in the American Navy brought him belated acclaim.
Photo: National Maritime Museum, Greenwich

Above: The *Bon Homme Richard* and the *Seraphis* off Flamborough Head in 1779. From an engraving by Laponière-Fittle. *Photo: National Maritime Museum, Greenwich* Below: The Battle of the Winter Storm in the Bay of Audierne, 1797: the *Droits de l'Homme* engaged by the British frigates *Indefatigable* and *Amazon*. From a painting by Mayer. *Photo: Musée de la Marine, Paris*

Above: The Battle of the Basque Roads, 1809. From an engraving by Robert Dodd. *Photo: National Maritime Museum, Greenwich* Below: The capture of the US frigate *Essex* by the British frigate *Phoebe* and the sloop *Cherub*, Valparaiso, 1814. From a painting by George Ropes. *Photo: Peabody Museum of Salem*

Chapter Ten

NEUTRAL AGAINST THE NORTH

The Career of Mystery Ship No.290, 1862–4

The Confederate States steamship *Alabama*'s record as a raider was unmatched. In twenty months at sea she sank or seized 69 vessels and did harm to Union commerce which far outdid David Porter's toll in the Pacific against the British. She had no base and was forced to live off the ships she took. For long she was a mystery ship, and especially so at her building, when she was simply job No.290 at the yard of John Laird & Sons at Birkenhead, near Liverpool in England.

The Southern States did not have the industrial resources to match the Union's shipbuilding programme. Therefore they initiated a programme of shipbuilding abroad, where the Yankee writ did not run—or, at any rate, not much. One of those places was England. Of course, there was a Neutrality Act by which foreign powers were not supposed to give aid to either side, but ways could be found to circumvent the Act; given the will there is always a way. And in England there was much goodwill towards the South and not just because of the importance of the cotton trade; in three days an appeal in Liverpool raised £30,000, a vast sum then, for the relief of the Confederate wounded. And every British-built raider that sank a Yank got a cheer.

In June 1861 a captain in the Confederate Navy, James Dunwoody Bulloch, arrived in Liverpool, the great port and ship building centre on the Mersey. In August he contracted with John Laird & Sons to build for him what was ostensibly a merchant ship, for the price of £47,000.

The American Civil War had occurred squarely in the middle of technological revolution. Timber was giving way to iron and although steam propulsion was now accepted, the early machinery was so inefficient and so heavy on fuel that it was installed in what were

basically sailing ships as auxiliary only—to claw off a lee shore, to
manoeuvre in difficult rivers or harbours—or to run away from trouble,
or to catch up with a prey.

No.290 had an oak-built hull sheathed in copper below the waterline;
that might indicate intended service in tropical waters, where wood-
eating organisms were a constant danger to timber hulls. She was 220
feet long with a beam of 32 feet, and rated at 1,040 tons. She was rigged
as a three-masted barque. She had two 300 h.p. steam engines which
gave her a useful speed of 13 knots in emergency, and she carried 350
tons of coal—eighteen days' steaming. And another pointer—No.290
carried condensing apparatus to produce fresh water. That, together
with her barque rig, would enable 290 to exist for a time independent of
bases.

The United States Consul in Liverpool, Thomas H. Dudley, kept a
watch on the construction, employing a spy, Matthew Maguire, who
must have been pretty obvious for no one would talk to him. All he was
able to report, in March 1862, was that 290 was a far better ship than
the *Oreto*, the first vessel built in Liverpool for the Confederates,
becoming the raider CSS *Florida*.

To enquirers, her builders stated that she was to become the Spanish
Barcelona; but when she was launched in May 1862 by an anonymous
lady, her name had become *Enrica*. A British captain, Matthew J.
Butcher of the Cunard line, was appointed to her, although during her
first trial runs in June it was reported that a number of American
gentlemen were aboard. The Union consul tried to get legal action
taken against what he claimed was clearly a warship, contravening the
Neutrality laws. The elaborate magazines and powder canisters were
too expensive for a merchant ship, and the purpose of the circular metal
rings screwed to her decks could be only to take swivel guns.

The consul's nagging, together with a rumour that the Union
warship USS *Tuscarora* was heading for Liverpool, helped to speed her
departure. On 28 July the *290/Barcelona/Enrica* came out of dock for
further trials, decked with flags. A party of guests were entertained to
lunch, but when it was over they were told that the ship was staying out
all night and that they must now go ashore in the tug *Hercules* which
accompanied them.

Bulloch, the Confederate agent, went with them in the tug; his next
task being to pick up a crew of Liverpool seamen to man the raider,
which was now lying off the pilot station at Port Lynas on the coast of

Anglesey. There was some trouble with the seamen's women, who wanted a share of the men's advance payments when they had signed articles. Then the mystery ship set sail, apparently for the West Indies. Bulloch transferred to a fishing boat off the Giants' Causeway in Northern Ireland and went back to Liverpool. There were still loose strings to be tied up. The mystery ship had no guns and no officers.

She went, not to the West Indies, but to the Azores. Off Terceira she rendezvoused with the brig *Agrippina*, which carried the raiders' armament. Shortly after, sailing from Liverpool in the steamship *Bahama*, Bulloch brought her real captain, Raphael Semmes, and other Confederate officers, as well as her permanent crew of British seamen.

Guns, ammunition and coal were transfered to the *Enrica*, which still flew the British flag; then, on 24 August, 1862, she sailed out into international waters, fired a gun, lowered the British ensign and hoisted the flag of the Confederacy, to the strains of 'Dixie'. Captain Semmes announced that they were now the commerce raider *Alabama*, but the men had a choice—go back to England in the *Bahama* or sign on with the Confederacy and expect danger, privation and naval discipline. The promised pay was higher than the average for the jobs, plus prize money, and most signed.

The CSS *Alabama* began her career of destruction with a crew of 27 American officers and 82 British seamen, mostly from Merseyside. Her armament now was six long 32-pounder guns plus one rifled 100-pounder Blakeley gun and one eight-inch 68-pounder shell-gun. Total weight of shot: 360 lbs. The *Agrippina* acted as her collier.

Semmes believed in spending no more than two months in any one area. This first cruise was in the Atlantic, starting from the Azores. The raider survived a cyclone, burned twenty ships and sank a warship, the USS *Hatteras*. Then she moved to the South Atlantic, operating off Brazil; ten prizes taken, one of them to be fitted out as a Confederate vessel. Then Cape Town in Southern Africa, then up the coast of West Africa. Her forays over twenty months included Java, India and the Mozambique Channel; the South China Sea, the Gulf of Mexico. The raider had no friendly base so supplied herself from the ships she captured, 69 of them in all—a world record. This one deadly ship was mainly responsible for the decimation of Union commerce, which dropped from 2,500,000 tons in 1861 to 1,100,000 in 1865. But it was not enough to offset the effect of the powerful Union blockade of the South.

In June 1864 the *Alabama*, in need of docking and refitting, put into Cherbourg, but the work had still not been authorised by the French when the Union sloop USS *Kearsarge*, under Captain John A. Winslow, arrived. Semmes decided that he had no option but to fight. The two vessels were not in theory all that unequal—the Union sloop was about the same size and armed with four short 32-pounders (as against the raider's six long 32-pounders), two eleven-inch smooth-bore pivot guns and one 30-pounder rifled gun (against the Confederate's one rifled 100-pounder and one eight-inch 68-pounder shell gun). The *Kearsarge*'s total projectile weight was 430 pounds, against the raider's 360 pounds. It is difficult in modern times to weigh these pieces of artillery one against the other, for this was a period of rapid change in armament, with no real guide lines because they were so rapidly superseded by other weaponry, in its turn almost immediately obsolete. Further, the raider's need to repair and refit is hard to appraise in terms of the battle.

It was a fine Sunday morning when the *Alabama* emerged from Cherbourg. The fight took the form of circling, the Union captain trying to cross ahead or astern of the raider, always the position of advantage, and Semmes denying him the chance and keeping his broadside guns in action. In an hour the *Alabama* fired 370 rounds, but scored only 28 hits. The *Kearsarge* managed to shorten the range to 500 yards, when her two big eleven-inch guns seemed to have gained the upper hand in the duel; there were now many dead and wounded on the raider's decks and she began to sink lower in the water.

The Union sloop could now cross ahead of the raider so as to rake her, and Semmes hauled down his flag. About noon a white flag was flown in the raider but someone obviously didn't agree, for he fired a gun. The *Kearsarge* replied, and a few minutes later the *Alabama* sank.

The battle, which had lasted from around 10 a.m. to just after noon, had attracted a number of spectators, one of which was the British yacht *Deerhound*. Captain Winslow asked the owner of *Deerhound*, Robert Lancaster, if he would kindly help pick up survivors. The *Kearsarge* herself took 70 prisoners, of whom 20 were wounded, three fatally; 12 other men had been either killed or drowned as a result of the battle. Lancaster, with the *Deerhound*, saved 42, of whom 14 were officers, including Captain Semmes; but instead of docilely handing them over to the victorious Americans, Lancaster took them to Southampton where they were given a hero's welcome. The *Kearsarge* had three wounded, one fatally. Clearly, there was some great discrepancy between the two vessels and their armaments.

The British had been so blatantly neutral in favour of the South that, after the war, what was now a theoretically united State of North America pressed the British Government for reparations, apparently threatening to invade Canada by way of reprisal. In 1872 their claim was settled by a payment by Britain of 15,000 dollars (over three million pounds by today's valuation) in gold.

From then on, until modern times, the story went into the history books. But with the rise of the 'Heritage Ships' industry the un-discovered wreck of the *Alabama*, like that of John Paul Jones's *Bon Homme Richard*, became a target for the Museum-orientated wreck-finders. But this wreck received great support in technical resources because, it was widely believed, Captain Semmes had built up a 'treasure' from the ships he had captured. Wreck-finding tends to be long, arduous and costly, particularly where a certain named ship is required and not just any old wreck, with which naturally the world's seabeds are littered.

It was the legendary 'treasure' which first attracted the French Navy to the search—and also perhaps the challenge of the difficulty. Most navies have teams of mine-hunters and divers whose vessels are equipped with various types of undersea detection gadgets, normally geared to finding quite small, specified objects—the average ground mine, for instance, might be a cylinder six feet long and perhaps 18 inches across. Once located by sonar or whatever, the object is in-spected by divers and, if positive, is then either made safe or, more usually, blown *in situ*.

Naturally, the French Navy had such a team stationed at Cherbourg, so the *Alabama* was a local wreck, right on their doorstep—if she could be found. They had most of them read Robert Stenuit's *The Book of Lost Treasures*, which devoted a chapter to the raider. His judgement was that the wreck would be either very difficult or virtually impossible to find. Stenuit, a Belgian diver, was a most experienced man in the wreck-finding business and was backed by Comex, the French firm involved in the revolutionary new deep-diving technology required by gas and oil exploration in the North Sea.

His assessment must have provoked the mine-hunting divers who also had the use of new, revolutionary technology—based on finding objects on the seabed (which is a totally different branch of the underwater business). Their search, with French naval gear, was carried out on a part-time basis, begun in 1978 and almostly certainly entered in the logs as 'training', the all-purpose standby in any Service. If that won't wash, then 'scientific research' (as with Japanese whaling vessels) is another gambit to be tried. 'Treasure-hunting', while sure of popular support, infuriates the archaeologists and is not to be recommended; at least not openly, but a few hints may suffice to bring in any particular type of equipment required, however costly.

The search area was centred on the three-mile limit, the extent of French ocean territory, where the *Kearsarge* had waited for the *Alabama*. It was a very large area indeed, at an average indicated chart depth of around 180 feet at low water; with low visibility and currents up to three knots. There were also far too many false targets littering the bottom, which will show as interesting anomalies to sonar and to magneto-meters. Many diving teams came and went during the eight years of unsuccessful search.

The first and obvious—too obvious—thing to do was to check on all wrecks reported by the hydrographic service. They were easier to find but by definition could NOT be the *Alabama*, which was a wooden wreck sunk around 125 years before. The ones that showed to the hydrographic vessels were virtually all modern wrecks standing fairly high off the seabed. But even when found, they could not always be identified by the means available—all that showed to the diver's eyes or the TV-camera's lens at any one time was a couple of feet of some structure or other. Sometimes, in the short dive-time available, they entirely failed to find the source of the sonar echo, let alone inspect it, let alone identify it.

A fresh search under Lt-Cdr Duclos, used a new method of navigation installed in the *Circe*. Their first wreck was found within thirty minutes and dismissed as a cargo ship from the Second World War. The second wreck to show on sonar proved to be another cargo ship, of uncertain date. While searching for the third wreck indicated on sonar, the divers swam across a quite different wreck which had NOT been shown by the sonar. This was all on the first day of the new search programme; by 2.30 p.m. the divers surfaced to report that the new wreck had a wooden hull and that they had brought up a plate from it.

Naturally, there was great excitement; but they came up with two distinct difficulties. Firstly, it was not enough to find a wreck which might well be the *Alabama*; they had to prove it. Secondly, they were

Navy divers, not archaeologists or naval historians and experts on the construction of historic vessels.

Capitaine de Vaisseau Max Gérout was sent to Cherbourg by the French Navy's Chief of Staff to analyse the findings. He concluded that it probably was the *Alabama* because (a) the remains were of a wooden-built steamship (witness reports of a funnel being seen and lumps of coal); and (b) there were a number of cannon of the classical type which were in outline standard for more than three centuries, and of which the *Alabama* had possessed six.

Gérout's conclusions had to be tentative because the divers' reports could not be wholly relied on. At the great depths involved a severe narcosis is experienced which affects the mental faculties (known to the crude English as 'the narcs'); the divers were not experienced either in archaeology or the construction of ancient ships and might well convince themselves that they had seen what they had been told to look for, and the plan they drew was not very precise, understandably because their time on the wreck was limited and no one diver had swum from one end of it to the other—15 minutes being their total allowed bottom time because of decompression requirements.

Further research on the three different types of plates raised tended towards the *Alabama* hypothesis. They were all made in Staffordshire, the English 'Potteries' near Liverpool, and the firms concerned had been in business for the period coinciding with the construction of the raider in nearby Liverpool. But as Gérout pointed out, these firms must have supplied many ships with pottery. Even if it was the raider, the plates might have been taken from a prize.

In May-June 1988 Géroux led a successful expedition which produced a good site plan and many usable photographs; the loan of a small submarine for a week and the work of an underwater film crew recorded the evidence for outsiders. It could now be seen that the remains were heeled thirty degrees to starboard, protected by a sandbank, but the port side is less well preserved and at the stern the depth of preservation is small—the boss of the propeller can be seen; similarly with the bow area. The central hull has been protected by the boilers; and a litter of debris lies all around. The receipt of builder's plans finally removed much of the doubt.

Two perfectly good models exist in Liverpool and the dock where she was built still exists. A maritime museum is proposed devoted to Liverpool shipping in general and the *Alabama* in particular. As a

centre-piece a full-scale replica of the raider is to be built. Hopefully.
Actually raising the wreck would not be impossible, merely very costly;
the conservation of a comparatively large hull and contents would
prove even more expensive, and then a large complex and staff to
display her would be required.

In December 1989 it was announced that another British-built
blockade-runner had been found and given Government protection.
This was the paddle-steamer *Iona*, built at Govan in Scotland in 1863,
intended in fact for the Confederacy but sunk off Lundy in the Bristol
Channel while on passage to America in 1864, the same year the
Alabama went down.

Chapter Eleven

THE LONG HAUL TO THE FAR EAST

And the Straits of Tsushima, May 1905

The Straits of Tsushima lie between Japan and Korea. When one looks at a map the names fairly leap out off the paper. On the Japanese mainland, one large port—Nagasaki. In Korea, several names—Pusan, Seoul, even the Yalu River. All these names again!

What Britain and America did between them, halfway through the nineteenth century, with some help from the Russians, was to let two genie out of their bottles—the two closed, superior societies (as they saw themselves) of China and Japan. The more volatile proved to be Japan, opened to trade through treaty ports after the visit in 1853 of two United States warships, the 3,000-ton paddle frigates *Mississippi* and *Susquehanna*, the only powerful warships that the Americans had at that time. When Commodore Matthew Perry's paddlers anchored near Tokyo that summer of 1853, the apprehensive Japanese described them as 'black ships of evil mien'. That is not how the Americans looked at it. Their imperialism was regarded as 'carrying the Gospel of God to the Heathen'.

In turn, for few seem to be exempt, the Japanese too turned expansionist; initially in China and Korea, where they clashed with Russian imperialism—the Russian naval base of Vladivostok nudges the north-eastern tip of Korea. The British, having just fought a war with Russia in the Crimea, made them an automatic enemy and Japan an automatic ally. As the leading industrial and naval power in the world, Britain was an attractive ally and it was British officers who helped form the new Navy and British shipbuilders who constructed her first battleships—they resembled exactly the latest British designs for her own Royal Navy.

In a war with China, Japan obtained territory in Manchuria

including the potential naval base of Port Arthur; but the Russians, with support from the Germans and the French, forced the Japanese to relinquish their gains. Then the Russians turned Port Arthur into a naval base for their Far Eastern fleet. Seething, in February 1904 the Japanese prepared and made a surprise strike without declaration of war. The Russian fleet was decimated, the first defeat of a major European power by an oriental one—and a foretaste of the future.

Port Arthur was important to both sides because, unlike Vladivostok, it was ice-free throughout the year. In Russian hands it closely menaced Japan's communications with her conquests in Korea; but the garrison was 5,500 miles from Moscow with a single one-track railway which did not run all the way, so that the enormous Russian army could not be quickly brought to the battlefield. The Japanese could not risk too much at sea, because their shipbuilding yards were in Britain; they had no facilities of their own to construct armoured vessels.

The Japanese landed their battle-experienced armies in Manchuria and assaulted Port Arthur. Here they discovered, as the British had in South Africa against the Boer farmers, that the magazine rifle made traditional infantry assaults suicidal, and were forced to besiege the fortified port. The Russian soldiers fought stubbornly, as their casualties showed, but their commanders were of uneven quality. Stössel, who commanded there, issued this order:

> To-day, near the church, I met two officers with a lady; she was wearing an officer's rifle forage-cap . . . I do not think that I need dwell upon how out of place it seems for one of the female sex to wear a military cap with a cockade, when even retired officers and reserves are not allowed by regulations to wear them.

On the Japanese side there had been astounding progress from a medieval society to a twentieth century one. For instance, Colonel Teruda, a regimental commander, had earlier begun his military career while wearing chain armour and carrying a battle axe. The Russians, on the other hand, were still wedded to the doctrine of naked steel, compelled to keep their bayonets fixed at all times, even though this contraption makes rifle shooting erratic and ineffective. The Russians were mentally stagnant whereas the eager Japanese were keen to learn.

The aim of the Japanese was to defeat the Russian army in the Far East and force a peace on their terms—total victory was not possible.

But Port Arthur had proved tougher than they thought, and they had lost two of their irreplaceable battleships to Russian mines; so the remnants of the Russian Far East fleet now in Port Arthur harbour, if united with a relief fleet already on its way from the Baltic, could well defeat the Japanese at sea.

The Russian Baltic Fleet consisted of ships either too new or too old. There were four modern battleships—*Borodino, Orel, Alexander III* and *Suvaroff*—armed with four 12-inch guns and twelve 6-inch quick-firers for close-in defence against torpedo boats. The main armament bore no relation whatever to nineteenth-century guns, even where they were 11-inch or more. Those were just smooth-bore muzzle-loaders of limited velocity and range; perhaps a mile effectively. The twentieth-century 12-inch had a range of ten or twelve miles, shortly to be doubled. Their engines, which could drive the battleships at up to 18 knots, were coal-fired; so frequent coaling stops were required. There were no sails any more; and no boarding.

With these brand new ships sailed older battleships and many smaller vessels including cruisers and torpedo boats; and something new—a fleet train (as it is now called). The warships were accompanied by a fleet of colliers and hospital ships. The Admiral was Rojdestvensky, aged 56, a veteran of a brief war with Turkey and mercurially temperamental. Many of the crew were raw and ignorant, others the type every CO wants to get rid of.

Japan had opened the war without warning by a torpedo boat strike against Russian warships lying off Port Arthur—a forerunner of the Pearl Harbour attack of 1941. And the menace of the torpedo boat was high in the Russian naval consciousness, particularly as reports in Danish newspapers told of a flotilla of improvised torpedo boats which the Japanese had somehow organised even inside the Baltic, ready to waylay the relief fleet.

The Tsar inspected the fleet at Reval on 9 October, 1904, and a week later it set out from the various Baltic ports, from Kronstadt to Libau. While still inside the Baltic various shadowy vessels were glimpsed and fire was opened on them by the Russians, who steamed on regardless for the North Sea where further enemy flotillas were rumoured to await them. Behind them they left a very angry Swedish merchantman and the startled crew of a German fishing vessel.

Steaming by night, the armada of some 40 Russian ships passed into the North Sea and, at a point where they were some thirty miles away from where they thought they were, a mass of torpedo boats was seen awaiting them. The Russians flashed on their searchlights to blind the attackers, who replied by firing a green flare. Then Rojdestvensky's warships opened a deadly fire. The thunderous bombardment lasted for twenty minutes as the battleships sought to sink or discourage their deadly little opponents. One was certainly sunk, many seemed to have been hit. It would have been unwise to linger within torpedo range so the Russian armada sailed regardless for its appointment off Korea.

Next morning what was left of the prowling torpedo boat squadron limped into the East Coast port of Hull with battle damage. First to return to base, their flags at half-mast, were the *Mino* of Captain Whelpton with sixteen shell holes in her above the waterline, followed by the *Moulmein* under Captain Hames, also carrying battle scars. They reported that a third vessel from their flotilla had been sunk by the shellfire with both the captain and the second officer killed and most of the men wounded. This unfortunate craft was the *Crane*; her dead were George Smith and John Leggot.

The deadly ambush which the Russian battle fleet had encountered had been in fact the steam trawlers from Hull peacefully fishing, which had fired a green flare to signify this. The reaction in England was of outrage and anger. But pity might have been a more suitable response. A battlefleet which had tried for twenty minutes to destroy a group of slowly moving unarmed trawlers, and had managed only to hit one and damage two, had a rendezvous with an implacable armed opponent at the end of their 18,000-mile journey.

In a considerable feat of organisation, they all got there, coaling at a number of ports *en route*, carrying out their own repairs far from any Russian base. And they arrived too late to join with the remaining warships of the Far East fleet in Port Arthur.

While the Baltic fleet was leaving Dakar in French West Africa, the Japanese army assaulted 203 Metre Hill, which overlooked the harbour of Port Arthur and, if captured, would enable the Japanese to sink the Russian ships still in port. The struggle lasted into December. When it finally fell to a tremendous bombardment by Japanese siege artillery followed by yet another assault by heroic Japanese infantry, a British newspaper correspondent wrote:

This mountain would have been an ideal spot for a Peace Conference. There have probably never been so many dead crowded into so small a space since the French stormed the great redoubt at Borodino . . . The Japanese are horrible to look at when dead, for their complexion turns quite green, which gives them an unnatural appearance . . . There were practically no bodies intact; the hillside was carpeted with odd limbs, skulls, pieces of flesh, and the shapeless trunks of what had once been human beings, inter-mingled with pieces of shells, broken rifles, twisted bayonets, grenades, and masses of rock loosed from the surface by the explosions.

On 6 December, 1904, the Japanese guns were emplaced on that horrible battlefield and within days the remnants of the Russian fleet in the harbour were wrecks. The Baltic fleet was still only at Madagascar, giving the Japanese admiral, the diminutive Heimachoro Togo, time to return with his fleet to Japan to refit for the coming battle.

On 27 May, 1905, the Baltic Fleet reached the Straits of Tsushima between Japan and Korea, knowing that Port Arthur had fallen and that they had no refuge until Vladivostok. Rojdestvensky had already left his colliers and other auxiliaries behind at Shanghai in the mouth of the Yangtse.

Togo's British-built battleships had a speed advantage over the Russian and French-built vessels of Rojdestvensky, and Japanese gunnery was faster and more accurate. The battle ended with the Russian battleships huddled in a crowd, guns silent; some were actually captured and entered in the Japanese Navy after repair. The only survivors to reach Vladivostok were the small cruiser *Almaz* and two destroyers. The Russians had fought bravely, but bravery is not enough. It was the most decisive defeat in history of one fleet by another.

British sympathy throughout had been with the Japanese, even before the outrage in the North Sea, for which the Tsar later apologised and paid £65,000 compensation. The only Russian success had been achieved by the small, unhonoured minelayers, which had earlier accounted for the only two Japanese battleship losses of the campaign.

It reads oddly now, but the heroism shown by the Japanese assault infantry at Port Arthur resulted in the writing of a popular song in England, about 'a little Jappy soldier, wounded and dying'.

The battle was decisive in two ways. A Russian naval witness wrote:

Far from assisting our army, Rojdestvensky brought it irreparable harm. It was the defeat of his squadron at Tsushima that brought about negotiations and peace at a time when our army was ready to advance—a million strong.

Although in fact both sides were exhausted, the Japanese physically, the Russians by unrest and riots at home, there can hardly have been a more decisive battle in history. An Asiatic power had thoroughly beaten a powerful European nation, by adopting modern technology and improving it.

Chapter Twelve

THE DOOMED ADMIRALS

Coronel and Falklands, November–December 1914

While Japan was beginning to shake the power structure of the East, the European balance had also been decisively altered by the emergence of a new nation—Germany—cobbled out of a patchwork of sleepy, courtly states. The new Germany of Bismarck, when allied to Austria, was the most populous grouping on the continent. Crudely expressed, for the approximate period of the two World Wars of the twentieth century the German nation numbered some eighty million, against the approximately forty million of France. So it was the threat of German domination which now replaced that of the French, and therefore England allied her population, also 40 million, with the traditional enemy against the traditional ally. She could also bring into the balance her Empire, just as the Germans could add Hungary and other East European states to their calculations of conscript classes and industrial resources. Both battalions were equally big and therefore the struggle had to be long and bloody. Of the two future superpowers, Russia was knocked out of the war early and the United States entered late.

On 2 October, 1905, less than half a year after Tsushima, HMS *Dreadnought* was laid down at Portsmouth and launched on 10 February, 1906, by King Edward VII, sailing for her trials on 6 October that year—little over a year to build a revolutionary battleship which immediately made all other battleships obsolete. She displaced 18,110 tons, mounted a main armament of no less than ten 12-inch guns, was protected by 11-inch armour, and could exceed 21 knots. She was the first of the 'all big-gun' battleships; no medium-guns, only small anti-torpedo boat pieces as secondary armament. Was it wise to build such a ship when Britain's fleet of now obsolete battleships was the largest in the world? Everyone now would start from scratch. And they certainly did, so much so that all modern battleships were for many years referred to as 'dreadnoughts'.

The *Dreadnought* was powered by Parsons turbines instead of the cumbersome, awkward reciprocating engines of the past. This, too, was a revolutionary move but it worked well. Admiral 'Jackie' Fisher had backed her and he was so pleased with the result that he invented a new class of warship called the battlecruiser. Her tonnage was to be about the same as that of the *Dreadnought* but the hull was designed to reach a speed of 25½ knots; this to be achieved by reducing the weight of the armament from ten 12-inch guns to eight, and reducing also the amount and thickness of armour protection. The first of the new type to be built was the *Invincible*. Fisher's idea was that while they were too fast to be caught by a battleship which could destroy them, they would be fast enough to catch a scouting or raiding armoured cruiser and well enough armed to dispose of her without much trouble. The *Dreadnought* had proved a winner. How would *Invincible* and her sisters perform?

All these big ships were still coal-fired or mixed coal and oil-firing. The first completely oil-fired capital ships were the *Queen Elizabeth* class battleships laid down in 1912. These carried eight 15-inch guns in four turrets and were excellent ships, surviving the whole of the First World War and two of them even surviving the Second, in spite of U-boats and dive-bombers. As built they reached 25 knots, almost as fast as the battlecruisers but without their inferior armour. The secondary armament was twelve 6-inch guns. Whereas with the pre-dreadnoughts, battleships carried a wide range of artillery, making spotting the shell splashes extremely difficult, a ship with a main armament of really big guns, and a secondary anti-destroyer armament of much smaller weapons, made for easy spotting. There was no doubt what had caused the great columns of water to erupt around the target.

While hulls, armour, engines and armament had changed radically in a very short time, the controlling system for the ships remained much as it had been in Nelson's time or Drake's. With one exception. Wireless telegraphy, although in its infancy, did give the possibility of issuing orders from Whitehall to the man on the spot. Instead of Admirals being sent out with broad directives to be carried out in the way they decided was best in the light of actual events and circumstances, the super-Admiral back home—or the Minister who supposed himself an all-purpose expert—could interfere and confuse. Further, the very idea of delegation, of creating a highly-trained and experienced staff to help a commander, was not likely to lend itself to dynamic and dominating personalities such as Fisher or Churchill. Yet the fact was that the complexities involved in handling such modern fleets was totally beyond the capacity of any one man.

In the British Navy this was not realised, although in armies it was widely recognised. Consequently, when a mistake was made it was often hard to find out, not so much who was to blame, but what proportion of blame was to be allotted to (a) the man on the spot, (b) the super-Admiral in London, and (c) the politician jogging his elbow. This proved to be exactly so when there arose a controversy similar to that expressed by the Elizabethan sailors regarding the wisdom or foolishness of Grenville's conduct in the Azores, which cost England the *Revenge*.

When war broke out in August 1914, Germany had a colonial empire and squadrons abroad to protect it. In an Austrian port for repair were the battlecruiser *Goeben* and the light cruiser *Breslau*. The British Admiralty handled the matter so badly that both ships got to sea, bombarded French ports in North Africa, evaded the much stronger British Mediterranean Fleet, entered the Dardanelles and reached Constantinople, a feat which brought Turkey into the war on the side of Germany. A noted British naval historian, Christopher Lloyd, judged the British admiral guilty of lack of enterprise, compounded 'by the divided objectives and contradictory orders issued by the Admiralty'.

The next most formidable force was the Far Eastern Squadron of Vice-Admiral Graf von Spee, based at the defended port of Tsingtao in China. He had the two most efficient large armoured cruisers in the German Imperial Navy, *Scharnhorst* and *Gneisnau*, the former having won the Kaiser's Prize for gunnery, together with three unarmoured light cruisers, *Leipzig*, *Nürnberg* and *Emden*. *Emden* was shortly despatched to the Indian Ocean to begin a most successful career as a raider, and was replaced later by a similar light cruiser, the *Dresden*. The ships were modern and the crews long-service professionals who had been working together for two years.

The British Admiralty's plans to deal with them revealed lack of forethought and then hasty orders shortly afterwards contradicted. There were a number of exceptional reasons which explain this. Of course, the German fleet in home waters was the first menace to be considered, but the British Navy alone had a great superiority in numbers and could rely on help from the French Navy from the beginning of the war and soon afterwards from that of the Japanese. But there was no properly thought-out plan to deal with these detached German squadrons which could be most dangerous on the Allied sea routes. The Assistant Director of the Admiralty was approached on 5 August, 1914, by Winston Churchill, who was First Lord of the Admiralty. 'Now we have our war,' said the latter. 'The next thing is to decide how we are going to carry it on.'

Lacking a staff, who should already have produced plans for all areas of operations according to different circumstances, the war at sea was run by the First Lord (Churchill) who should not have interfered, and by the First Sea Lord (Prince Louis of Battenberg), a most able officer. But both, during the time leading up to the battle of Coronel on 1 November, 1914, were badly distracted by other events nearer home.

Battenberg, whose family was German, was at that time the victim of an unscrupulous derogatory campaign in the popular 'yellow press', implying that Britain's early set-backs at sea had occurred because the man in charge did not wish resolutely to prosecute the war against his own people. Of course, the British Royal Family were also of German origin, related to both the German Kaiser and the Russian Tsar. Nevertheless, this was a time when English mobs stoned German dachshunds and patriotic ladies gave white feathers to young men in civilian clothes. Had Battenberg managed to ignore this, he would have been superhuman (but it does help to explain the suicidal naval actions carried out in the Second World War by his son, Lord Louis Mountbatten). He also had to contend with a forceful and interfering First Lord. On 28 October, 1914, he resigned, and was succeeded by 'Jackie' Fisher who, in spite of his tremendous talents and superb energy, was sometimes wrong—and when he was wrong he was resoundingly wrong—and had split the Navy during his earlier quarrels with Admiral Lord Charles Beresford. It was not possible, apparently, to argue with Fisher; anyone who did not agree with him, instantly and wholeheartedly, was a troublemaker and must be got rid of. He was a hard-driving despot and got on very well with the First Sea Lord, Winston Churchill, the former journalist turned cavalryman, who actually took part as a combatant in the wars he covered for the newspapers. This desire to participate personally distracted him from doing the job he was paid for.

In October the First Lord of the Admiralty was obsessed with the advance of the German armies into Belgium, despatched a Naval brigade to their defence, left London to visit the front at a critical time for the Admiralty and actually suggested that he should assume personal command of the Naval brigade in Belgium, letting the sea war get on by itself. And that is more or less what it did do, to the undoing of the naval force sent to engage Graf von Spee with, as it happened, a much inferior force (although this was not fully realised at the Admiralty). The commander of the British force was unfortunately not very good at communicating, and as the Admiralty had really no very clear ideas of their own, he went to his death as a result and was blamed for it.

Rear-Admiral Sir Christopher Cradock was in charge of the force ordered to destroy Graf von Spee's Far East Squadron. He was to base himself on the Falklands, where there was a British coaling station and an enclosed harbour, and to go into the Pacific in search of the Germans. The very considerable naval forces available in the Pacific, including an Australian battlecruiser and several Japanese capital ships, were diverted by the Admiralty to operations connected with taking over German colonies in the Far East.

A powerful armoured cruiser, the *Defence*, had been ordered to join him; but the order had been countermanded by the Admiralty (but without notifying Cradock) so that his squadron of five ships contained only a single efficient modern vessel, a small, unarmoured light cruiser. Three of the rest were obsolescent vessels due to be scrapped, crewed mostly by reservists who had not had time to work up to full efficiency. His flagship was the armoured cruiser *Good Hope*, 14,100 tons, built in 1902, with two 9.2-inch and sixteen 6-inch guns (the latter in the hull so that they were unsighted half the time and half-drowned the rest of the time, especially in the heavy seas off the tip of South America). A similarly old ship, the armoured cruiser *Monmouth*, 9,800 tons, mounted only 6-inch guns, similar in layout to that of the *Good Hope*. The fast modern vessel was the unarmoured light cruiser *Glasgow*, 4,800 tons, built in 1911, armed with two 6-inch guns and ten 4-inch, and capable of 25 knots. Lumbering on behind was the old pre-Dreadnought battleship *Canopus* of 12,950 tons, armed with four 12-inch guns and twelve 6-inch, but built in 1899 and far too slow to support Cradock in trying to catch the faster Germans. The Admiralty convinced themselves that Cradock could anchor his squadron on her and so should be quite safe if anything went wrong; but they had also ordered him to find and engage the German squadron. Finally, there was an old liner, the 12,000-ton *Otranto*, armed with eight 4.7-inch guns and slower even than *Canopus* at about 15 knots. Her only use would be in a search screen proceeding slowly; in battle she would be a liability.

The German squadron, which had moved south away from the possible threat of Australian and Japanese warships, was now off the coast of Chile, not too far from the area where the American raider *Essex* under David Porter had come to grief. As we have seen, Graf von Spee's force consisted of two sister-ships, the 11,400-ton *Scharnhorst* and *Gneisnau*, each with eight 8.2-inch and six 5.9-inch guns, supported by the light cruisers *Leipzig, Nürnberg* and *Dresden*, of between 3,200 and 3,600 tons, built in 1906–8 and armed with ten 4.1-inch guns. *Scharnhorst* and *Gneisnau* had been built in 1907. It was a modern force and von Spee kept it concentrated.

Cradock did the best he could with what he had, sending the fast *Glasgow* ahead to seek the enemy, while he followed with his old cruisers and, far astern, the ancient nineteenth-century battleship lumbered after with the squadron's colliers. Towards the end of October, off Coronel on the coast of Chile, the *Glasgow* kept picking up messages which seemed to be from the *Leipzig*. In fact, von Spee was using the call-sign of a single ship to give the impression that there was only one of him instead of a full squadron of five. In his turn, he intercepted *Glasgow*'s messages, assumed that he was faced with a single ship only, and steamed south to cut her off.

The two squadrons did not come together as two compact groups, since they were dispersed to search wide areas of ocean. The seas were heavy and the light was fading. The enemy might still escape, if he wished. Neither Admiral so wished. Cradock tried to obtain the advantage of the sunset light to illuminate the Germans and keep his own ships in shadow; but the Germans were faster and he failed. The afterglow of sunset kept the British ships silhouetted and clear; the Germans shadowy and indistinct. At about 7 p.m. on 1 November, the Germans opened fire.

Over the darkened gale-torn sea, yellow gun flashes winked from *Scharnhorst* and *Gneisnau*, the former firing on the *Good Hope*, the latter on the *Monmouth*. Three salvoes and *Scharnhorst* had *Good Hope* bracketed. The Germans were steaming twenty knots into a head sea and firing at a range of five miles; it was good gunnery. *Leipzig* engaged the *Glasgow*, *Dresden* the *Otranto*. The armed liner turned away, wisely; the *Glasgow* was surrounded by shell splashes but suffered few hits, none serious. It was otherwise with the British armoured cruisers.

The German Admiral recorded his impressions:

> On board *Good Hope* and *Monmouth* many fires broke out. A tremendous explosion occurred in the former, which looked like gigantic fireworks against the dark evening sky—white flames with green stars reaching higher than the funnels. I thought the ship would founder but the battle continued uninterruptedly. Darkness came on.

It appears that the forward 9.2-inch gun of *Good Hope* (she only had two) was knocked out before it could fire a shot; the after 9.2 could only get away one shell per minute; the German ships were firing four salvoes each every minute. Cradock's hope now must have been to inflict such damage on the Germans as could not be repaired locally; in fact both *Scharnhorst* and *Gneisnau* were hit; in the latter there were some slightly wounded, in the former a 6-inch shell which penetrated, fortunately for the Germans, did not explode.

The German Admiral, writing next day, set down his impressions:

> Fire was continued against the ships made visible by the fires burning on board, but ceased when the gunlayers were no longer able to sight their guns. The enemy's fire had ceased. I therefore ordered the light cruisers to continue in chase, but as the enemy had apparently extinguished his fires nothing was to be seen. The action had lasted fifty-two minutes.
>
> At 8.40 p.m. when steering north-west, we observed gun-fire ahead at a great distance, estimated at ten miles . . . It turned out to be *Nürnberg* which had come across *Monmouth*. *Nürnberg* closed her and finished her off with her guns. *Monmouth* capsized and sank. Unfortunately the heavy sea forbade all attempts at saving life. I do not know what became of *Good Hope*. Lieutenant G----- thinks she had a heavy list. This appears quite possible, although I thought it was due to the movement of the ship in the heavy seas. It is possible that she also foundered—she was certainly *hors de combat*. *Glasgow* we could hardly make out. It is believed that we got several hits on her, but in my opinion she escaped.
>
> I know not what adverse circumstances deprived the enemy of

every measure of success ... *Good Hope* though bigger than *Scharnhorst*, was not so well armed. She mounted heavy guns, but only two—while *Monmouth* succumbed to *Gneisnau* as she had only 6-inch guns.

He added that had 'the battleship carrying 12-inch guns' been present also 'we should probably have got the worst of it.'

On 3 November, the day after von Spee wrote this letter, the Admiralty decided to countermand their order for the big armoured cruiser *Defence* to remain in the Atlantic and instead send her at once to reinforce Cradock's squadron; and they wirelessed Cradock to that effect. But, as Churchill was to write: 'We were already talking to the void.' Cradock had been dead for two days; there were no survivors from either *Good Hope* or *Monmouth*. No one knows where or how she sank. *Monmouth*, however, was seen by two ships—*Glasgow* which closed her but was unable to help; and the *Nürnberg*, limping along behind the rest of von Spee's squadron because of her worn-out engines and boilers and the loss of blades from her screws. She was attracted to the spot by what must have been the smoke from the departing *Glasgow*. The British armoured cruiser was listing and damaged but still under way, and when *Nürnberg* shone a searchlight on her she began to turn, perhaps to ram, possibly to bring her disengaged guns into action. Her ensign was still flying and the captain of *Nürnberg* had no option but to sink her, which he did. Then more funnel smoke was seen (which on investigation turned out to be from another German) and for this reason and the state of the seas running there, no attempt at rescue could be made. In these two ships 1,418 British sailors had died, without achieving anything of importance.

Cradock was criticised, of course; the main charge was that already voiced by von Spee. Why didn't he wait for the *Canopus*? Firstly, because of her slow speed and unreliable engines; if Cradock had been tied to her the Germans, if they wished, could simply have passed round him out of range and gone into the Atlantic to raid British commerce. Secondly, her old guns were pretty certainly out-ranged by those of the two German armoured cruisers; she did not in fact offer the comfort-able, if slow, protection, which the British Admiralty and the German Admiral both believed she did.

The only person involved who absolutely absolved the Admiralty from all blame for the disaster of Coronel was the then First Lord,

Winston Churchill. After a much more costly shambles at the Dardanelles, he had to go and was succeeded by another politician, Arthur Balfour. In 1916 Balfour had to dedicate a memorial to Cradock in York Minster, and added this to his tribute:

> Why, then, you will ask me, did he attack—deliberately, designedly, intentionally—a force which he could not have reasonably hoped either to destroy or put to flight? . . . Remember what the circumstances of the German squadron were. They were not like those of the German High Seas Fleet . . . close to their own ports, capable of taking a damaged ship to their own dockyards, and their own protected bases. The German admiral in the Pacific was very differently situated. He was far from any port where he could have refitted. No friendly bases were open to him. If, therefore, he suffered damage, even though in suffering damage he apparently inflicted greater damage than he received, yet his power, great for evil while he remained untouched, might suddenly . . . be utterly destroyed. If Admiral Cradock . . . judged that his squadron, that he himself and those under him, were well sacrificed if they destroyed the power of the hostile fleet, then I say that there is no man . . . but would say that such a judgement showed not only the highest courage, but the greatest courage of unselfishness: and that Admiral Cradock, by absolute neglect of personal interest and personal ambitions, had shown a wise judgement in the interests of his country. If I am right there never was a nobler act.
>
> We shall never know the thoughts of Admiral Cradock when it became evident that, out-gunned and out-ranged, success was an impossibility. He must have realized that his hopes were dashed for ever to the ground, that his plan had failed. His body is separated from us by half the world, and he and his gallant comrades lie far from the pleasant homes of England. Yet they have their reward, and we are surely right in saying that theirs is an immortal place in the great role of naval heroes.

Churchill attempted to have the last word in his book *The World Crisis.* His claim that no blame attached to the Admiralty led to severe criticism, as did his subsequent endeavours (in the *Morning Post*) to justify his verdict. A leader stated that in 'attacking the memory of an heroic martyr to his duty (and his orders)' the former First Lord had

put the blame 'upon the principal victim of his own error of judgement
. . . He would have been wiser to have left the reputation of the dead
sailor alone.'

*   *   *

Two days after Coronel von Spee put into the neutral port of Valparaiso
with three ships (the most he was allowed and then only for 24 hours).
Chile was neutral against the British, as in the time of David Porter's
Essex, and moreover there was a German colony there; the victors
received a tumultuous welcome. For the first time in one hundred years
the British Navy had suffered a major defeat, and from the guns of a
new navy. In the roadstead were thirty-two merchants ships, 'an
exhilarating sight', noted von Spee, 'but alas all of them confined to the
harbour by the seapower of England.' Von Spee had one over-riding
preoccupation—coal. Coal for five warships which might have to
steam at speed. Starting with full bunkers, they might be able to cruise
for a week; not enough to get home, and in any case the way home was
blocked by the mightiest battle fleet in the world. Anyway, half their
ammunition had already been expended—on Cradock's ill-fated ships.

The Admiral paid a call on the German minister in Valparaiso, von
Erckerdt, who believed he could continue to supply the squadron with
coal from Chilean ports; although he had bad news regarding the
Japanese fleet. A telegram from Berlin contained even worse news. The
rendezvous points with German colliers in the Atlantic had been
compromised; all routes home were being strongly patrolled by the
enemy. But groups of warships might get through. Von Spee's reactions
were recorded:

> I am quite homeless. I cannot reach Germany; we possess no other
> secure harbour; I must plough the seas of the world doing as much
> mischief as I can, till my ammunition is exhausted, or till a foe
> superior in power succeeds in catching me.

There was a festive dinner at the local German club which von Spee
had to attend. A German civilian got up and proposed a toast:
'Damnation to the British Navy!'
Von Spee raised his glass.
'I drink to the memory of a gallant and honourable foe.'
Before embarking in the *Scharnhorst* to put to sea once more, a female

wellwisher handed von Spee a bouquet of arum lilies, and the admiral replied:

'Thank you, they will do very nicely for my grave.'

By the time the news reached England a German battlecruiser squadron had raided the North-East coast. People were asking: 'What is the Navy doing?'

The effect on the Admiralty was galvanic. Churchill and Fisher (the new First Sea Lord) decided to do what ought to have been done originally—send battlecruisers, the very ships created by Fisher in his first term of office as the solution to this very problem. Who was to command? That had not been decided when on 4 November Fisher so informed his chief of staff, Admiral Sir Doveton Sturdee, an officer whom Fisher much disliked because he had refused earlier to take part in intrigues against Fisher's opponent, Admiral Charles Beresford. Sturdee now made things worse by receiving Fisher's news with the comment that he had himself proposed the very same thing before Coronel, but had had the idea turned down. Fisher went fuming to Churchill, that he would not tolerate 'that damned fool as chief of staff one day longer.' So Churchill suggested to Fisher that Sturdee be given command of the new, more powerful squadron to be sent to hunt von Spee in the Pacific.

Admiral Jellicoe, who commanded the Grand Fleet at Scapa Flow, was to supply the two battlecruisers, at a time when a decisive battle with the German High Seas Fleet was expected in the North Sea. But Jellicoe made no objections. And finally Devonport Dockyard, with very little time, was ordered to prepare the two selected battlecruisers for extended foreign service.

The two battlecruisers chosen, *Invincible* and *Inflexible*, were the first that Fisher had ordered to be built; completed in 1908 they displaced 17,250 tons and gave 25 knots (as against the German armoured cruisers' 22 or so knots), achieving this speed by having protection equivalent only to that of an armoured cruiser. But their armament was almost the same as that of battleships of the time—eight 12-inch guns backed by a secondary anti-destroyer armament of 4-inch guns. They left England on 11 November, ten days after Coronel, with clear orders:

Your main and most important duty is to search for the German armoured cruisers *Scharnhorst* and *Gneisnau* and bring them to action. All other considerations are to be subordinated to this end.

They were joined by a force under Admiral Stoddart in the cruiser *Carnarvon*. Coal took them to the Falkland Islands, where there was a British depot and wireless station. Coal and the wireless station took von Spee to the Falklands one day later. His aim was to hit the British Navy by firing the coal stocks and blowing up the wireless station and, as a reprisal for the capture by the British of the German Governor of Samoa, himself capture the British Governor of the Falklands. Some of his captains had advised keeping well clear of the Falklands and then going north to destroy British commerce off the River Plate, the old 'Silver River' of Spain. But up to now, during his squadron's career in the Pacific, von Spee had attacked only warships and enemy bases. Sinking unarmed merchantmen, no matter how desirable on economic grounds, did not seem fitting.

David Porter, in deliberately inviting a clash with his inevitable pursuers off Valparaiso, may have felt the same; but in his case, his only previous victims having been whalers, the desire to fight a real enemy must have been stronger; and there was besides a strong personal element in that desire for 'glory'. Whereas Graf von Spee was a gentleman doing his duty. The fires glowing redly inside the riven hulls of *Good Hope* and *Monmouth* as they drifted away in the darkness spoke truly of the agony, mutilation and death which was the reality of war.

The Falklands are like the Orkneys, a ring of bare hillsides, sparsely populated, enclosing a naval anchorage. A barren and forlorn sort of place, home to penguins, seals, sealions and sheep farmers. On 7 December, 1914, the ships of Sturdee's fleet lay in the anchorage or in the adjacent Stanley Harbour. Apart from the two battlecruisers with their distinctive tripod masts, there were the three armoured cruisers of the county class, the *Carnarvon*, *Cornwall* and *Kent* (similar to the ill-fated *Monmouth*), two light cruisers *Bristol* and *Glasgow* (the latter having escaped from Coronel), the armed liner *Macedonia*, and beached as guardship the wobbly old battleship *Canopus*, which had two funnels and two straight masts. Some were coaling, others were waiting to coal, one was undergoing engine repair. Mines had been laid across the eastern entrance, and *Canopus* was placed to give an arc of defensive fire to the south-east. The Governor had formed an emergency defence force, supplanted by Royal Marines from the old battleship.

Humphrey Pakington was Admiral Stoddart's flag-lieutenant in the *Carnarvon*. That night, their first in the Falklands, he and his admiral dined with Sturdee in the *Invincible*. So far Pakington had not had an exciting war. The high point had been the capture in mid-Atlantic of a German cargo ship laden with lager and black silk petticoats. Over the port, Sturdee told them his plans. The enemy was thought to be in the Pacific, so after they had finished coaling tomorrow they would sail in the evening for the Horn. At that moment the signal bosun entered the cabin. A masthead lookout had reported three puffs of smoke on the southern horizon. But perhaps in the twilight he had been imagining things? The Germans were 2,000 miles away, after all.

Next morning, while Pakington was shaving, a signal was brought to him from the flagship:

Prepare to weigh anchor. Raise steam for full speed.

Pakington had plans to go riding that afternoon, having been promised the loan of a horse. No doubt the panic would be over by then. But he duly reported the signal to his admiral. It was a peaceful, even beautiful summer's day; with vessels coaling or waiting to coal. A quarter of an hour later there was a report of strange warships sighted to the south of the Falklands; first seen by an old lady living up in the hills, she had sent her servant galloping on horseback to the Governor. Now Sturdee's force was caught at anchor and unready. At least the wonderful weather had enabled the watchers to sight the Germans while they were still far away.

The leading German force consisted of *Gneisnau* and *Nürnberg*, whose boats would take the landing force in and clear the expected minefield at the entrance. No real opposition was expected. Once the mines had been cleared or neutralised, first *Nürnberg* and then *Gneisnau* would follow their boats into the anchorage, put parties ashore, capture the Governor, destroy the coal stocks and the signal station. Leutnant Kotthaus would command.

Dense columns of smoke were seen rising from behind the hills in various places—coal stocks being burned, thought the Germans. Then where the hills declined to low-lying land, masts could be made out. Very briefly, so that he could not be quite sure, the first lieutenant of the *Gneisnau* thought he glimpsed a tripod mast, and reported it. He was told that there were no battlecruisers nearer than the Mediterranean.

As the two German ships steamed on—one armoured cruiser, one light cruiser—they could make out a number of vessels in the harbour. Captain Maerker of the *Gneisnau* estimated two armoured cruisers like the *Kent* or *Monmouth*, two light cruisers, possibly *Glasgow* and a sister ship, and two heavier ships like the old *Canopus*; and he so signalled to von Spee who was 15 miles away with the covering force.

Shortly after, the upper works of an armed merchant cruiser—the converted liner *Macedonia*—were seen going into the harbour (for safety) while a *Kent*-class ship was coming out. The Germans were faced by a force very like the one they had met off Coronel. At 9.20 a.m. two huge waterspouts rose from the sea, followed by the sound of the shells approaching, followed by the thump of the 12-inch guns firing. But nothing could be seen of what was in fact the *Canopus* because she was hidden by the land, and firing at high elevation directed by an observation post on a hill. Maerker moved to cut off the *Kent*, which he believed to be escaping. Almost at once he received a message from von Spee:

Do not accept action. Concentrate on course east by south. Proceed at full speed.

There was still confidence in the German squadron, but at 10 a.m. two observers in the *Leipzig*, their glasses trained on the harbour, separately identified tripod masts and then, conferring, made the horrifying discovery that they had not been looking in the same arc. Two battlecruisers, not one, were coming out!

Raising steam at all, let alone for high speed, was a long drawn-out process; not at all like modern warships propelled by what are virtually jet aircraft engines; indeed much, much slower in getting under weigh than with a sailing ship. Hence, the British feared that von Spee might decide to take his ships inside the harbour. No one now can tell why he chose to run; but possibly because the reported presence of so many ships in the anchorage also implied that the expected minefield at the entrance (which did exist) would be covered by both small arms fire and by light guns which would at least hinder if not prevent the German ships' boats dealing with it.

Sturdee's reputation was that he never got rattled, and this morning he proved it; then, when his force was at sea, he did not rush matters but handled the massacre with care, not giving von Spee's heavy guns the chance to hit him much, turning away if they seemed likely to or to give his own gunners clearer shooting unobscured by smoke. The old-style cannons in old wooden warships tended to hit most of the time because the ranges were so short and the ships so slow. But now the ranges were in many miles and both ships moving at not far short of 30 m.p.h. From a rolling, pitching platform, the guns had to fire, not direct at the enemy but at some point ahead of him where he would be when the shells finally arrived, provided that he hadn't changed course in the meantime.

At 1.20 p.m. von Spee signalled: 'Light cruisers part company and endeavour to escape.' He intended to sacrifice both *Scharnhorst* and *Gneisnau* to save them. But Sturdee had already issued his own orders to cover the contingency, and so the British cruisers and light cruisers turned away to chase the fleeing Germans. The slow *Carnarvon* continued after the battlecruisers. Aboard her, Pakington witnessed an unbelievable sight—a full-rigged sailing ship appearing near the German cruisers; it seemed, he wrote, 'that the ghost of an ancient line-of-battleship had come for a lesson in modern warfare.'

Everyone in the British ships, from Sturdee downward, commented on the perfection of the German fire: rapid, steady controlled salvoes almost to the end; both the battlecruisers were hit. Their gunnery officers found themselves just as much professionally interested in the damage done by the German shells as the havoc their own were creating in the enemy. One of *Scharnhorst*'s funnels was gone, there were fires redly glowing inside her; but the volume of return fire from her surprised the British. The noise was of course incessant. One witness found fascinating the behaviour of men he knew well. There were solid-appearing officers who, one would swear, must be stalwarts in battle, but proved cowards; and there were mild and apparently ineffective, far from forceful men who behaved with unexpected heroism. For most, except the crew of the *Glasgow*, this was their first experience of war.

Of *Scharnhorst* both masts were gone, her bridge was gone, the first two funnels were leaning against each other, her boats blown to matchwood, but her ensign still flying from a jury mast aft. Around 4 p.m. her fire ceased 'as if a light had been put out', and she turned, bow down and listing, towards the British battlecruisers. Von Spee had signalled to *Gneisnau* to escape while he tried to close the British for a torpedo attack. Sturdee turned the *Invincible* towards the dying German flagship but never reached her. By 4.10 p.m. *Scharnhorst* was lying right over on her starboard side, dipped her bows, her stern rose in the air, and she disappeared leaving a vast cloud of smoke. 'Her gallant company,' wrote Pakington, 'were going down to sleep among the sea-monsters on the unsounded bottom.'

The *Gneisnau* could not escape. She had lost all steam from her boilers, and when her ammunition ran out only a single gun was still capable of firing; 600 men had been killed and wounded, so Captain Maerker gave the order to scuttle. At 5.30 p.m. the British ceased fire, as the German ship was listing heavily and about to roll over; but she did this slowly, so that many men were able to get up from below in time. The two battlecruisers and the *Carnarvon* closed the scene. Some two or three hundred men, dressed in grey uniforms, were in the water, which was bitterly cold, clinging to hammocks, lifebelts and pieces of wreckage. It took about half-an-hour for the British ships' boats to pick them up and by then there were less than 200. Sturdee's only impatient gesture of the day was to signal *Carnarvon* to get all her boats in the water.

A midshipman from *Carnarvon* stated that the water temperature was 46°F and air temperature about 51°F—really bitter conditions—and that many of the men in the water were wounded. 'A great many were drowned . . . a horrible sight.' An officer of the *Inflexible* noted that the prisoners were

> very nice fellows . . . most of them could not sleep that first night, the scenes in their ships had been so terrible . . . But we were all good friends after the fight, and both agreed that we did not want to fight at all, but had to.

To the senior German survivor, Commander Pochhammer, Sturdee wrote, praising their good gunnery and ending:

> Unfortunately, the two countries are at war, the officers of both navies who can count friends in the other have to carry out their country's duty, which your Admiral, Captain and Officers worthily maintained to the end.

This was literally true in the case of the *Carnarvon*, Admiral Stoddart's flagship. A survivor from *Gneisnau*, Leutnant Aneker, as he swallowed his cocoa, told his rescuer, 'I believe I have a cousin in one of the British ships. His name is Stoddart.'

These were the officers of course, writing at the time. The ratings' views were less well recorded. One of them had his verses on the battle printed on the 50th anniversary of the battle, which included the lines

> They steamed around the harbour's mouth and the sight that met
>   their gaze
> Filled their craven hearts with fear and their Admiral with surprise.

'Craven' is not the first adjective that comes to mind, but perhaps he
was down below (as most were) and saw little or nothing, and as the
war went on the influence of 'hate the cowardly Hun' propaganda was
heavy. But this was still December 1914—the Christmas Truce in the
trenches was only weeks ahead.

It was now about six in the evening, and miles away the cruiser chase
was coming to a climax. *Leipzig* and *Nürnberg*, which had been with the
squadron in the Pacific since they had left China and were badly in need
of engine and boiler overhauls, lagged behind the *Dresden*, which had
joined them only recently. The three pursuers, *Glasgow*, *Kent* and
Cornwall, caught up with the slower German light cruisers. *Nürnberg* was
overwhelmed first, then *Leipzig*, both flying their colours to the end,
even when no resistance was possible. The faster *Dresden* got away.

The sinking of all but one of von Spee's squadron was received in
England with enthusiasm by almost everyone, with the notable exception of Fisher, who sent needling telegrams to Sturdee and tried to prevent him being received at Buckingham Palace by the King. The effect
on the war was more important, in that the battle freed many ships
engaged in protecting trade routes against the possibility of attack.

The *Dresden* passed into the Pacific south of the Horn, hiding in
remote, fogbound bays and always crippled by the need for coal. One
day the *Kent* was searching for her in fog, when it lifted—and there was
the *Dresden!* She got away into another fogbank, but not before it had
been seen that she was riding high in the water; clearly, she had to coal
soon. And where was she likely to go? An intercepted wireless signal
showed a German collier heading for the Juan Fernandez group of
islands (where Alexander Selkirk had been marooned). On 14 March,
1915, *Glasgow*, *Kent* and *Orama* found her there, at anchor, the crew
ashore cutting wood to fuel the ship's engines. *Dresden*'s captain had
received a last signal from Germany, telling him that he could accept
internment in a neutral port; these were in fact neutral waters, but as
the British opened fire, *Dresden* replied. She was at such a complete
disadvantage that she hauled down her flag after three minutes and
began a parley. This was designed to gain time not merely to scuttle her
but, because she was in shallow water, totally wreck the ship.

At 10.45 that morning *Dresden*'s forward magazine blew up, and she sank, to the cheers of her crew assembled on the shore and from the watching British sailors. The last of von Spee's squadron had gone, the most complete victory to be won by the British Navy in the First World War.

That is, if one excludes the light cruiser *Emden* detached from the squadron at the start of its raiding cruise to create individual havoc in the Indian Ocean.

Above: Another American attempt at a submarine: the CSS *Hunley*, used by the Confederates off Charleston in 1864. From a drawing by R.G.S. Kerrett. *Photo: US National Archives* Below: The sinking of the CSS *Alabama* by the USS *Kearsarge* off Cherbourg, 1864. Engraving from a sketch by Frank Beard. *Photo: US Naval Historical Center, Washington*

Above: Togo's flagship at Tsushima in 1905: the predreadnought *Mikasa*, built by Vickers in 1902. She had four 12-inch guns backed by a mixed secondary armament.
Photo: McKee collection

Left: Admiral Cradock, commander of the British fleet at Coronel and the Falklands, 1914.
Photo: Imperial War Museum, London

The heavy cruiser *Monmouth*, sunk with all hands at the Battle of Coronel.
Photo: McKee collection

The German raider *Emden* aground off North Keeling Island, 1914.
Photo: Imperial War Museum, London

The submarine E11, one of the fleet which solved the secret of the Dardanelles in 1915.
Photo: Royal Navy Submarine Museum, Gosport

The old pre-dreadnought battleship *Majestic* sinking off Gallipoli in 1916 after
being torpedoed.
Photo: McKee collection

Chapter Thirteen

THE CRUISE OF THE RAIDER *EMDEN*

August–November 1914

The European nations in the Far East had frequently been allies during the minor colonial wars and rebellions, especially in China. Indeed the light cruiser *Emden*, under Captain Karl von Müller, had become something of a hero ship by replying to fire from Chinese batteries while his vessel was passing up the River Yangtse, and silencing them. Ashore the relations between the crews of the warships was cordial, particularly between the British and the Germans. They could indeed count many friends in the other's fleet. For instance Admiral Jerram, of the armoured cruiser *Minotaur*, went shooting snipe with Admiral von Spee of the *Scharnhorst*. The Far East was a pleasant backwater, not much bothered by rumours of yet one more war crisis in Europe. The others had been resolved, so too might this.

Von Spee's squadron was based on the German-built and defended port of Tsingtao, facing Korea across the Yellow Sea; the equivalent British base was a little to the north at Wei-hai-wei, facing Seoul in southern Korea. Shanghai and the mouth of the Yangtse were well to the south, and farther south still was the British commercial centre of Hong Kong. In the expectation of war, Admiral Jerram's plan was to base himself at Wei-hai-wei and so keep a close watch on the German ships in Tsingtao. His plan might have resulted in the destruction of the *Emden* at the very start of her career, before she had sunk a single ship; but as one of her officers wrote: 'Happily, we had in the First Lord of the Admiralty, Churchill, an involuntary ally.'

A political appointment, the First Lord of the Admiralty should not interfere in operations, especially when he had a very experienced and competent First Sea Lord, Admiral Battenberg; nevertheless Churchill ordered Admiral Jerram, the man on the spot, who had a thoroughly thought-out plan, to change it and go far south, to Hong Kong, with the British Asiatic Squadron. Jerram obeyed but noted: 'I must confess that I was reluctant to do so, as it placed me almost 900 miles from what I conceived to be my correct strategical position.'

Jerram had concentrated at Hong Kong by 5 August, 1914, but six days later again received firm orders from the Admiralty, half a world away: 'Practically certain Japan declares war against Germany on 12 August . . . You may leave whole protection of British trade north of Hong Kong to Japanese . . .'

But Japan lingered in declaring war. The *Emden* got out of Tsingtao on 31 July, 1914, without even being shadowed by the British or French, and on the 1st of August, heard on her radio messages from Admiral Jerram's ships passing south for Hong Kong, where they would be well out of the way, and even passed through their distant wakes so close had been the possibility of confrontation. The situation—who was at war with whom?—took a week to clarify. On 28 July Germany and Austria (the Central Powers) declared war on Serbia; on 1 August against Russia; on 3 August against France, on 4 August against Belgium; and on 23 November against Great Britain (but as Britain had already declared war on Germany on 5 August this was a mere formality). The Japanese did not enter the war until 23 August.

On 1 August Karl von Müller, captain of the *Emden*, had to decide what to do. He was now allowed to make war on Russia. Their nearest base was Vladivostok, north of Korea, and they did have an armoured cruiser, the *Askold*, capable of sinking him, and a light cruiser of approximately equal force; both the French and the British also had armoured cruisers in the Far East which could destroy him easily, if they came into the war. Von Müller did not see his job as that of fighting warships but of waging the far more effective warfare of a commerce destroyer. He consulted Oberleutnant Lauterbach, a merchant navy officer doing his reserve service aboard the *Emden*. A fat, jolly individual, quite determined not to lose a single kilo, Lautenbach knew the routes intimately and most of the ships plying them. He suggested the Tsushima Straits, between Korea and Japan, as a cruising station to prey on Russian sea routes.

Von Müller was a Prussian gentleman from a Service family; he was the first to join the navy rather than the army. His speech to the crew on 1 August was restrained and not very informative. Their first duty was to raid the enemy's commerce so they were going towards Vladivostok;

if they happened to meet warships, he was confident that all would do their duty. (This is what Nelson *would* have said before Trafalgar, if the signal book had allowed it.)

They met bad weather in the straits where Togo had beaten the Russians (soon to be their allies) in 1905; and on 4 August they sighted a fast steamer with two golden funnels, which tried to escape them. Naval officers are generally indifferent at merchant ship recognition, but Lauterbach identified her at once—the *Rjasan*, Russian mail steamer, 3,500 tons, 19 knots. It took a dozen warning shots before she stopped, then Lauterbach was told off to lead the boarding party. Von Müller had decided to take her to Tsingtao to be converted into a raider. Apart from mail, she carried nothing of importance, except eighty passengers, most of them Russian women on passage from Nagasaki to Vladivostok. Singly or in groups the women set out to make Lauterbach's life a misery by constant complaints. And by turning their cabin lights on they might be alerting French or British forces in the vicinity. Lauterbach had the necessary generators turned off but could not still their complaints. One can imagine them telling him that if stupid men wanted to have their silly war, then get on with it, but don't inconvenience us, we want to go home.

On 5 August the news of the British declaration of war was received, together with an intercepted Reuters newsagency report that the *Emden* had been sunk. That was very good news—it might make their enemies less watchful. Another signal was received, this time from Berlin. The *Emden* was to rendezvous with Graf von Spee's Far Eastern Fleet which was concentrating in the Marianas group of islands far out to the south-east in the North Pacific. On 12 August she joined the armoured cruisers *Scharnhorst* and *Gneisnau*, the light cruiser *Nürnberg*, and their fleet of colliers and support ships. Von Spee had already made up his mind that, because China and the other Eastern countries produced rice but no coal, the only practical area of operations for his squadron was off the western coast of South America, where coal could be had. And he preferred to keep all his ships together rather than let them be separated and then mopped up one by one. But he listened to an alternative suggestion, that the *Emden* be detached to prey on the much richer pickings undoubtedly to be found in the Indian Ocean on the British trade routes. She might not survive long—indeed, there was no forseeable long-term future for any of these ships—but while she lasted the *Emden* would certainly cause the British a great deal of trouble and tie up many times her strength in enemy warships. She was assigned the collier *Markomannia* as her immediate source of fuel supply.

The *Emden* sailed, her decks piled high with coal loaded in the Marianas, in addition to full bunkers. Anything further she would have to obtain from the enemy, for all ports would be either neutral at best or enemy at worst; and coaling at sea was anyway difficult and sometimes impossible, apart from being filthy, hard labour for the crew.

Her objective, the sea routes of the Indian Ocean, were in effect a British lake with entrances easily guarded; von Müller planned to go in via the Dutch East Indies. He did not expect to come out. The Dutch made it clear that coaling was forbidden in their waters to all belligerents; it would not be possible to play hide and seek. Indeed no belligerent ship would be allowed even to enter Dutch waters more than once every three months, and then only for 24 hours.

The *Emden* entered the Indian Ocean through the Straits of Lombuk opposite Bali, and by night with extreme caution. A 3,650-ton ship capable of 24½ knots, she was armed with ten 4.1-inch guns and classed as a *kleiner ungepanzerfer Kreuzer* (small, unarmoured cruiser) because, although built of steel, her plates were thin. She was designed as a corsair, for commerce raiding, and constructed at Danzig in 1907–8. Like all ships on the Far Eastern station, she was painted a grey so light that it was almost white and her crew wore white tropical rig. With her three tall funnels and distinctive superstructure she was clearly German. This had to be altered, so a fourth funnel, a dummy, was erected which made her resemble a British light cruiser such as the *Glasgow*.

Their first steamer sighting was on the night of 8 September. The *Emden* fired two shots over her bows and signalled in Morse: 'Stop engines. Don't use wireless.' Again, Lautenbach was the prize officer. To the captain, he spoke first in English. 'What ship is this?' No reply. So he tried French. 'Ah! A British cruiser.' 'No!' replied Lautenbach. 'A German cruiser.' At this, the captain declared his nationality. Greek. 'I am a neutral.'

Lauterbach asked to see the ship's papers and bills of lading, and the captain said he did not have them, they were being sent by train. He was just carrying coal from Calcutta to Karachi. Lauterbach, a former shipmaster himself, did not wear that one. He told the Greek he was a liar. Eventually the papers were produced. The prize was indeed a neutral, the Greek *Pontoporos*, her cargo was indeed coal—6,500 tons being transported from Calcutta to Bombay for the British government. The ship was neutral but the cargo was British. A tricky question so early in what was still a 'gentleman's war'. Lauterbach decided to let von Müller decide; he brought the Greek captain on board the *Emden*, where von Müller, not unexpectedly, ruled that the Greek ship was his prize because she was carrying contraband. He needed that coal. The Greek said he needed the money and as far as he was concerned, German cash was just as good as British. It made no difference to him who he supplied. The *Pontoporos* temporarily joined von Müller's little fleet until an opportunity came to transfer the coal.

The next ship they encountered was the SS *Indus* and her captain was so confident that the four-stack light cruiser overtaking him was British that he ran up his flag instantly. The *Emden* put one shot over his bows and was so close that they could clearly hear the shout from the bridge of the merchantman: 'Damned German!'

This case was clear cut. The 3,400-ton ship was owned by the British government of India and chartered by them to the British government in London to transport men and horses from Bombay to Europe to take part in the fighting on the Western Front. The white-painted stalls for the horses were evidence of this. Had the cargo been private but the ship owned by the enemy government, the ship would be considered an enemy but the cargo untouchable, which would have brought all sorts of problems. As it was, von Müller had the crew of the *Indus* removed to the *Markomannia* and detained there under guard; while their ship was ransacked of supplies wanted by the *Emden*'s crew, particularly soap (because coaling was a dirty job!), navigating instruments and food, even some live chickens. And then she was sunk. But her boats remained floating as evidence of the spoor of the *Emden*.

Her next victim was the *Lovat*, a British merchantman bound for Bombay to pick up troops destined for the Western Front. She was sunk immediately without being ransacked. Von Müller could not afford to stay too long in any one area. But newspapers were found aboard her and from them it could be learned that the British did not yet know that they had a raider in their midst.

Next to be stopped was the *Kabinga*, 4,600 tons. She was a British ship, but her cargo of jute was bound for New York; the ship was enemy but the cargo was neutral; if he sank her, Germany might have to pay the owners of the jute. Von Müller's solution was to use her as a *Lumpensammler* (literally 'rag and bone man'). The crews of both the

Indus and the *Lovat* were transferred from the *Markomannia* to the *Kabinga*; she was now the prison ship of his little fleet, which still included the *Pontoporos* carrying all that useful coal.

After that came the *Killin*, a British collier carrying 6,000 tons of Indian coal from Calcutta to Bombay; but the *Emden* already had the Greek collier, so he sank this one, transferring her crew to the *Lumpensammler*. Next came the *Diplomat*, 7,600 tons, carrying a thousand tons of tea from Calcutta to London. So he sank her too, putting her crew into the prison ship *Kabinga*. The boarding officer chosen for the next victim was Prince Franz Joseph von Hohenzollern, nephew of the Kaiser, serving as second torpedo officer. But this ship turned out to be the *Loredano*, an Italian merchantman. Now that was awkward. Italy was still officially a member of the Triple Alliance of Germany, Austria-Hungary and Italy, but when she later entered the war it was to be on the side of Britain, France, Russia, and Japan. Von Müller let her go, as he did the next ship, which also proved to be Italian, although in this case von Müller did not bother to board. But he changed course once she was out of sight.

Next morning von Müller spotted an unusual structure on the horizon but the unknown ship turned out to be the pagoda of the great temple of Puri, which lay on a shallow water coast. He hurriedly reversed course.

On 14 September he took the 4,000-ton collier *Trabbock*, and after transferring her crew to the *Kabinga*, sank her. The *Lumpensammler* was now overcrowded and short of provisions so von Müller reluctantly decided that she had to be released although this would mean giving away the position of the *Emden*. Worse still, when the demolition charges exploded in the *Trabbock* they set fire to the coal dust and she burned like a beacon against the evening sky until she sank.

That night they encountered yet another steamer, which was suspicious and ran from them, increasing speed. This one did not intend to give in. Like the Russian *Rjasan* under Captain Austin, she ignored the warning shots fired by the light cruiser until one landed very close and the *Emden* warned that the next would be aimed at her hull.

That stopped her, and on being hailed her captain gave her name as the *Clan Matheson*, on passage from Southampton to Calcutta.

'English?' queried the *Emden*.

'British,' replied the captain, Scots being especially resentful of being described as Englishmen, for reasons no Englishmen and few foreigners can understand.

His cargo consisted of Rolls Royce motor cars, railway locomotives, typewriters and a prize racehorse. This animal and the other horses had to be shot, before the prize was sunk. Initially, the Emden's crew had not proved very good at sinking their prizes quickly, but by now they had had plenty of practice. The *Clan Matheson*, her luxury cars, locomotives and freshly killed racehorses, went to the bottom in 45 minutes, including the time to transfer her crew to the *Markomannia*.

That night they intercepted a message to all shipping made in clear rather than in code, warning that the steamer *Loredano* had reported the German cruiser *Emden* at a given position and the sinking of the *Diplomat*, the *Kabinga*, and the *Pontoporos*. Her captain, as well as breaking his word not to mention the *Emden*, clearly had creative imagination of a high order.

Next day it was flat calm, so von Müller tried the expedient of coaling at sea from the *Pontoporos*, and soon wished he had sunk her instead of one of the other captured colliers. Her Indian coal was of poor quality, sure to cause excess smoke, and so compacted in the holds that it took the men thirteen hours' work to shift 450 tons of it to the cruiser.

On 18 September the *Emden* sighted a steamer and came up with her after it got dark. She was the Norwegian *Dovre*, a neutral. Still, her master might agree to take the captain and crew of the *Clan Matheson* off von Müller's hands. The Norwegian agreed but wanted payment to cover their keep; the German offered 100 Mexican dollars and this satisfied him. In the wake of 1939–1945 (the War Criminals' War, which succeeded the First Cads' War of 1914–1918) the Prussian officer's conduct must appear almost indecently sloppy and unrealistic, but it had after all only just begun, following the Last of the Gentlemen's Wars (in South Africa). The crew of the *Clan Matheson*, however, would not have agreed. They gave three cheers for the *Emden* as she steamed away.

Von Müller was equally pleased. He had learned from the Norwegian that at the port he had just left, Penang in Malaya, lay the French armoured cruisers *Montcalm* and *Dupleix*, a menace von Müller was anxious to avoid. What he had now decided to seek was a target on land which could be bombarded from the sea with maximum morale effect on ocean traffic. As he had learned from the newspapers, the English were concealing or playing down the presence of a German raider. He must now strike a blow which they could not ignore. He chose Madras, a port on the south-east coast of India, far from Malaya and far also from the British armoured cruiser *Hampshire* whose wireless transmissions he was picking up clearly. She was so close that at one point she could not have been more than ten miles away from the blacked-out *Emden*.

The *Markomannia* was sent away, to rendezvous later; the hammocks and awnings were brought down below and stowed; the crew were to have freshwater baths, to reduce the danger of infection from wounds; the fourth funnel, not much used until this time, was erected; the ready-use ammunition supply was doubled. This time, the *Emden* was really going to war. The oil storage tanks of the Burma Oil Company, the main military target, were at the south end of the harbour, overlooked by a battery mounting 5.9-inch guns. Madras was a city of half a million people and stretched for sixteen miles along the coast.

No one there even dreamed of attack. As the *Emden* approached the city after dark on 22 September, Madras was lit up as if at peace like any neutral port, even the channel and harbour lights burning helpfully. The cruiser slowed from 17 knots and stopped 2,500 yards out; her searchlights flashed out, played for and found the red-striped white tanks of the Burma Oil Company. The first salvo overshot and plunged into the battery of 5.9s. Then one by one the oil tanks began to burn.

The return fire was so late, feeble and inaccurate that some of the *Emden*'s crew did not realise that they had been under fire at all. At a celebratory dinner at the European club the shelling was not discerned among the cheerful roar of good fellowship, for they were all celebrating the news—that the *Emden* had been sunk. Only when an Indian servant padded in with the later news—that the *Emden* was shelling Madras and the oil tanks were burning—did anyone suspect that the newspapers were not to be relied on.

The *Emden* got away 125 rounds before von Müller decided that that was as much ammunition as he could afford to spend on this target, and steamed off at high speed. For many hours the fires burning in Madras could still be seen glowing against the night sky. He was now heading for Colombo, a port in what was then called Ceylon, a large island lying off the Indian coast south of Madras province.

On 16 September Admiral Jerram had word of the *Loredano*'s experiences and, in addition to the *Hampshire*, already in the area, he had sent a Japanese cruiser to join the hunt. The latter was directed to coal at

Colombo and then rendezvous with the *Hampshire* off Madras on 19 September. Jerram was very close to success when another report came in, placing the raider at Akjab in Burma, far away to the North-East. He sent the British cruiser to Akjab, so there was no rendezvous with the Japanese ship off Colombo. The coast was literally clear when von Müller arrived, anxious above all to learn the results of the Madras raid. The searchlights fingering the sky made it clear that this harbour at least was on the alert.

They took the *King Lud*, 3,600 tons, but in ballast, and sank her, taking off her crew; then moved closer to Colombo whose watchful searchlights proved useful—the bulk of a steamer coming out of the port was silhouetted. When she was well clear of the land they hailed her. She was British and her cargo of sugar was bound for England. She was the *Tymeric*, her master being Captain Tulloch. For the first time, the fat and jolly Lauterbach met resistance. Tulloch would not command his ship under German orders. His chief engineer refused to man the engineroom and stokehold. Tulloch added that he would order his men to refuse to obey any order from the 'damned Germans'.

It seemed that it was not only the Germans who had got under Captain Tulloch's skin. Only two hours before, he had sat in the King's Harbour Master's office at Colombo being told that the *Emden* was a thousand miles away and that it was safe for him to sail on to Aden. Worse still, his sole reason for putting in to Colombo (rather than steaming straight past) was to learn the whereabouts of the *Emden*. If he had simply not bothered, he would have been well clear and away before von Müller came up. Lauterbach could sympathise but also, being a former merchant marine master himself, sensed for once that this captain and his officers meant trouble. Lauterbach recommended that this prize be sunk at once, which was done. But she did have the very latest newspapers with the English version of what had happened at Madras.

The *Emden*'s first two salvoes, it said, had fired the oil tanks. A number of buildings were damaged, including the telegraph office. Two policemen on duty at the oil tanks were wounded. Eight of the crew of the British India Company ship *Chupra* had been wounded. 'The principle result of this incident has been to stop the return of confidence of shipping men, of which the signs are already visible.' And that was what von Müller wanted to hear. British seaborne commerce was being paralysed by the operations of one small cruiser.

For the officers and men generally there was even better reading in the captured newspapers. The daring of the *Emden* was acknowledged, as was her captain for his humane treatment of captured crews—he was compared to a knight in the days of chivalry. The most telling sign of their success, however, was that the name of the *Emden* was being used in a British advertisement for soap. 'Even the crew of the *Emden* use our soap,' it claimed, referring to the captures taken from the *Indus*.

Now, what the *Emden* really wanted was some good old high-quality coal from Cardiff, as one of her officers remarked; coal which wouldn't signal her presence 50 miles or more away by dense clouds of smoke. She soon got it by borrowing from supplies intended for Admiral Jerram, sailed from Britain in the collier *Buresk*. What was good enough for British warships should be good enough for a German. This ship too was added to the little fleet as well as the *Gryfevale*, 4,000 tons, which was in ballast and so would make a convenient *Lumpensammler* or dump ship in which to keep the ever-growing number of new prisoners. Von Müller ignored altogether a ship passed in the night with all lights blazing which announced herself in clear to be the Dutch motorship *Fionia*, although Lauterbach told him he suspected it was really a British passenger liner. Under no circumstances was the German captain prepared to attack any liner and then have to deal with a mass of passengers, many of whom were bound to be women and children. Even a year or two later, not to mention throughout World War Two, this fastidiousness would have resulted in mockery at the least, if not court martial for dereliction of duty, regardless of which side the culprit was on.

By 28 September the *Emden* had sunk or taken 15 ships and by studying the wireless traffic her officers could estimate that they were being closely hunted by at least an equal number of warships. Von Müller, a quiet man who rarely raised his voice and did not indulge in dramatics, had at the start of their voyage told all officers and men that they could not expect to see Germany again. This did not have a depressing effect, because it promised action. And as the cruise became clearly ever more successful until even the enemy praised their heroism, and they must surely by now be the talk of Germany, morale became ever higher. But they were tired, as was their ship. The men were getting little sleep and the underwater hull was becoming encrusted with barnacles, while the bad coal meant constant work on the boilers and in the engine room. The only amusement was provided by the playfulness of the *Emden*'s cats—named Pontoporos, Lovat-Indus, Kabinga, King Lud, and Diplomat after some of their prizes. But a sentry, the kitten-watcher, had to be put over Diplomat, who seemed convinced that the sea was solid and that it might be interesting to jump down onto it and play there.

Having raised enough havoc in the Bay of Bengal, von Müller steamed west into the Arabian Sea and found a quiet spot to coal in the Maldives, a straggling group of islands south-west of the southern tip of India. The men could relax mentally, if not physically—for coaling was desperately hard and filthy, dirty work—but never the captain. Von Müller had an armchair brought from the wardroom and placed on the bridge; and there he dozed, ready at any moment to take command if they were discovered—as one day inevitably they must be.

On 30 September the *Emden*'s first officer, Hellmuth von Mücke, told the men that they could write letters home. The now almost empty *Markomannia* would carry them to a Dutch port, where also some provisions might be bought. Then she would rendezvous with the cruiser in November at a designated point. In his own letter, which like all the others might be captured and read by the enemy, Captain von Müller could only hint.

> I see with calmness what fate will bring to my ship and to me. Sadly, I give thanks to you, dear mother, that on your birthday you must go through so much difficulty . . .

The crew's letters, which of course were censored, expressed great admiration and liking for their captain. But, knowing that they would be read by an officer certainly and by the enemy possibly, their style also was a little cramped, although some were stridently dramatic and patriotic.

From the Maldives, von Müller sought an even lonelier group of islands to carry out engine repairs and boiler cleans, and to scrape off the worst of the barnacles; and also to tidy up the *Emden* which now had hardly a trace of her once-smart grey-white paint. Loading coal by the sackful, thousands of tons of it over the months, had bent stanchions, torn the linoleum covering of the decks, and mixed dust with rust on her sea-stained hull. Far south in the Chagos Archipelago the cruiser was made more presentable, although far from yachtlike, and then moved to another island of the group for the hull to be canted over, first on one side and then on the other, so that the wetted areas might be scraped and cleaned of barnacles and growth which slowed her speed. This island was called Diego Garcia, and had a bay enclosed by high hills which would conceal the raider from seaward while the work was done. As the *Emden* steamed in, the British flag was run up ashore.

Then a boat rowed by natives came out to the raider, carrying one white man—an old Frenchman beaming all over his face, with gifts of eggs and vegetables for the German ship. He spoke only French, which was lucky. Translation gave the Germans sufficient time to learn that neither he nor an Englishman ashore—they both managed an oil company station—had any news about the progress of the war, simply because they did not know there was a war on. The Frenchman, beaming, recalled that the last German ship which he had seen come to the island was *Bismarck*; that was in 1899. Normally they only had a visit from a sailing ship once every three months, so they were delighted to see the *Emden* and anxious to know what was happening in the world. The Pope was dead, said the Protestant von Müller.

Like any ambassador, the captain was now required to lie for his country, inventing peaceful happenings in an untroubled world. A few whisky-and-sodas made his task easier with the old Frenchman, but when the Englishman who managed the station came out, he eyed the state of the *Emden* with suspicion. It was not only that positive things were wrong, but negative ones, too. For instance, traces in the ward-room where furniture had once been and wooden panelling—all of it thrown overboard long ago as too combustible in battle. And the anti-splinter netting shrouding the guns. And the ragged, unpainted state of the deck, and the repairs being made. This, said the Germans, was because the cruiser had only just come through a typhoon which had almost capsized her. Suspicion was finally removed when the pair requested help with the repair of their motorboat and von Müller speedily set men to work on it.

The *Emden* sailed on 10 October and two days later the British armed liner *Empress of Russia* sailed into the bay, while the heavy armoured cruiser *Hampshire* patrolled outside. It was von Müller's careful custom to alter course as soon as he was out of sight of potentially hostile witnesses, so the now indignant oil men's description of the course the *Emden* had taken led to the German light cruiser steaming round one side of the island while the British armoured cruiser steamed the other way. Even so, Admiral Jerram's dispositions for the hunt can hardly be faulted. He simply lacked the luck which attended Admiral Sturdee when hunting for Graf von Spee.

Intercepting a British wireless transmission which gave the news that the Aden to Colombo route was safe now that the *Emden* had been gone a week, von Müller returned to the Indian Ocean. On 15 October he took the *Clan Grant* and appropriated part of her cargo—live cattle, beer and cigarettes. After that, there was a distinct farmyard smell aboard the warship, although the menus now were an improvement on the monotonous previous diet of rice and corned beef.

Next day the ransacking of the *Clan Grant* for new crockery, table linen and firebricks was halted by a smudge of smoke on the horizon. A ship was approaching but her silhouette was unusual. Certainly not a merchantman, perhaps some new type of destroyer? But when the vessel could be seen broadside on, it was clear that she was an ocean-going dredger. No prize crew was required, her own crew were delighted to be captured by the *Emden* and eager to be taken off what they described as that 'rolling coffin'. They had started out for Tasmania with another dredger which had capsized, and feared the same fate; but as prisoners in the *Emden* they expected, from newspaper reports, to be well treated and then sent home.

Apart from two quiet days, a hectic series of captures followed. It took time to transfer passengers and crews to dump ships which would shortly be released; to transfer coal and stores to the *Emden*; and in one case—a tribute to British shipbuilding—a captured vessel took hours to sink. Then, still escorted by two colliers and all ships blacked out, the little German fleet observed two ships travelling fast with only side-lights on; these, they learned later, had been the pursuing *Hampshire* and *Empress of Russia*, which had actually overtaken their quarry without spotting them in the dark.

But they were going north and the *Emden* was going south, and would later turn east for the Nicobar islands where she would coal before entering Penang harbour in Malaya to attack the warships believed to be there. It would require skilful seamanship, for the navigable channel was narrow and curving, and the target would open up to view only at the last moment, so that von Müller would have seconds only to scan the shipping inside and choose his targets, risking torpedo boat attack. When the crew were told, they were enthusiastic; there had been some quiet grumbling that a real warship was being wasted on a job that an armed merchant cruiser could do. The *Emden*'s dummy fourth funnel was erected, to help confuse enemy reactions. The port was British but it might well hold French and Russian warships.

They came up the channel in darkness, the lights of Penang bright ahead and all the buoys lit. There was even a pilot boat heading for a steamer which had stopped and was waiting to enter. At 4.50 a.m., just before first light the *Emden* went to action stations, searchlights, guns and torpedo tubes manned.

In the uncertain visibility of the pre-dawn, the lights on shore still shone out. To port a row of bright lights, regularly spaced, seemed to indicate a row of houses, but as the sun tipped the horizon the men on the bridge of the *Emden* began to make out a row of large funnels and a ship superstructure—a warship. Von Müller had the battle flags run up and turned hard to port to bring the tubes to bear. Now they recognised the ship—the Russian light cruiser *Yemtschuk*, similar to their own vessel. No one was stirring aboard her. From 300 yards the first torpedo was loosed and a track of bubbles racing away across the harbour marked its underwater path. A few men began to move on her decks. A huge column of water rose behind her second funnel, followed by the muffled boom of the explosion.

Immediately, the *Emden*'s guns opened up on the Russian, which in her turn opened fire and was joined by the guns of the French destroyer *d'Iberville*. The *Emden* turned to launch a torpedo from her starboard side. This one raised a high column of water beneath the bridge of the Russian ship, resulting in a second explosion which seemed to break her in two, although the details were obscured by vari-coloured smoke and the red of fires. Minutes later, only the tops of her masts showed above the water. Seeing what appeared to be a torpedo boat speeding towards him, billowing black smoke, von Müller headed out of harbour. In fact, it was only a pilot boat.

Later that morning, while the *Emden* was dealing with an ammunition-carrying cargo ship, she had to break off when she was intercepted by a fast-moving destroyer flying the tricolour of France. She loosed two torpedoes at the *Emden*, which evaded them, and then overwhelmed her smaller opponent with gunfire. *Emden* lowered boats to pick up survivors, one officer and thirty-six seamen, many wounded. One man's entrails were hanging out, another had both legs so badly smashed that the German doctor had to amputate. The French captain, who had gone down with his ship, had also had his legs smashed and had had himself lashed to the bridge. Presumably, the immediate shock had dulled the pain. The survivors said that their ship had been the *Mousquet* and that they had seen the *Emden* entering Penang but had taken her for a four-funnelled British light cruiser.

On 30 October von Müller captured the 3,000-ton *Newburn* carrying salt, and decided to put his French prisoners into her and then let her go, because some of the wounded might die if they did not receive shore hospital treatment. The *Emden* had suffered no losses whatever.

So far, they had captured or sunk twenty-three merchant ships, sunk a Russian light cruiser and a French destroyer, and attacked the tanks of the Burma Oil Company at Madras. In three months they had covered 30,000 miles and consumed 6,000 tons of coal. Some 78 ships were involved in the effort to hunt them down and British merchant shipping had been seriously disrupted and delayed.

Von Müller's next target was the wireless and cable station on Direction Island. This was where the undersea cables crossed—the Australia-India link and the Australia-Zanzibar-Africa link. His officers suggested that they begin by shelling the wireless station and put it out of action before any messages could be sent. The Captain refused because this would endanger civilian lives; instead the landing party would go in early and take the British by surprise. In any event, monitoring of wireless traffic indicated that the nearest enemy warship was 250 miles away.

The landing party was carefully chosen, mostly long-service men led by two young officers well trained in infantry tactics. As well as rifles and revolvers, they had four light machine-guns. On the night of 8 November the raider lay fifty miles out to sea with her collier the *Buresk*. Before going in, the *Emden* erected her fourth funnel. The last two miles to the landing place had to be made in cutters and a steam launch, because it was shallow with many coral heads. The British civilian staff of the station made no resistance, indeed they met the invaders on the beach and politely gave them directions, and even congratulations at their award of the Iron Cross recently made by the Kaiser. The reason was that they already had reserve equipment well hidden on the island and could re-activate the station in short order. The only resistance came from a Chinese mechanic who defended the 'fridge with the words: 'This no b'long electric light, this b'long makee ice.' On the other hand, when the British saw the Germans placing explosives to fell the wireless mast, they asked for it to be felled away from the tennis courts, please; which was done. Then they heard quick blasts from the *Emden*'s siren. The recall signal.

Kapitänleutnant Hellmuth von Mücke, first officer of the *Emden* and commander of the landing party, assembled his men at the beach; there was no time now to blow up the little white schooner tied up at the quay, as they had at first intended. The *Emden*'s anchor flag was flying at halfmast, which meant she was about to leave. They piled their captures—mostly documents and files—into the three boats and set off. The British waved them goodbye and some even took photographs.

Hellmuth von Mücke assumed that the *Emden* was reminding him that he had over-stayed his time ashore, as indeed he had—destroying the undersea cables had proved a more difficult task than anyone had thought. But he was not all that late, only half-an-hour or so. Then, as he saw the raider getting under way, he thought that she must be going to meet the *Buresk* for coaling to begin. What he did not know was that a Chinese employee had sighted a strange ship off the entrance to the lagoon hours ago and that the four-funnel disguise had not worked for long. The British wireless station had then got off a message: *S.O.S. Strange ship in entrance*. And then, when an unknown station started to jam the British transmission they sent a shorter message: *S.O.S. Emden here*. They had only stopped sending this when von Mücke's men burst in.

Still assuming that he could catch up when the *Emden* stopped to load from the *Buresk*, von Mücke piled his men into the three boats and set off through the coral shallows of the lagoon. But, strangely, the raider was increasing speed to perhaps sixteen knots; and then he saw her black-white-and-red battle ensign go up. That explained it, then—she was intercepting yet another enemy freighter. His guess seemed confirmed when yellow flashes winked out from the *Emden*'s sides and a few seconds later the sound of the firing rolled across the water to him. The land hid whatever the raider was firing at. Then five tall columns of water volcanoed up around the *Emden*. The enemy vessel was a warship!

Their luck had run out. But it was not entirely luck. Firstly, von Müller had refused permission to shell the British radio station for fear of hitting civilians—and now some of his own crew were going to die because of it. But secondly, he had made that decision based on the belief that there were no warships in the vicinity and that he had plenty of time to get clear even if the British did give the alarm. And that belief was based on a report from his own wireless staff that the distant transmissions they were picking up were from ships some 250 miles away. In fact, they had been fifty-five miles away but transmitting on low power. And 55 miles at 25 knots or so is less than two hours. Thirdly, there had not even been early visual warning of the approach of a warship, so that the *Emden* could work up to full speed; by some quirk of vision the enemy had been mistaken by the lookouts for the collier *Buresk*, which was expected.

The warship was the brand new cruiser *Sydney* of the Royal Australian Navy, built 1911–1013. Her full load displacement was 5,945 tons. She had a protected deck against plunging fire and for 175 feet amidships the hull was made up of three-inch plating extending some distance below the waterline. Her main armament was eight 6-inch guns all mounted high up in the modern fashion to cover both sides of the ship. And she could do 25½ knots. Her 6-inch gave her an overwhelming advantage over the *Emden*'s little 4.1s, not just in hitting power but in range. Because the *Emden* had not had time to get up full steam, the *Sydney* had an initial speed advantage, which she kept and increased as her fire steadily crippled the raider.

There was no reason for Captain Glossop of the *Sydney* to risk unnecessary casualties, and he didn't. The object in war is to win at the least cost to one's own side, not to have a jolly good fight. So the Australian pounded the *Emden* to pieces while keeping out of the raider's effective range and also out of torpedo range, while von Müller kept trying to close.

The *Emden* began to move off soon after 9.30 that morning; her fourth salvo got a lucky hit on the *Sydney* and knocked out her fire-control room; and that was the last luck the raider had. Captain Glossop opened the range to 7,000 yards, where the *Sydney* could hit but the *Emden* couldn't. After that it was pure punishment. Gun after gun was knocked out, steam pipes were pierced, the radio room destroyed, fire broke out aft, the bridge steering system was out of action and orders were given verbally, the ready-use ammunition began to run out and there was lack of men to bring up further supplies; the torpedo flat down below was still operative but the torpedomen waited in vain for the order to fire—the *Sydney* evaded all von Müller's efforts. At 10.45 a.m. a shock was felt throughout the ship—the foremast had fallen. Then the torpedo flat, which was below the waterline, was holed and had to be abandoned. Two funnels fell and the third lurched over at a crazy angle; the smoke from the boilers could not be drawn off fully, and so the *Emden*'s speed slowed still further. The electrical system failed. Few guns were now firing, one of them being commanded by a boatswain's mate who had had an arm torn off. But it was the flooding of the torpedo flat which caused von Müller to make his fateful decision. As there was now not the remotest chance of sinking the *Sydney*, he faced the same basic situation as had Grenville in the *Revenge*.

In spite of the wounded strewn about his upper decks and the close to 100 sick men confined below, Grenville was for scuttling not surrender. Von Müller, however, decided in favour of his crew. He turned the *Emden* towards North Keeling Island and deliberately ran her hard aground on the coral reef fringing the shore. This would save not only his wounded but also the men still on duty down below, men who rarely have time to climb the ladders to the deck but usually go down with the ship, still alive, sometimes trapped for days in an air pocket from which there is no hope of escape, with the hull capsized.

When the *Sydney* saw that the raider was hard aground, she stopped firing, but put duty before mercy and steamed away after the collier *Buresk*. A few more wounded were found in the riven hull and then collected on deck; but parts of the ship were too hot still to enter. Worse, the supplies of drinking water had been either ruined by shellfire or were now underwater and out of reach. In that climate, with so many wounded, this was serious, particularly as there was no shelter from the sun as all the awnings were in flooded compartments. Further, the wounded on deck had to be guarded because the great seabirds of the region, which the Germans called *Döskoppes*, would swoop down on any helpless man and feed on his eyes.

It was four o'clock in the afternoon before the *Sydney* reappeared, towing the boats of the *Buresk*, which had scuttled herself. She stopped 4,000 yards away and hoisted a signal which none of the Germans could read. They made a flag signal in Morse spelling out *No signal book*. The Australians may not have understood; anyway they opened fire and continued to fire for half-an-hour until von Müller hauled down the German ensign and hoisted the white flag. Then they stopped. In the same circumstances the Germans had been compelled to fire on the floundering wreck of the *Monmouth* and the British on the sinking *Nürnberg*. The first duty of a captain is to his own ship and his own men; it is difficult to see what else they could have done, so long as their enemy remained potentially lethal.

Nearly two-thirds of the *Emden*'s crew were casualties, with 141 killed and 65 wounded; among the dead were a civilian cook, a civilian barber and three Chinese laundrymen. There were only 117 unwounded survivors. On a small scale the situation was not unlike that immediately after the battle of Waterloo (except that there were no tourists or scavengers to witness their agonies). The *Sydney* sent them the boats of the *Buresk* manned by Germans from that ship, and then sped off for Direction Island intending to capture the men of the landing party under the first officer, Hellmuth von Mücke, a very cool and determined man, more like a Prussian than a Saxon, which in fact he was.

He had seized the 90-ft long schooner *Ayesha*, named after the favourite wife of Mohammed, and normally manned by five men. Von Mücke had ten times that number and four machine-guns. Knowing that the British would certainly land on Direction Island within days, if not hours, he had quickly provisioned her and set off for home across what was nothing but a British lake. In May 1915 the survivors of his party reached Constantinople, having come partly by sea in various craft, party riding on camels across Arabia while harassed by Bedouin, and finally by train. At the last railhead they were met by Admiral Souchon, commanding the German fleet in Turkish waters, to whom von Mücke could say:

'I report the landing party from the *Emden*—five officers, seven petty officers, and thirty men.'

Chapter Fourteen

THE KEYS TO THE MARMARA

The Dardanelles, 1915

Because the Admiralty had failed to catch the battlecruiser *Goeben* and the light cruiser *Breslau* at the outbreak of the conflict in August 1914, Turkey had come into the war at the end of October. A British force was sent to watch the mouth of the Dardanelles in case the two warships tried to break out into the Aegean. In December the weakest and most obsolete vessel of the British force—the tiny, outdated coastal submarine B11, powered by a petrol engine—entered the Straits and sank a Turkish heavy cruiser, the *Messudieh*, sometimes described as a battleship.

The area of the Dardanelles was famous but unknown. The current large-scale Admiralty chart showing the entire region, from the mouth of the Dardanelles and the Gallipoli Straits to the Sea of Marmara and thence to Constantinople (shown as Istanbul) and so into the Bosporus and the Black Sea, was No. 224 'surveyed by Commander W. J. L. Wharton and the officers of HM Ships *Shearwater* (1872) and *Fawn* (1879–80)'. What this chart showed was a generally narrow strait, 35 miles long, fairly deep (40–50 fathoms), overlooked on both sides by rugged hills up to several thousand feet high.

This strait was really a submerged river valley with a river of fresh water flowing very fast to seaward all the time, which to the north opened into a great freshwater lake, the Sea of Marmara, which held several rugged islands and was very deep indeed (up to 600 fathoms in places. A fathom is six feet). At its most northerly point lay 'Stambul and the Golden Horn, once the capital of the Eastern Roman Empire, Byzantium. On the shores of the Black Sea were many former Greek colonies.

At the southern end of the Dardanelles, on the Asiatic shore, is the

Plain of Troy immortalised by Homer's splendid tales of Hector and Achilles, the long siege and the abandoned 'wooden horse' (probably a siege tower), and the mound covering the layered ancient cities excavated in the 1870s by the German Heinrich Schliemann, and showing Homer to have been an historian rather than a teller of tall tales about the early Bronze Age. So the scene was set for war from stories of battles long ago. The Greeks had had to sacrifice a princess before the gods would grant them a wind strong enough for them to breast the current with their ships. Much greater sacrifices were soon to be asked here of many men.

Nearer to modern times, in the age of Classical Greece, in 448 BC, the Persian King Xerxes with his huge imperial army found the Dardanelles a great obstacle (it was called the Hellespont then) and built a floating bridge by the usual method of floating it on moored boats, but the current swept the boats from their anchors before a walkway of planks could be nailed across; to punish the waters he had them struck with 300 lashes, cursing the 'salt and treacherous stream'. This may seem an odd way of describing a freshwater river, but then he knew more than the British did in 1915. Indeed the few British representatives in Turkey with full information of conditions on the spot were not consulted beforehand.

There were exceptions, as there always are. The Army commander eventually chosen complained to Lord Kitchener that his knowledge of the Dardanelles and of the Turks was *nil* and of his own forces, *next to nil*. The Navy commander eventually chosen demanded a large force of battleships and sufficient ammunition to carry out prolonged bombardment. Lord Fisher who, despite certain faults, was no amateur, had rueful recollections of the poor performance of naval gunfire against the forts of Alexandria in the 1880s, while Kitchener favoured seeking a decision in Europe and was keen on a Baltic invasion. It was Churchill who favoured the more subtle eastern approach without fully appreciating the resources required to capture Constantinople and force Turkey out of the war. The matter is still argued, but it seems probable that if a large-scale, properly thought-out, professionally mounted sea and land operation had been carried out early in the war, without first alerting the Turks and before the efficient Germans had taken over the direction of the Turkish army, a success might have been achieved and German pressure on the Russian front notably weakened.

But this did not happen. Instead, the sequence of events was a British raid in November which served to alert the Turks and Germans, then the daring penetration of the Straits (but well short of the Sea of Marmara) by Lieutenant Holbrook's tiny submarine B11 in mid-December, followed by consideration in London of a scheme to force the Dardanelles by battleships only and by actual attempts to do this in February and March of 1915. The first day's sea bombardment was astoundingly successful; but never afterwards rivalled. The army was then brought in and full-scale landings begun on 25 April; it was evacuated in December 1915, less the 44,000 or so soldiers—British, Dominion and French—who remained there; and are there still.

This was the background to the only successful eruptions into the Sea of Marmara—by the newer E-class submarines. The battleships failed utterly and with heavy losses. The Germans had taken over the previously inadequate defences—a process described as *Deutschland über Allah*—which relied on mines to destroy them and on hidden and mobile guns to destroy the minesweepers which must precede the battleships. Heavy naval guns proved none too useful even against formally emplaced artillery and less so against the hidden mobile batteries, the naval observers frequently hoodwinked by false theatricals representing non-existent guns which drew fire.

Only the frail, vulnerable submarines eventually hit hard at the Turkish supply lines. Their crews, and those of the even tinier steam picket boats, exhibited a heroism to match that of the men who stormed the heights and stony gulleys ashore. At one point, early on, the record stood at one to five. Five submarines had attempted to pass through the Straits; four had not returned. Of the lost boats, two were French, and one Australian.

In December 1914 the success of Holbrook's short-ranged and obsolete B11 had led the naval commander, Admiral Carden, to ask for a flotilla of the new E-class boats; this was refused initially because the Western theatre had priority; but Russian requests for help reversed the decision. The E-class had a much longer underwater endurance and should be able to reach the Sea of Marmara, once the hazards of the Straits had been survived. Apart from the fast-flowing currents and eddies, the Turks had laid new minefields and their reinforced artillery commanded the narrow waterway at close ranges.

By March the first E-class boats were arriving at Mudros, the submarine base, led by E14 (Lt.-Cdr. Courtney Boyle) and E15 (Lt.-Cdr. T. S. Brodie, twin brother to C. G. Brodie who was on the staff of

Commodore Roger Keyes, effectively controller of the undersea fleet. Limping along behind was E11 (Lt.-Cdr. Martin Nasmith) with clutch trouble. Nasmith, a leading submariner before the war, had not fulfilled his promise; his commands were plagued with mechanical troubles or unfortunate acts of the elements—he had once missed torpedoing a German battle ship because a wave threw his boat off just as he was firing. Now it seemed to be happening again.

When E11 tied up alongside the depot ship at Mudros, there was only a single E-class submarine there, E14; E15 under T. S. Brodie, eager to be first into the Marmara, had made the attempt on 17 April. His twin brother, C. G. Brodie, had flown over the straits as a passenger with Cdr. Sampson and was witness to failure; a current had somehow swept E15 onto a sandbank directly under the guns of a Turkish fort. A brand new British submarine of the latest design, virtually undamaged, was likely to fall into the hands of the Turks and, through them, to the Germans.

She had to be destroyed and attempt after attempt was made without success. The little B6 under Lt. Birch was sent in to torpedo her in daylight; under a hail of shell splashes, he missed. That night, two destroyers were sent in. Brodie's twin brother went in one of them, the *Scorpion*. Searchlights dazzled, and accurate shellfire drove them back. In the morning Cdr. Sampson's seaplanes tried to destroy E15 by bombing, and failed. Shortly afterwards, Holbrook was asked to do the job with B11 in daylight, but there was a mist which hid the stranded submarine but did not conceal Holbrook from shore guns; this attempt also failed. Then the big card was played—two old pre-dreadnought battleships, *Triumph* and *Majestic*, were despatched to destroy the submarine with heavy gunfire, but the Turks had moved up extra guns to cover the scene and their fire was so effective that it kept the battleships at bay; at 12,000 yards they could survive but could not hit a target as small as a submarine. But if they couldn't hit a stranded 700-ton submarine in full view in broad daylight, what hope did battleships have against mobile guns hidden in rough, jagged country? This question seems not to have been asked, yet an answer to it was central to all the naval plans. For if the battleships could not knock out the guns, the minesweepers could not clear the mines—and the way through the Straits was barred, except perhaps to submarines.

It was Admiral de Robeck (who had succeeded Admiral Carden) who made the suggestion: an oldfashioned cutting-out expedition, like

Basque Roads or Barfleur. Why not use, not the battleships, but the battleships' boats? More precisely, the 19-ton steam picket boats which each ship carried for ferrying senior officers—or children out to the ships at Christmas for their parties. They could be fitted to take 14-inch torpedoes, were small, fast and handy.

At mid-day on 17 April, hours only after E15 had been reported aground, de Robeck summoned Lt.-Cdr. E. G. Robinson to select two boats for an attack on the night of 18–19 April, should all the other methods of destruction fail. Robinson decided to use two 56-ft boats, one from the *Majestic*, one from the *Triumph*. Normally a crew was six, but volunteers were asked for to provide a double crew for manning the 3-pdr gun and the maxim—and a hundred or so men came forward. Sets of torpedo launching gear were fitted, two to each boat, and a torpedo officer appointed. To get the utmost speed, their hulls were cleaned and greased, machinery checked, and hand-picked coal for twelve hours' steaming loaded. Fourteen knots was their usual trials speed, and they would need every part of a knot they could get, for their hulls would not stop even rifle bullets.

At 9.30 a.m. on 18 April the two picket boats steamed off for a rendezvous to await the final order. Lt.-Cdr. Robinson was in *Triumph*'s boat as overall commander of the mission. This boat had been built at Cowes in the Isle of Wight in 1894 and had a 200 h.p. engine. With their curious fluted single funnel they were distinctive. At nine o'clock that night a coloured flare came up in an arc from where the battleship *Majestic* lay. That signalled that all attempts so far had failed; now it was up to the picket boats.

De Robeck's hope had been that the two small boats could approach silently and unseen to where E15 lay aground off Kephez Point, where the Straits were about one and three-quarter miles wide; a little farther on, they narrowed to a mere three-quarters of a mile. If all went well, they would launch their small 14-inch torpedoes head on from 250 yards, and then retire in haste. Identifying the target might be difficult, but air reconnaissance indicated that now and then the Turkish searchlights involuntarily threw the stranded E15 into relief. This was what they hoped for, but in case of early discovery the boats stayed some distance apart; one might be picked up by the lights, the other perhaps not. There were eight searchlight points covering the spot and nine gun positions, all the guns being 6-inch.

However, almost as soon as the two boats had separated, a searchlight picked up *Majestic*'s boat commanded by Lt.-Cdr. C. Godwin, who changed course to mislead the Turks about the objective. Then they picked up the *Triumph*'s boat too and the whistling roar of approaching shells announced the arrival of the projectiles, some striking so close that the boats were half-swamped by the columns of water they threw up. Each boat was held by not less than three searchlights at a time.

Triumph's boat, with Robinson aboard, fired one torpedo at the estimated position of E15; but there was no resulting yellow flash; she turned away with one in hand to let *Majestic*'s boat commanded by Godwin have a go; and then, for seconds only, a Turkish searchlight lit up their target, allowing Godwin to make a last-minute change of course to bring their bows dead on E15. Godwin let both torpedoes go, then turned sharply to clear the way for another approach by Robinson.

But it was unnecessary. With a flash and a roar a torpedo—or possibly both torpedoes—struck the submarine. Godwin turned instantly for home and Robinson, aborting what would have been his final torpedo run, followed him.

Minutes later the *Majestic*'s boat was struck by a shell which blew off the transom and rudder and probably the screw as well. With three watertight compartments, picket boats are not all that easy to sink, but this one began to fill slowly. The scene was floodlit by the white glare of the searchlights' fingers and screaming shells continued to plunge into the black water, throwing columns of spray, but Robinson's boat came alongside the sinking boat of the *Majestic*, took off the crew and carefully lifted one wounded man over the gap and into the cockpit of the *Triumph*'s boat.

Then the amazing happened. The bulk of the Turkish fire fell on the slowly sinking but empty picket boat they had left behind, and although two searchlights tracked them and the occasional shell was fired in their direction, the *Triumph*'s boat was allowed to escape without further damage, although the wounded man rescued from Godwin's boat died during the run back.

He was T. Hooper, the armourer, one of whose tasks in action was to make a tick on an armpad for every shell he could count which had been fired at them. The number of ticks made up to the time he was fatally wounded was 217. He was the only casualty out of the 24 men led by Robinson.

De Robeck wanted confirmation of the success and as the naval seaplanes could not get low enough to observe properly he sent in B6 under Lt. MacArthur, with C. G. Brodie as passenger. On the morning of 19 April B6 entered the wide mouth of the Straits which narrowed towards Kephez Point and made the final approach at 80 feet. When MacArthur calculated that he was near the wreck, he came up to periscope depth for a visual check. And at that point the little submarine was pushed sideways as if by a giant hand, overpowering the weak electric motors which had to be used when they were submerged; there was a sinister sh-sh-sh-sh underneath them. They were aground 100 yards from E15, which was truly wrecked, deposited there by the same unsuspected current and, as soon as the Turks spotted them, likely to share the same fate.

MacArthur was about to apply the usual method of getting a grounded submarine off a sandbank; that is, lighten it by blowing ballast tanks. But Brodie, suspecting now what had led to the death of his brother in E15, suggested that the opposite method should be used. That is, admit water and make the boat heavier, so that she was not instantly driven farther up the bank by the current; and in this state of negative buoyancy, use the electric motors to pull the boat down the slope of the bank.

For a moment, Brodie had had the horrifying vision of making it a double for the Turks; two Brodie brothers, in two different British submarines, wrecked side by side, to the shame of the Navy and the delight of the enemy. But there was deep water to port and MacArthur steered into it as the submarine slid off the bank sternfirst. Then B6 did something extraordinary: once over deep water she stood on her nose so that Brodie had to hang on with both hands to prevent himself falling forwards, and the depth gauge flicked from 70 to 80 feet in spite of all the cox on the diving rudder could do. Then, before any orders by MacArthur could take effect and as the depth gauge registered 90 feet, B6 came level and the speed became normal. Some giant, unknown forces were at work in the Dardanelles and must be discovered before a penetration into the Sea of Marmara beyond could be made.

For the moment there was an embargo on further attempts by the submarines, but like them all, Nasmith was gaining as much information as he could. Lt.-Cdr. Pownall, commander of the submarine flotilla, had Holbrook's report, but he had penetrated into the Straits only as far as Sari Siglar Bay and even so, had returned with batteries completely flat. The French submarine *Saphir* had tried but had been lost at Nagara Point—strong currents were thought to be the cause. Then had come T. S. Brodie in E15. Brodie had been chosen by Commodore Roger Keyes on 14 April, when Keyes had asked everyone, one by one, if they thought the operation feasible. One by one they had all answered 'No' until the last man to be questioned said 'Yes'. That man was Brodie and not unnaturally, Keyes chose him. Keyes was a well-known fire-eater from the colonial wars and believed that the answer to everything was keenness and enthusiasm—what a later war generation would call 'bash on regardless'. To be fair, this view was widely held in both military and naval circles and had often proved correct. A less optimistic and impulsive officer might have noted that T. S. Brodie was in a very small minority of one, and sparked a general discussion of the difficulties. However, he was in other ways thoughtful and afterwards brought to C. G. Brodie in person a translation from a Turkish newspaper regarding the fate of his twin brother: '. . . the captain and three of his crew were killed outright by a direct hit on the conning tower . . . they were buried on the beach with military honours . . .'

Pownall was the source of a weird but significant story. Long before Chicago gangsters disposed of awkward colleagues by weighting them with concrete for a dip in the nearest lake, the Sultan's court at Constantinople stuffed such people into sacks and chucked them into the handy Marmara which ran beneath the seraglio walls down to the Dardanelles. But according to this story, one such sackful, long after it should have been carried down by the current, actually came back again, popping up under the walls of the seraglio, almost at the spot at which it had been disposed of.

The Admiralty charts showed only the surface currents, flowing continually towards the Aegean, a river of fresh water. Nasmith asked about the former British Naval Mission to Turkey under Admiral Lupus; but Brodie could say only that Admiral Lupus had been shunted off to Malta, apparently for some diplomatic reason. But if the legendary story of the returning corpse of the seraglio was true, then there must be an inward current moving as a layer under the outgoing freshwater; and if the inward current was salt, then the change in densities would be ruinous to a submarine's trim. A fighting submarine needs to be slightly heavier than the water it displaces, the final trim being obtained by using the hydroplanes. If it comes into an area of heavier water it will tend to go up, perhaps uncontrollably; but if this layer is light, the boat may descend rapidly to depths which will implode the hull.

Nasmith's E11 was still not operational, waiting for spare parts to arrive from Malta, but what preceded them was the Australian submarine AE2 under Lt. H. G. Stoker, fully repaired. And so when the embargo was lifted and the next submarine to go in was chosen, it was Stoker's AE2. She sailed on 25 April, 1915, two hours ahead of the Allied invasion force which was to capture the forts the Navy had failed to subdue.

The Australian boat had trouble with currents, and twice went aground; partly as a result of obeying an order by Keyes to surface off Chanak to search for minelayers. There were no minelayers but there were a lot of gunboats which spotted the periscope. However, by 9 a.m. on 26 April, Stoker could signal that he was in the Marmara.

This signal was received at an opportune time. A conference was considering a report from General Birdwood, Commander of the Australian and New Zealand Army Corps, on events ashore and suggesting that a re-embarkation might be necessary. Brodie broke into this conference, ignoring furious gestures by Keyes, and read Stoker's signal to the assembled brass gathered in the new battleship *Queen Elizabeth*. Keyes was now ablaze with enthusiasm:

> It is an omen—an Australian submarine has done the finest feat in submarine history and is going to torpedo all the ships bringing reinforcements, supplies and ammunition to Gallipoli.

The generals did not think to ask how one boat, with a limited load of torpedoes, could do all that; they caught the enthusiasm and there was no further thought of evacuation. The bitter fighting just begun would go on through the unendurable torrid summer and the deathly cold of a Turkish hillside in winter.

Only hours later Lt. Courtney Boyle of E14 was on board the *Queen Elizabeth* being briefed by Keyes. Keyes, as Brodie put it, communicated enthusiasm but no orders and no information. However, Boyle had his own solution to the problem of fighting the unpredictable currents with the limited life of the weak electric motors: he would dive only when strictly necessary. Most of the time he would take the risk of unknown minefields by travelling on the surface, using the powerful diesel engines, but trimmed down so that the boat was barely awash. It was a method similar to that employed by the Confederate 'Davids' so long ago. At 3 a.m. on 27 April, E14 entered the Straits. On 30 April she was followed by the French submarine *Joule* under Lt. du Petit-Thouars. People were queuing up to go through the Straits and Nasmith was at the end of the queue and still pondering the problems.

A few days after entering the Straits, there were no less than two submarines hunting in the Marmara, the Australian AE2 and Courtney Boyle's E14. They rendezvoused and their captains compared notes. Boyle had torpedoed a transport but AE2's torpedoes went underneath their targets. Boyle also had the best story. One of his attacks had been interrupted by the complete blacking-out of his periscope, as if it had been shot away. Then he recalled that there had been a Turkish fishing boat in the vicinity—the fisherman, attracted by the valuable bit of brass sticking out of the water, had grabbed it, seeking to hoist it inboard. Then, it must have seemed to him, the brass had acquired magic powers, for it slid down out of his grip, as Boyle ordered, 'Down periscope!'

On 1 May the bad news came to the British base at Mudros. The enemy announced tht they had sunk the *Joule* with all hands (apparently on a mine); and a few hours after that the German light cruiser *Breslau* signalled Admiral de Robeck in English that AE2 had been sunk by a Turkish gunboat but that all her crew had been picked up. It was later learned that AE2 had entered an area of dense water, which affected her trim so that she went up and down between the depths and the surface like a bucking horse. A waiting Turkish gunboat holed her pressure hull, and her career in the Marmara was over.

E15, *Saphir*, AE2, *Joule*—four boats out of five sunk, because Courtney Boyle in E14 not only got in, he got out again, the first captain to do so. E11 was still in Mudros harbour, her engines dismantled while repairs were done. Nasmith, still seeking information, conned a free ride in a Farman out of Commander Sampson. From above, he had hoped to see the mines, but the sun's glitter on the waves hid everything. Nevertheless, the lighthouses were clearly visible and they would be important checks to his navigation seen for a few seconds only through a periscope; that proved valuable, and a distant glimpse of the Marmara did wonders for his spirits.

E14 got back on 18 May and there was a celebration dinner in de Robeck's flagship, attended by the Army commander, General Hamilton, and other senior officers, together with Roger Keyes and the submariners Boyle, who had just returned, and Nasmith, who was next to go. There was a political crisis at home; Fisher had resigned and Churchill was expected to do so. There were eighteen guests and, of them all, Keyes was the most excited, bubbling with eagerness and delight. The Admiral asked Boyle to describe for them his visit to the Marmara.

Boyle made the error of giving a factual and far too modest account of the patrol. Consequently he was frequently interrupted by generals asking deep technical questions about underwater operations, with Keyes butting in and trying to explain, and the generals no doubt no wiser than before. Boyle was not allowed to get a word in until the Admiral asked if he had sunk any ships, apart from the gunboats he had mentioned. Boyle replied carefully and quietly that he had hit several, one being a large transport, but he had not actually seen her sink, although he thought she must have. Another had given off yellow smoke, she had definitely been on fire. And he had had to sink a small gunboat which had been firing at him all the time; possibly she was a minelayer.

That sparked off other gigantic hares, because so many battleships had been sunk recently, and few could be sure whether it had been by mines, by shellfire or by shore-mounted torpedo tubes.

'Did you observe any (torpedo) tracks?' Keyes asked.

'No—there were only guns.'

'I don't care about guns!' snapped the fire-eating Keyes. 'Were there any torpedoes?'

'No, sir.'

Keyes then queried Boyle as to why he had not sunk a Turkish battleship operating in his neighbourhood, when he had been ordered by wireless to do so. Boyle replied simply:

'I was asleep.'

That got a round of laughter and a whisper by Brodie to Nasmith:

'Keyes doesn't realise that submarine commanders ever have to sleep.'

Afterwards, Keyes took Nasmith aside. Two Turkish battleships were bothering the beach-heads with fire from newly installed howitzers as well as shells. They should be priority targets for him. Stay in the Marmara until E14 gets back from her refit. 'Well, then—go and run amok in the Marmara!'

Books could be—and have been—written about what Nasmith did

in the Marmara in the course of three deadly patrols, which included the sinking of a battleship, as ordered. But he also found the keys to operating there, so that he could repeat his visits and others could use his methods.

As he had suspected, there was a river of fresh water flowing out of the Marmara through the Straits into the Aegean, and underneath another river of denser sea water flowing up the Straits into the Marmara to Constantinople. By going down until the submarine was riding on that in-flowing current, instead of stemming an outgoing stream, the boat's progress was faster over the ground and quicker in time. It was this lower layer of dense water which had brought B6 out of her uncontrollable dive and prevented other submarines from going low enough to get under the moored mines. It explained the return of the corpse to the seraglio and it made sense of the furious Xerxes and his cry that the Hellespont was 'a salt and treacherous stream'. Yes, it was salt deep down—but how did he know that in the fifth century BC?

Of course, there were further losses—the British E7 and E20, the French *Mariette* and *Turquoise*—but now that the principles were known it was mainly the hazards of wartime which took their toll—nets, mines and, later, U-boats. But Nasmith reached Constantinople—the first enemy vessel to enter the harbour for 500 years—and Turkish supply lines to their troops in the Gallipoli peninsula were harried almost at will. Holbrook, Boyle and Nasmith all won the VC. There were countless heroes at Gallipoli, most of whom were sent there to die in vain. Their sacrifice is remembered and is still a cause of bitterness; almost the only bright light is the memory of the submarine campaign.

Chapter Fifteen

CARNAGE IN THE NORTH SEA

Jutland, May 1916

One footnote regarding the submarine campaign in the Dardanelles is of general application. When Holbrook torpedoed the *Messudieh* she sank in ten minutes, the Turkish gunners as usual firing until the last; and like all too many large warships, she capsized, taking most of her crew down with her, still alive. But she was in shallow water. Next day holes were cut in the hull and most of the trapped men got out at last. When this happens in deep water, most of the men are still alive, and may then climb and crawl up—where before they would have been going down—to as near the keel plates as they can get; all terribly disorientated and breathing the foul air at far more than atmospheric pressure—three or even four times more. And there they would hammer on the hull and wait in vain for rescue, not knowing how impossibly high above them was the surface of the cold sea. The most badly wounded might never get there, but some of the injured men might be able to struggle past the jumble of displaced gear, up the narrow ladders at their now unfamiliar angle, and all in the dark. Until hope—and the oxygen—ran out. And the hammering died away.

This fate awaited the losers when the great dreadnoughts finally clashed; it was a terrible facet of twentieth-century technology which historians tend not to dwell on, but as typical of its time as the whistling grapeshot and slash of cutlass had been in the days of sail. And steam has its own drawbacks and its own special, horrific injuries: picture scalded, screaming men with the skin peeled off them; that, too, was the twentieth century.

The German Navy was new and without tradition. The British Navy looked back to Trafalgar and had immense prestige, but for most of the nineteenth century the effectiveness of its battle fleets in actual war had

Admiral
Sir John Jellicoe.

Hats off to the Flag
we all love and adore,
And give it a mighty
great cheer,
For with gallant Commanders
like this to the fore -
Old England has
nothing to fear.

Portrait of Admiral Jellicoe on a patriotic postcard of the First World War.
Photo: McKee collection

The battlecruisers *Indomitable* and *Inflexible* steaming in the North Sea. Both took part in the Battle of Jutland where their sister ship *Invincible* was sunk.
Photo: McKee collection

Commander Peck's big destroyer *Swift* with her heavy and unusual armament. In 1915 the two forward 4-inch guns were replaced by a single 6-inch gun whose flash blinded her captain at a critical moment during the night action in 1917.
Photo: McKee collection

The Q-Ship HMS *Dart* looks like a merchant vessel but has finer lines.
Photo: McKee collection

German photograph of the breach in the mole, taken the morning after the raid on Zeebrugge.
Photo: Royal Navy Submarine Museum, Gosport

Above: The USSR battleship *Marat* during a review at Spithead in the 1930s. An unbelievable relic of Tsarist Russia, she was built as the *Petrapavlovsk* and sunk at Kronstadt by CMB88 in 1919. Afterwards she was salvaged and rebuilt.
Photo: McKee collection

Left: German photograph of the *Glowworm* sinking off Norway in 1940.
Photo: Imperial War Museum, London

not been fully tested. Indeed, there was to be only one major action between rival fleets of battleships during the First World War, and that was off the coast of Denmark over the shallow Jutland Bank, in May 1916. The British admiral, Jellicoe, knew that British shells were defective and that this fault had not been corrected. He rightly feared underwater weapons—the mine and the torpedo—but did not know that the cordite charges used to propel the shells were more unstable than those used by the Germans. With one notable exception, his admirals and senior captains failed to realise the importance of promptly signalling their commander-in-chief the whereabouts of the enemy. On a dull misty afternoon with variable visibility and with enormous fleets of huge ships covering many miles of sea at the speed of a motor car, this made Jellicoe's task even more difficult.

The forces engaged were uneven. The British had 37 capital ships (battleships and battlecruisers) against the German total of 21. The British could count 344 12-inch and 15-inch guns against the Germans' 241 11-inch and 12-inch. Against this, German guns out-performed British guns and the German optical equipment for range-finding was superior. In numbers of cruisers and destoyers the British again much outnumbered the German. Air reconnaissance was ineffective on both sides, the Germans using a huge Zeppelin, vulnerable to gunfire, and the British using primitive seaplanes from an improvised carrier. The German reconnaissance submarines were equally ineffective. The British, however, had to a great extent broken the German naval codes (largely thanks to the Russian capture of a code book from a wrecked cruiser), but this information was not properly tied in to operations and in some cases senior officers did not take code-breaking seriously.

The disparity in numbers was, however, central to the strategy of both sides. Admiral Sir John Jellicoe, if he lost, could simultaneously lose the war for Britain. Admiral Rheinhold Scheer, if he lost, would hardly affect the British blockade of the Central Powers, but if he won crushingly, could raise that blockade and win the war for Germany. Jellicoe, if he won, would hardly alter the position (although it has been suggested that such a victory might have exposed Germany to an invasion via the Frisian Islands or in the Baltic—which seems far-fetched).

Because of the mine and the torpedo, close blockade was no longer possible; and because Germany was the enemy, not France or Spain, the British had to set up new bases in the north and east—Scapa Flow in the Orkneys, 700 miles north of the previous main naval base of Portsmouth, and the Scottish ports of Cromarty and Rosyth. Harwich, near the mouth of the Thames, became a base for light craft and saw also the 'Wobbly Eight'—the squadron of old pre-dreadnoughts which was supposed to guard the east coast against raids by the fast German battlecruisers. The German main fleet base on the North Sea was at Wilhelmshaven at the end of the Jade estuary. This was a generally shallow coast, once home to the Frisian pirates of medieval times, and guarded far out to sea by the red rock island of Heligoland. Many of the Saxon invaders of England had come from here, and had long since settled.

The spirit of the times provided impetus for a battle, for the soldiers were dying by the hundreds of thousands on land while the great battle fleets, the pride of their respective nations, swung round their buoys in danger of grounding on their discarded bully beef tins. The battleship had become the symbol of might, and morale both of the crews and of the public might suffer if they were not employed. So they were employed—just once, at Jutland—but with caution and with cunning. Both sides set out to trap the other. And both succeeded.

If the German High Seas Fleet met the British Grand Fleet, the German force, totally outnumbered, must be crushed. So the German policy was to reduce their enemy's numbers by using submarines, mines and entrapment of smaller British forces by larger German forces. The British lost one battleship to a mine and three cruisers to a single small submarine early in the war. The clashes between light forces were not favourable to the Germans but some useful lessons were not learned by the British, and they ought to have been, especially inferior signalling techniques and personnel and the danger of unstable cordite.

There was also the legacy of Lord Fisher—the battlecruisers. They were an excellent idea for their time: they could catch and overwhelm anything smaller, and yet run away from any battleship. They were not designed to fight battleships, but because they mounted big guns there was always the temptation to use them in a fleet action, particularly now that the enemy had battlecruisers also. As soon as Fisher resigned for the first time, new ideas were aired, including the fast super-battleships of the *Queen Elizabeth* class, four of which were to be present at Jutland. They had 15-inch guns throwing one-ton shells, as opposed to the German 11- and 12-inch barrels; and by removing one turret and going over to all oil-fired turbines, they were almost as fast as a battlecruiser. An ordinary dreadnought could do about 20 knots, compared to the battlecruisers' 26 knots or so. The fast battleships did 24 knots and their armour was formidable. It was to be fully tested at Jutland.

The German battlecruisers' previous bombardments of English East Coast towns had failed to bring out the Grand Fleet, so Scheer planned a lure further north off Norway. His U-boats were withdrawn from patrols against cargo ships to lie across the routes that Admiral Beatty's battlecruisers were most likely to take from their base at Rosyth; with luck, he might get one or two by torpedo or by the mines which some of them would lay. The German battlecruisers under Admiral Hipper, would take care to be seen off Norway, but they would be followed by the main body of the High Seas Fleet at a distance of some 60 miles.

Jellicoe's plan was almost identical. Beatty's battlecruisers were to be seen by the enemy, and they would retreat, enticing the Germans towards the British Grand Fleet some 60 to 70 miles behind.

The line-up on this day was: 28 British battleships to 22 German; 9 British battlecruisers to 5 German; 34 British cruisers to 11 German; 78 British destroyers to 61 German. Six of the 22 German battleships were pre-dreadnoughts, older and slower than the modern vessels, thus complicating Sheer's problems.

The British were not fielding their full strength. The efficient light forces at Harwich were to be held back because of unfounded fears of a German dash for the Channel, and of course the stock of British pre-dreadnoughts were held back at home for the same reason.

The vital element in all conflicts—the quality of the officers and men on both sides—was, as near as makes no matter, equal.

In spite of the eagerness of both Beatty and Hipper to engage, the immediate cause of the battle was a neutral ship, a Danish steamer. Beatty sent the cruiser *Galatea* to investigate her, while Hipper despatched the *Elbing*, a German cruiser. So both admirals got the message 'Enemy in sight' at about the same time, and both admirals believed that they had only the enemy's battlecruisers to deal with. Misty weather had hampered the Zeppelin and the U-boats failed to report on the German side, while Admiralty undervaluing of the code-breakers' work prevented clear warning being given that the whole High Seas Fleet was out. Apart from being independent of the wind, which brought with it the penalty of dense smoke from their funnels obscuring the battlefield and visual signals, recent inventions had placed them all hardly in advance of Nelson and Villeneuve. The speed and complexity of the combats were much greater, however, making matters more difficult for the commanders. At two knots there was plenty of time to think.

It was already afternoon of a misty day in May; in sailing ship days there would have been no time to get the two fleets together. But even at modern speeds there was hardly time enough. The light was now very important. No longer did ships fight side to side, at ranges down to as little as ten feet or so; the ranges were in miles and for the range-finding instruments to work properly there had to be clear images. So the position of the sun was as important as the wind direction had been a century earlier.

Beatty's line, consisting of the six battlecruisers—*Lion, Princess Royal, Queen Mary, Tiger, New Zealand* and *Inflexible*—closed on Hipper's five battlecruisers—*Lützow, Derfflinger, Seydlitz, Moltke* and *Von der Tann*. Although screened by scouting cruisers, poor signalling had left ten miles behind the four formidable fast battleships under Evan-Thomas—*Barham, Valiant, Warspite* and *Malaya*—which, by cutting corners, managed to close up to six miles by the time the battlecruisers engaged. Hipper, grievously outnumbered, turned towards the High Seas Fleet, still over the horizon, leading as he thought the impetuous Beatty into the prepared trap. The two battlecruiser lines converged, British port side to German starboard side, with the Germans to the eastward, their superstructures indistinct, and further blurred by the smoke of the ninth British destroyer flotilla which was attempting an ill-judged torpedo attack. By another piece of bad management one of the German battlecruisers, the *Derfflinger*, was not engaged by any of the battlecruisers of Beatty's superior force. She was for ten minutes allowed to blaze away undisturbed. The Germans opened fire first.

At 4 p.m. Beatty's flagship, the *Lion*, received a 12-inch shell on one of her turrets; the 9-inch armour plate was penetrated and the flash exploded the cordite charges, killing 70 men. A gun turret revolved on top of a cylindrical construction which led to the magazines, down almost at the level of the keel, connected by a hoist which brought up as separate items the shells and the bagged cordite charges which propelled them. Later, more cordite charges in the hoist caught fire and exploded, sending flames as high as the masthead. Major Harvey of the Royal Marines, with both legs blown off, nevertheless managed to order the closing of the doors and flooding of the magazines, which saved the ship.

The other 'big cat', the *Tiger*, was also hit on a turret. A midshipman who survived it was told later that two of the battlecruisers had been sunk, and did not believe it, assuming his informant was suffering from shellshock. But when he was able to go out onto the forecastle, there was no *Queen Mary* ahead and no *Indefatigable* astern. The six battlecruisers had been reduced to four. Most men were below and had no view of the action and only rarely were they told what was happening. They could only follow the course of the battle by the firing of their own guns and the shock of enemy shells hitting their ship or thundering into the water alongside.

Another witness, who was stationed on the upper deck of the light cruiser *Fearless*, denied that the *Indefatigible* had been sunk by the *Von der Tann*, as generally believed; she did not haul out of the line when hit, but fired her forward turrets and then just blew up with no German shells apparently causing the explosion. A few minutes later the *Queen Mary* exploded, her masts and funnels falling inwards to the seabed, her bow and stern as separate pieces resting on the shallow bottom and rearing up out of the water, and a 56-ft steam picket boat turning circles in the air above her. Out of her 1,266 crew, only twenty men survived. More than two thousand men had died or gone down alive in those two ships in the space of a few minutes.

The British superiority of six to five had been turned into a German superiority of five to four, for no German ship had even been badly damaged, let alone sunk. Beatty's reaction to disaster was typical. To his Flag Captain, Chatfield, he remarked, 'There seems to be something wrong with our bloody ships today. Turn two points to port.' That is, towards the Germans, shortening the range.

The battlecruisers racing to war were a splendid sight, going 30 miles an hour, bow and stern waves piled high, funnel smoke pouring upwards under forced draught. From the enemy line rippling yellow flashes, puffs of cordite smoke. Then the sight of the shells, black shapes against the sky, the whine of their approach chilling the blood, the bang like doom when they hit; armoured turrets torn open like tin cans, the great guns lolling uselessly. The 100-ft high columns of water roaring up from the ones that missed. And around the enemy ships, the rearing columns of white, under, over or—flash—a hit!

The four *Queen Elizabeth*-class fast battleships under Evan-Thomas in the *Barham* came into the fight, too late to save Beatty's battlecruisers but not too late to punish Hipper's. The shells they threw weighed a ton each, three times as much as those of the Germans. And their shooting was unlike Beatty's—it was accurate. *Barham* hit the *Von der Tann* at 4.12 p.m., and twice more in ten minutes.

A British destroyer flotilla put in an attack and Hipper countered by sending in his own destroyers and turning his big ships away from the oncoming torpedoes, considered by both sides the best option as it presented the huge hulls end-on to the torpedoes and going away towards the limits of torpedo range. So, with the ranges now opening out, the light craft of both sides clashed between the mastodons.

In the light cruiser *Southampton*, on scouting duty ahead of the battlecruisers, Stephen King-Hall was a young lieutenant. What he and all the others on her bridge saw now was a line of more than twenty battleships coming at them at a speed of 17 knots. They were Admiral Scheer's main force—the whole High Seas Fleet. But Commodore Goodenough did not turn away; he pressed ahead to make quite certain of the facts for his reports and not a single gun fired at the *Southampton*! Not until she turned away, that is—for then the Germans realised that she was an enemy and not one of their own. Then the Commodore did something extraordinary for a British commander this day. He wirelessed the Commander-in-Chief:

Urgent priority. Have sighted enemy battle fleet bearing south-east. Enemy's course north. My position 56° 34' N. 6° 20' E.

In all other cases, Jellicoe had actually to plead for information as to where, late in the afternoon of a dull misty day, the enemy was. And getting either no answer or most unhelpful ones, such as '*I am engaging the enemy*'. Clearly, most senior officers had been badly trained and believed that if they just engaged the enemy, like Nelson, they could do no wrong. The attitude was not confined to the Navy. There is the true story of the Army *CO* who told young officers that his motto was: 'Damn your writing, mind your fighting'.

But Jellicoe needed to know where the High Seas Fleet was, so that he could make the correct deployment from cruising formation to fighting formation. All he could actually see himself was about seven miles, when vision was not obscured by mist, and there were hundreds of ships loose covering a vast stretch of ocean. In the event, on inadequate and sometimes inaccurate information, he made the right decision. Hipper and Scheer followed Beatty into the jaws of the trap.

Admiral Scheer confidently ordered: *General Chase* of the apparently fleeing battlecruisers and fast battleships. Jellicoe signalled to the Admiralty: *Fleet Action Imminent.* This was an agreed signal to alert the dockyards to receive damaged ships.

On the vast battlefield the light forces were clashing as they attempted to attack the enemy's capital ships. The Britrish destroyers *Nomad* and *Nestor*, stopped or crippled after their torpedo attack earlier, were in the path of the High Seas Fleet; they fired their last torpedoes in vain and were overwhelmed.

The cruiser *Chester* turned to attack an enemy cruiser accompanied by destroyers which loomed out of the mist; then three other three-funnelled cruisers appeared in her wake. The four were the *Frankfurt*, *Wiesbaden*, *Pillau* and *Elbing*. Their fire overwhelmed the *Chester*. About 80 men were killed and wounded on the upper deck; of one gun's crew, only one individual remained on his feet, the Boy Seaman John Cornwall, who was a sight-setter. Although fatally wounded and all the others dead, he still stood to his post.

Minutes later, the German light cruiser squadron in their turn were overwhelmed by the appearance out of the mist of three new British battlecruisers, *Invincible*, *Inflexible* and *Indomitable*, the first two veterans of the Falklands battle under Admiral Sturdee. They had been previously detached for much-needed gunnery practice with the Grand Fleet. Now, as they passed the fleeing *Chester* surrounded by the splashes of German shells tearing the water around her, their 12-inch guns blazed out retribution. The *Wiesbaden* became a smoking wreck, stopped, with both engines out of action. The *Pillau*, on fire with four boilers out of action, made her escape through a smokescreen, limping after the remaining two light cruisers. The sudden appearance of three new British capital ships into the action prompted Commodore Heinrich, who commanded a force of light cruisers and destroyers, to attack them; and he was met by the four British destroyers which had accompanied the battlecruisers. Commander Loftus Jones, in the destroyer *Shark*, also decided it was time for a torpedo attack, and led the three other boats under his command. As he was up against light cruisers as well as destroyers, he did not last long. *Shark* went down in a few minutes, only six men surviving; Loftus Jones, one leg blown away but still directing the one remaining gun, went down with her.

He, and also Boy Seaman Cornwall, received posthumous Victoria Crosses.

The disabled *Wiesbaden*, lying between the speeding battlecruisers of both fleets, became a target for everyone who passed. The British Third Light Cruiser Squadron was succeeded by a solitary destroyer, the *Onslow*, whose captain realised that she might possibly be a torpedo threat to Beatty, and poured fifty-eight salvoes into her, to which the German light cruiser, flag still flying, replied with the occasional shot. Then the *Onslow* steamed on to try to torpedo the German battlecruisers.

Next on the scene from the British side were Admiral Arbuthnot's heavy cruisers. *Defence*, *Warrior* and *Black Prince* pounded the *Wiesbaden* and in their turn were taken under fire, out of the mist, by the approaching German battlecruisers which, seeing no other target, sent their heavy shells into the two leading cruisers. *Defence* went up in flames, billowing smoke, before her magazines exploded and she disappeared from the surface of the sea. *Warrior*, also riven and ablaze, wreathed in the smoke of her own fires, limped off into the haze.

In the very variable visibility and lack of light the stopped *Wiesbaden* came into view from some of the British battleships of Jellicoe's fleet engaged in closing the trap on the Germans, and they too fired at her in passing. Then the damaged *Onslow*, returning from her torpedo attempt against the German battlecruisers, also passed by. Her captain, Lt. -Cdr. Tovey, saw to his astonishment that the floating ruin which was the *Wiesbaden* still had not sunk, so from 3,500 yards he put a torpedo into her. It struck below the conning tower of the smoking wreck, which still refused to sink.

It was now after 6 p.m., with a dense curtain of mist lying between the battleships of the two main fleets. Beatty had skilfully led the whole of the High Seas Fleet to Jellicoe who was beginning to deploy into line behind the British battlecruisers which had now turned in their tracks to engage Hipper once more. No one man saw the whole of the battle, not even one-tenth part of it: the area was too vast, the ships too many, their speeds too great, the mist too confusing. Only the outlines of the major actions may be attempted.

The low and rapidly changing visibility confused Evan-Thomas leading the fast battleship squadron, and at an embarrassing moment the *Warspite*'s helm jammed and she began describing circles on her own in full view of the battleships of the High Seas Fleet. Although hit by heavy shells, her engines were not affected and all her turrets continued in action. Luckily for the disabled *Warrior* limping away, the manoeuvres of the apparently mad battleship masked the battered cruiser and also drew fire which otherwise must have destroyed the smaller ship. Meanwhile the three battlecruisers which had come up under Admiral Hood had taken up position at the head of the deploying Grand Fleet's line-ahead array.

Only those few officers and men in the open saw any part of what was happening. In the modern battleship *Royal Oak*, immediately following Jellicoe in the slightly older *Iron Duke*, Albert Parker was down in the boiler-room where men were getting impatient to know what was going on. Being young and impetuous, he was easily persuaded to leave his post and find out. He crept up towards the light, closing every water-tight door behind him, and at length reached the Marines' mess room, opened the inner case of a porthole and looked out. For a few seconds he glimpsed a scene quite unforgettable, a line of battleships to starboard of the flagship, the *Superb*, the *Canada*—a massive new vessel painted almost white—and following her the remarkably long *Agincourt*, built to foreign order but taken over by the Royal Navy, with her array of no less than fourteen 12-inch guns, some of them firing.

Vice-Admiral Sturdee, now in the battleship *Benbow* under Jellicoe, soon after saw through his field glasses what he thought must be the great hull of a wrecked Zeppelin in the water disturbed by the wakes of so many ships. He looked once, then turned away. He had read the word *Invincible*. His flagship at the Falklands.

Under Admiral Hood, the *Invincible*, *Inflexible* and *Indomitable* had taken station ahead of Beatty's four remaining battlecruisers, and were engaging Hipper's battlecruisers to such effect that Admiral Hood used the voice-pipe to Commander Dannreuter in the spotting top to say: 'Your firing is very good. Keep at it as quickly as you can. Every shot is telling.' They must have been his last words.

Dannreuter saw a shell hit the starboard turret and blow its armoured roof clean off into the sea. Vast clouds of smoke welled up, then the battlecruiser broke in half, the sunken middle ends coming to rest on the seabed. Dannreuter was unhurt, but the conning tower came down into the sea and the water pushed him out. The two halves of the 567-foot long ship stood up like tombstones over the dead and dying. As the battle fleet swept past the wreckage they cheered, believing that the ship must be German.

Dannreuter was covered in oil and believed that this was what kept him warm in the sea for 20 minutes before he was picked up by the destroyer *Badger*. One of the destroyer's officers was astounded at the way Dannreuter came aboard, 'as cheerily as if he were simply joining a new ship in the ordinary course of events'.

He was one of the six survivors out of the 1,026 men in the *Invincible*. In the *Indefatigable* there had been two out of 1,017, and from the *Queen Mary* 20 out of 1,266.

The Germans had realised that new ships had joined Beatty but not at first that he had the whole of the Grand Fleet behind him, arrayed in a line which 'crossed the T' of the High Seas Fleet, so every British gun could be brought to bear, but only a few of the German guns. In spite of confusion, bad reporting, dud shells and bad luck with his battle-cruisers, Jellicoe had managed to place his giant fleet in the position of advantage which admirals have always sought.

Scheer was facing annihilation. He ordered a manoeuvre which the British believed impossible in the circumstances but which the Germans had often practised: the Battle Turn Away. Instead of each ship turning in succession after the leader, which takes a long time, the ships turn individually, starting with the rearmost. It took ship-handling of a high order, and it was covered by the German light craft going in with torpedoes and making smoke. And that caused Jellicoe to make the safe reply. The Grand Fleet turned away, presenting their sterns to the torpedoes, so both fleets were going in opposite directions at high speed, and were soon out of sight of each other.

It was at this point that the British battleships passed the still-floating wreck of the *Wiesbaden* which, it must be remembered, was a light cruiser without armoured protection. There being no other Germans ship in sight, the battleships turned their huge guns on her. And somewhere amid the raging fires in the riven hull some unknown Germans—whose names will never be known—prepared a torpedo tube, trained it on the battleships, and fired. The torpedo ran true and struck the *Marlborough*, flagship of Admiral Burney, reducing her speed to 16 knots so that momentarily she was virtually out of the battle.

Belching flame but still afloat, the *Wiesbaden* drifted off into the coming night and disappeared, her end witnessed neither by friend nor foe.

Jellicoe's aim was to get between the Germans and their bases, and Scheer's to break off and get home as soon as possible. But nevertheless the High Sea Fleet once more blundered into the Grand Fleet and once again Scheer had to order a 'Battle Turn Away', but this time much later and in great confusion. To save his battleships the German Admiral signalled to his battlecruisers the desperate order:

Battlecruisers at the enemy! Charge! Ram!

Their flagship, the *Lützow*, was absent, so badly damaged that later on, when she could no longer steam, she had to be sunk and her crew taken off. The remaining four ships, led by the *Derfflinger*, had scarcely a working gun between them, had been repeatedly punished, some of them so holed that they had thousands of tons of water aboard, but they obeyed as far as they could. In German legend, they called it 'The Death Ride'. It was supported once again by the German destroyers making smoke and attacking with torpedoes. But in spite of the blizzard of fire and shell-torn water around them, no German battlecruiser actually sank during the 'ride', although the *Seydlitz* went down in shallow water when she reached home, and had to be salvaged.

Using their initiative, the German battleship captains got round and away somehow or other, even if it meant turning to starboard instead of port, by reversing engines to avoid collision, or by jinking round other ships. The British battleship captains (and admirals too), however, remained paralysed by pre-war rigidity and discipline. The Germans in a fair state of chaos were in range of the British Second Battle Squadron under Admiral Jerram (who had so narrowly missed the *Emden* earlier in the war), but not a shot was fired at them. Even a 17-year-old range-taker in Jerram's flagship, *King George V*, remarked afterwards that the Admiral seemed afraid of opening fire without direct permission from the Commander-in-Chief.

Once more, Jellicoe played safe and turned away from the torpedoes (which was his previously stated policy) rather than turning towards them, which was not quite so safe. And so the High Seas Fleet escaped a second time, in spite of Beatty's signal:

Submit that the van of the battleships follow me; we can then cut off the enemy's fleet.

But the two battle fleets had seen the last of each other for the duration of the war, although in escaping from the British trap, the Germans ploughed through some of the British light forces at their rear and the night was rent by the yellow flashes of gunfire and the white and wavering fingers of searchlights. But quite deliberately Jellicoe did not engage. The Germans were trained in night fighting, the British were not; and all night operations are a chancy business, where mistakes in recognition can have fatal consequences. Jellicoe was between the Germans and their base; he thought he still would be in the morning. Had the Admiralty done their job and transmitted to him the results of their wireless decodes, so that he knew which route through the minefields the Germans would take, there might still have been that annihilating victory for which the Navy and the nation longed.

There were little bursts of sudden action in the night as the Germans broke through. There were collisions, of British with British and of British with German. Blinded by searchlight beams, the destroyer *Spitfire* did not see the looming sides of the battleship *Nassau* and scraped past, the German guns firing directly over her, their blast wrecking the *Spitfire*'s bridge, mast and funnel. Her hull torn open for most of its length, the destroyer carried away with her twenty feet of side plating from the battleship.

The British destroyer *Broke*, uncertain of a possible opponent, made the challenge and never got the chance to fire; her bridge wrecked and all on it killed, the wheel jammed hard to port, she went out of control and drove into the side of another British destroyer, the *Sparrowhawk*, which was just about to torpedo the German ship which had done the damage. The destroyers knew they were fighting battleships as well as cruisers, but they kept it a dark secret. No one bothered to inform Jellicoe. Some of the British battleships also saw what was happening but regarded the information as confidential to them, apparently. The destroyers did manage to torpedo the old pre-dreadnought battleship *Pommern*, which sank with all hands.

Steering south astern of the Grand Fleet was the *Southampton* with three other light cruisers, when the faint shapes of five ships were detected to starboard, steering a parallel course. British or German? A line of coloured lights suddenly glowed on the signal yards of the five strange ships. Presumably the reply would be a similar display, for the British used morse code. As the British order to fire came through, King-Hall found himself surrounded by blinding light. All five had concentrated their searchlights on the *Southampton* as the leading British ship. They concentrated their guns on her too, following the search-lights, and the hail of shells within seconds killed or wounded all the gun crews near King-Hall. Two giant columns of flame leaped up and King-Hall found himself surrounded by unstable cordite charges which were just beginning to catch fire. And more cordite charges were being sent up from below by men who did not realise that there was no one left on deck to load the guns. As a third column of flame leaped up, King-Hall ran for the quarterdeck. Having seen about four British ships blow up, he expected that the *Southampton* might be next.

He was not at all sure what to do about the prospect of being spirited hundreds of feet into the air and then dumped in the sea. There was a whizzing noise just over his head, which was a shot-away searchlight falling. For perhaps ten seconds he stood alone apparently among the dead.

The uncertainty was broken by a tremendous explosion in the second or third ship of the German line. She 'opened up like a sardine tin' and King-Hall could see right inside her—an extraordinary sight. *Southampton*'s torpedo lieutenant had fired a torpedo into what turned out to be the *Frauenlob* and this providentially convinced the Germans that they had heavy ships to deal with; they switched off their searchlights and turned away into the night.

King-Hall then realised what he ought to have done 30 seconds earlier. He shouted down for a fire party and was rewarded by the appearance of the wardroom cook and some other men with a hose. The three fires died down quickly and the ship was pitch-black again. Then he became aware of a new sound which had been lost in the hissing and roaring of the fires. Cries and groans were coming from some of the bodies lying around the guns. Stumbling forward with a torch, he came on a Boy Seaman whose name was Mellish. He had lost both legs. King-Hall took the mangled lad in his arms helplessly. The boy smiled and said 'Just slip me overboard, sir.' Then he died.

When they worked it out afterwards, King-Hall had been standing on a patch of deck about three by four feet which was the only part not scored by splinters. He was the only man on the afterpart of the *Southampton* who had not been killed or wounded in those few minutes. When King George V visited the ship at Rosyth, King-Hall was asked to stand on this patch of untouched deck and a string representing the fall of the searchlight stretched down just above his head. The monarch remarked, 'Well, King-Hall, you and I can agree there are some advantages in being on the short side.'

Commander Dannreuter, whose escape from the *Invincible* had been even more miraculous, found himself fêted at home as a 'Jutland Hero'. But first, Beatty asked to see him in the *Lion*, also lying at Rosyth. For Dannreuter it was extremely embarrassing. Beatty was in a state of near 'frenzy', railing against Jellicoe, his Commander-in-Chief, who, he declared, had let him down. There seems little doubt that the flamboyant publicity-seeking Beatty, like many others, saw himself as a potential rival to Nelson, and that the expectations of another Trafalgar governed his actions.

Shortly afterwards, Jellicoe was relieved of command of the Grand Fleet and replaced by Beatty, who looked like a hero, tough and dashing (and not at all like Nelson). He now had access to the records of Jellicoe's time as Third Sea Lord and Controller in 1910, when he had discovered by tests the ineffectiveness of British shells. Jellicoe had written a memorandum to the Board of Ordnance asking for an armour-piercing shell which would penetrate even when it struck obliquely and thus always burst inside the enemy ship. He had then been sent to sea and left the task to his successor, who had done nothing. At Jutland the British had scored far more hits than the Germans but too many of their shells had either been duds or had broken up on the enemy's armour. Jellicoe had known this at Jutland, Beatty had not. The new Commander-in-Chief proved just as cautious as his wise predecessor.

The ghost of King Henry VIII, if he was still around, must have been grieved. He had initiated the policy of putting really big guns into battleships and the gun had reigned at sea for over 400 years; but not for much longer. The result on the German side was far-reaching, the decision to back the U-boat as a war-winner necessarily resulted in a campaign of what, by earlier standards, was atrocity; for no submarine could take large numbers of prisoners, indeed even to surface might mean its own destruction. And the British Navy was not ready to combat this weapon either. The truth was that, as with bayonets, you can do anything with your laurels, except sit on them.

The Germans proclaimed Jutland a victory for them on the basis of ships sunk and men killed. The British lost three battlecruisers, three heavy cruisers and eight destroyers; the Germans lost one battleship (an old pre-dreadnought), one battlecruiser, three cruisers and five destroyers. The British losses in men were far greater than those of the Germans—6,097 killed, 510 wounded and 177 taken prisoner, as against 2,551 Germans killed and 507 wounded. The British proclaimed a victory because the enemy had avoided battle, and finally their surface fleet mutinied, eventually turning up at Scapa Flow to surrender. At the beginning of the Second World War Jellicoe's flagship *Iron Duke*, demilitarised, was bombed at Scapa Flow by the Luftwaffe and run aground where, with a concrete bottom, she became prison ship and post office for the Orkney garrison. Meanwhile the German battlecrusier *Derfflinger* lay bottom up in a geo, after her salvage had been interrupted.

The British Navy longed still to re-fight Jutland, and this time to win it conclusively, a desire which distorted naval policy. The battleship was obsolete, the U-boat had not been rendered impotent by the new sonar (or Asdic), and the bomber could, alas, sink battleships far bigger than any that fought in the North Sea in 1916. It took longer than necessary for these facts to be appreciated, and for this the unsatisfactory conclusion of Jutland was responsible.

Chapter Sixteen

EVANS OF THE *BROKE*

The 'Shoot and Scoot' Raids, April 1917

From boredom, bad food and barracks-type discipline the crews of the battleships were to mutiny in 1918. But not the men of the cruisers and destroyers, who found themselves fully employed on warlike work. There were several British disasters to their convoys from the Shetlands to Norway, their escorting destroyers being sunk together with many of the merchantmen. But these battles took place far away. Much nearer home—and therefore more newsworthy in England—was German destroyer activity in and around the Straits of Dover.

The British supply routes for men and war material to the Western Front in France lay mainly through the ports on the Kentish coast; and there was the so-called 'Dover Barrage' of nets and drifters and guard vessels designed to catch or destroy or deter U-boats from entering the Channel from their bases on the Belgian coast, and there was the great storm weather anchorage off Dover called the Downs. All these offered tempting targets for the fast German destroyers to dash over during the night on what came to be called 'Shoot and Scoot' operations.

They were helped to success on occasion by alterations in their codes which were hard for 'Room 40', the Admiralty wireless interception and decoding unit, to crack; added by much senior Admiralty indifference to the importance of their work. 'Damn your decoding, why aren't you fighting?' was the motto of many.

But Room 40 scored a success on the night of 22–23 January, 1917, when the move of a German destroyer flotilla to Zeebrugge on the Belgian coast was detected in time and intercepted by a British force. On 25 February the Germans obtained surprise but did little damage; and on 17–18 March Room 40 gave timely warning of a destroyer raid, which was driven off. A much larger raid by a dozen German destroyers on the night of 20–21 April was intercepted by a British force consisting of two exceptionally large British destroyers which may be classed as flotilla leaders. The result was to discourage the Germans for ten months.

After a British destroyer, the *Paragon*, had been sunk on 23 March, the Admiralty formed a force of four flotilla leaders, *Botha*, *Faulkner*, *Swift* and *Broke*. On this particular night it was the last two which were on patrol. The *Swift* had a 6-inch gun forward, an enormous piece worthy of a cruiser; her captain was Commander A. M. Peck. Keeping station astern of her was the *Broke*, with a new bow; she had lost the first one by ramming another British destroyer at Jutland, losing her captain at the same time. She was now to lose her bow a second time, and bring her captain fame.

The *Broke* had been built by Vickers-Armstrong in 1912 for the Chilean Navy and been requisitioned in 1914 for the British Navy. Her original name of *Almirante Uribe* had been changed to *Broke* after Philip Broke, captain of the frigate *Shannon* when she took the American frigate *Chesapeake* north of Massachusetts Bay in 1813. She displaced 1,850 tons and had a crew of 214 including Royal Marines, an unheard-of thing in a destroyer at that period. In command was Edward Evans who commented that she had 'beautiful accommodation for the captain and rotten quarters for everyone else'. She was armed with six 4-inch guns, four of them sited to fire ahead, and four 18-inch torpedo tubes.

Evans had a father whose hobby was painting ships; he had entered the Navy the cheap way as a boy of 15 in January 1895, through the training ship *Worcester*, which prepared lads for the Merchant Marine but from where cadetships to the Royal Navy might be obtained by promising youngsters. Evans was a small, tough little lad who gained high marks for everything except good conduct, being classed as a 'ruffian'. Becoming bored with life in the Royal Navy in peacetime, he volunteered for the Polar Expeditions then being conducted under Scott, Shackleton and others, took part in three of them, and gained material for a book of adventures. It was while lecturing on his three Antarctic expeditions that he met Elsa Andvord at Christiana in Norway. This would not have been popular in the British Navy at any time, for obvious reasons, so Evans was commanded to report to the Admiralty where he was told that Their Lordships did not like naval officers 'contracting marriages with foreigners in wartime'. Evans told

Admiral Sir Reginald Hall, the head of Room 40, 'I don't care if she's a Hottentot, I'm going to marry her.'

Hall told Evans that he was impudent, but he may have told him a good deal more. For on the night of 20 April, 1917, his biographer noted that Evans said he had 'passed word round' about an expected German raid, blaming 'an extraordinary instinct'. To his wife he had said: 'The Germans will come out tonight. We're ready for them.'

Evans had previously told his crew what his tactics would be in a night action, '. . . to strike direct for the enemy after firing the first torpedo and to drive right in among them ramming or being rammed, as the case may be.'

Of course, it was not a good idea to be rammed, but quite likely because in a high-speed night action, if you missed the ship you tried to ram, the next astern of her would probably ram you. And if you missed ahead, you also would be the one to be rammed. If Room 40 were right, they were in for an exciting night.

The *Swift* and the *Broke* left Dover for the ninth night in succession at 7.45 p.m., having loaded 233 tons of coal during the crew's rest period. At forty-five minutes after midnight seven miles east of Dover, they sighted an enemy flotilla steaming fast towards them 600 yards away. The fire-gongs sounded in the German ships and in the British, who were out-numbered apparently six to two.

Sub-Lieutenant Peppe went onto the bridge. The German destroyers, whose gun flashes they had seen as they shelled Dover an hour earlier, could just be made out, passing swiftly down the starboard sides of the two British flotilla leaders.

> Simultaneously, *Swift*, ourselves, and the enemy opened fire and a ripple of flame ran along their line as blinding flashes lit the dark night. A roar denoted *Swift*'s mighty six-inch gun firing.

It was the great flash from that gun, firing from just forward of the bridge, which momentarily ruined Commander Peck's night vision at the critical moment when he was turning his ship to ram. He missed, but avoided being himself run down by a German. Then he turned onto a course parallel to the Germans and fired his torpedoes, going 25 knots. One of them seemed to hit.

Of the six men around the *Broke*'s forward gun a few moments ago, only two were left; but they were still loading and firing. A ball of

burning cordite landed on the bridge, lighting up the *Broke* and making
her a target for concentrated fire. Lieutenant Max Despard, the first
officer, picked out the second ship in the German line; as his torpedo
sight came on, he fired; and hit. But when he ordered the second tube to
stand by, there was no answer. 'See what's happened, Sub,' he said to
Peppe.

When Peppe reached the tube, he saw the torpedoman lying dead
astride it and amidships there was steam pouring from the ventilators.
The main steam pipe had been carried away by a shell and all the men
there had met an agonising end, scalded to death. Another exploding
shell threw Peppe against the ladder leading to the bridge, from where
he could hear Evans giving orders to attack the third ship in the
German line.

'Stand by to ram.'

'Hard over and ram, Quartermaster.'

The impact (reflected Evans later) 'must have been a dreadful
moment for those aboard' the German destroyer G42. In the *Broke*'s
engineroom the artificers believed that they had been torpedoed. Lt.
Peppe remembered:

> The crash when it came was terrific. Straight into the enemy the
> *Broke* cleaved her way. For a few moments the doomed ship was
> carried alongside, then slowly she heeled over and sank underfoot.
> On our lower bridge there was carnage, only the Quartermaster
> (Leading Seaman Rawlings) survived, grasping the wheel from a
> kneeling position because his back and legs were riddled with
> shrapnel. Now the Midshipman (Giles), grasping a revolver in
> each hand, was preparing to lead a boarding party armed with the
> cutlasses always kept in readiness, but he was knocked down by
> shrapnel over the eye. Three Germans managed to crawl aboard
> over the stockless anchor, more ready to surrender than to show
> fight.

In this carnage a shell splinter shattered the compass and struck the
binnacle against which Evans was standing, a fragment cutting his
tunic. Otherwise he was unharmed and, taking no chances, he ordered
the 'boarders' to be thrown back into the sea, and then for the *Broke* to
follow the *Swift* in her pursuit of the Germans. On being told that the
loss of boiler feed water meant that the speed was cut by half, so that

pursuit was impossible, he tried to close a disabled German destroyer which was stopped and burning some distance away. This was G85, possibly the ship torpedoed by the *Swift*.

On her way, more drifting than steaming, the *Broke* with ruined bows passed German survivors in the water calling for help. Lt. Despard suggested lowering a boat, to which Evans replied: 'We're not here to look after midnight bathers.'

To the desperate cries from the water of '*Hilfe! Hilfe!*' the British sailors roared back:

'Hospital ships!'

'*Lusitania!*'

When they reached the burning, drifting G85, cries of 'Kamerad!' came out of the smoke. Then the forward gun of the German ship opened fire, possibly because the gun's crew had not heard an order to give in, or perhaps merely did not agree with it. Anyway, the British regarded this as rank treachery and fired back with four rounds of 4-inch and a torpedo, taking no prisoners except a single man in a boat who came alongside. The seamen were in favour of hanging him, according to Lt. Despard. The *Broke*, by now out of action, anchored near the mine barrage, when HMS *Mentor* turned up to offer help. Her sub-lieutenant recalls the Germans swimming in the water and Evans leaning over the bridge, shouting 'Remember the *Lusitania!*' (which may have been an injunction to the men not to save life).

However, between them the *Swift* and the *Broke* rescued 140 Germans. The *Swift* had had one man killed and four wounded. When the battered *Broke* was towed in to Dover to roars of cheering and the wild noise of hooters, there were 21 flag-covered bodies on her upper deck and 27 wounded down below in the sick bay. Evans, on visiting the seamens' messdeck, found scores of German sailors being fed with bacon and eggs by British sailors 'as if they were entertaining a visiting football team'. Nelson would have approved ('May humanity after victory be the predominant feature of the British Fleet.') But not everyone can swiftly discard the ruthless determination to kill which is essential to the winning of battles.

Two days later the dead were buried in a hillside cemetery above Dover. Evans then reflected, 'how hateful war is . . . We who had come out unscathed were not unmindful of the poor relatives . . . their drawn cheeks, dimmed eyes, and pale faces one cannot forget.'

A local Court of Enquiry arrived at the view that 'the total number of enemy vessels engaged was five. We consider that three were sunk.' The Admiral commanding at Dover disagreed: six enemy engaged, only two enemy sunk. Notoriously, high-speed actions at night are difficult to dissect; it is hard even for witnesses to remember everything that happened, let alone the order in which they occurred, or to be absolutely sure of all that they observed.

Commander Peck, who was the senior officer and, according to Evans, 'the most modest man in the Royal Navy', gave Evans a glowing report. However, a naval member of the London Press Bureau came up with the title of 'Evans of the Broke', which had a bold, dramatic ring to it, whereas 'Peck of the Swift' would have sounded merely silly. A fellow destroyer captain recalled that this publicity made Evans unpopular with a certain group of officers who considered him a self-advertiser. 'What they did not realise was that to the newspapers he was news.' So 'Evans of the Broke' it was.

'Evans of the Broke' sounded the very man to choose as a liaison officer to go over to Queenstown in Southern Ireland to welcome the first division of United States destroyers, under Rear-Admiral Sims, to arrive in Europe. His style went down well with the Americans and also with the merchant seamen serving at Queenstown with 'Q' or Mystery Ships.

By September 1917 he was senior destroyer officer at Dover (Captain Peck having been given a cruiser), an early assignment being to proceed to Calais (which in this war was still French and not German) to pick up a load of gold, amounting to five million pounds, consigned anonymously to the Bank of England. He was to load the gold on board the *Broke* and then wait for an escort. While at lunch, the quartermaster, in dripping wet oilskins, entered to say that there was 'somebody out there on the wharf asking for you, sir'.

There were indeed no less than three drenched figures trying to shelter simultaneously in a sentry box. In order of seniority they were the Prime Minister (David Lloyd George), the Chief of the Imperial General Staff (Sir William Robertson) and the Secretary of the Cabinet (Sir Maurice Hankey). It appeared that they were queuing for the cross-Channel steamer. So Evans offered them a lift in his own cross-Channel steamer (of the Grey Funnel Line).

On being taken down to Evans' cabin, Lloyd George was startled to find the floor covered with little green bags containing gold. 'Do you trust me with all this wealth?' he asked.

'I suppose I shall have to *say* I do, sir!' replied Evans.

The *Broke* made the crossing in rough seas which made her appear a submarine rather than an outsize destroyer, but when Evans had seen his passengers safely packed away in a special train (no queuing at Dover for them) he returned to his gold-laden cabin to find an agitated official of the Bank of England exclaiming: 'We're one bag short!'

Evans laughed loudly. The Bank official snapped that he was being 'too casual'. Evans shrugged off responsibility on the grounds that it was many years since the Admiralty had abolished its kindly custom of paying a percentage to the Captain of any bullion he carried. Then, perhaps to plant a seed in fertile ground, he admitted that 'a man named George with a small attaché case' had been in this cabin during the crossing. Before the Bank of England could arrest the Prime Minister, the bags were recounted—and found to be correct.

In October 1917 Evans was appointed Flag Captain to Admiral Bacon, who ran the Dover Patrol. Bacon was soon replaced by a more energetic figure, Roger Keyes, who had started the war as a Commodore, Submarines, had played an enthusiastic part in urging decisive action at the Dardanelles, and was soon to plan what might be a decisive action against the U-boats now that the command was in his hands. But Keyes brought in his own staff and was thought to be a bit of a snob, and so Evans, who had joined via the Merchant Navy, had to go. Later, he became Lord Mountevans, but 'Evans of the Broke' he remained at heart.

Chapter Seventeen

Q-SHIPS AND U-BOATS

Western Approaches, April 1917

On 1 February, 1917, Germany began an intensified submarine campaign. No longer were German submarine captains required by their government to establish if merchant ships were carrying cargoes helpful to the British war effort before sinking them (while making provision for the safety of their passengers and crews). Most ships were now likely to be sunk on sight if in the war zone.

Sinkings of Allied and neutral merchant ships rose dramatically —and for Britain, terribly—while the risks to the attacking submarines were lessened. In April 1917 over 545,000 tons of British shipping were sunk. Adding the numbers of Allied, neutral and fishing craft sunk, the total for the month was 875,000 tons. If sinkings continued at this rate, Britain would have to sue for peace. What the formidable German armies had failed to do, what the German High Seas Fleet had, not surprisingly, failed to do, a quite small fleet of cheaply built and inexpensively manned underwater craft seemed about to accomplish. After many hesitations on the part of the German government, because of the unfavourable effect of killing civilians or neutrals—particularly the United States—these risks were accepted. The Gentleman's Wars were over. Nowadays, everyone wages—or plans to wage— unrestricted submarine warfare; no one now may opt out; neither sex, nor age nor status can confer immunity. But in 1917 there was still a horrified reaction to this attitude.

Very old means of defence, such as convoy, were resurrected (in spite of the British Admiralty), Keyes at Dover set to work to create an impenetrable barrier to U-boats entering the Channel and pondered attacking their bases in Flanders; the Americans created a gigantic mine barrier in deep water to shut U-boats off from the Atlantic; and the decoy ship was reintroduced. Basically, the latter came under the 'dirty tricks' department of Admiralty which was traditional: ambush under false colours was as old as sea warfare itself. Indeed, there had been a few so-called 'Mystery Ships' as early as 1914; but the crisis of 1917 gave the idea new emphasis when it was already almost too late.

By 1917 the enemy were well aware that the Allies had decoys, which could be anything from a liner to a small sailing ship, so that complete surprise was difficult to achieve. Most, however, were either tramp steamers converted or warships specially built to look like tramp steamers. They were of course armed with hidden guns which could be unmasked instantly, for the time in which to disable or kill a submarine was short indeed, even if the captain was kind enough to surface at all.

Keeping the secret started at the dockyards where the ships were built or converted; it was almost impossible to prevent leaks in dock-yard towns. Then, when built, armed and manned, all sorts of bureaucratic procedures could point the finger at an apparently inno-cent tramp as being anything but what she seemed. In Southern Irish ports where the Mystery Ships were likely to be stationed, a proportion of the population must be 'shinners', the comparatively honourable ancestors of the IRA, to whom England's current enemy must be an ally. To keep the secret, the Admiralty decided to stop calling them SS (for Special Service) and instead gave them numbers prefixed by the letter 'Q'. That made the spy's work easy: every ship with a 'Q' in front of its number was a decoy and not just any old newfangled idea; just as a B or a D or E meant submarine.

Every man aboard was required to be a split personality. Publicly, he wore civilian clothes (with a bowler hat, if appropriate) and used merchant navy terminology—'Master' instead of 'Captain', for in-stance; but when under cover he was pukka navy, on duty 24 hours a day like any other serviceman. He was always conscious of his duty which was, first, to go and get torpedoed, and then, if he could innocently tempt a naïve submarine to the surface, kill it in seconds. Even the first part wasn't easy, finding U-boats being a hard art; the second requirement demanded constant practice at drills and lightning reactions, as well as the self-discipline to remain concealed even if wounded. The skills required could be considered as a difficult and dangerous branch of angling, even if the cargo consisted of loads of lumber or other buoyant items.

The enemy used three classes of submarine. Plain U-Boats were big and had a long range—the ability to visit New York, Madeira, and so on—and were armed not only with torpedoes but with guns as large as 5.9-inch. The UB class were small and handy, designed to operate in the North Sea. The UC class carried mines mainly, as well as torpedoes.

Since their battery power for underwater travel was limited, submarines spent most of their time on the surface, and definitely had to surface to recharge batteries. They were actually surface vessels with an occasional diving capability. Their torpedoes, which were really small, unmanned submarines, travelled ten to twenty feet down, leaving a trail of bubbles on the surface; they could, if seen early, be dodged, and for this reason submarine commanders preferred to fire at close range. The warhead in the nose contained sufficient explosive to blow a hole some 40 feet square in the hull of an unarmoured merchant ship.

Probably the most successful of all the Q-Ship captains was Gordon Campbell, who began as a Lt.-Cdr. and ended up a Captain. He endured a year of this stressful work, which was highly unusual. He was to write:

It was not always the successful actions that called for the most courage and subjected the crews to the greatest ordeal: it was frequently that the unsuccessful actions called forth the best in men.

When a Q-Ship met a U-Boat it was infrequent for both captains to survive and be able to compare notes afterwards on their duel. An exception was the action between HMS *Tulip* (Q12), a 1,500-ton sloop built to resemble a merchant ship, under Commander Lewis, and the 1,000-ton ocean-going submarine U62 under Commander Ernst Hashagen. The date was 30 April 1917, the place some 200 miles off the western coast of Ireland. A brilliant spring day and a calm sea.

Hashagen had got his first command in February 1916, the little 262-ton UB21, just completed by Blohm & Voss at their works beside the Elbe in Hamburg. After carrying out firing exercises in the bay of Eckernförde in the Baltic, he took her out on the first of three patrols he made in her. She finished the war as a training boat at Eckernförde, listed number 20 among the top-scoring boats, was surrendered in 1918 and sank in 1920 off Portsmouth while in tow to the breakers. Some careless fellow had left a live G7 torpedo in the starboard tube.*

By November 1916 Hashagen was an experienced commander and was given the ocean-going U62. His second cruise in her began on 21 April 1917, when she left the advanced submarine base at Heligoland, the red rock island which had been a British possession from 1807 until 1890. His new boat could do 16 knots on the surface, had a crew of 40 men and mounted two guns—a 4-inch and an 18-pounder. It lacked, however, the quick-diving capabilities of the smaller UB21. Correspondingly, its commander had to be more careful not to blunder into situations where he might have to dive in a hurry. She even had a doctor on board, Staff-Surgeon Dr Sonntag, who was to study crew health on a long cruise.

The big ships, which might go to a real war for 24 hours in four years, had doctors of all ranks; the small ones, such as destroyers and submarines, which did quite frequently take casualties, had initially no more than a coxswain trained in First Aid. By this time, in the British destroyers, a scheme had been instituted whereby a medical student did six months at university followed by six months at sea, then back to university, then back to sea; better than nothing, if you were wounded, but you would still be tended by a learner-doctor (Surgeon-Probationer being the cunning British term).

In fog banks and high seas alternately, U62 rounded the Shetlands, another group of desolate islands north of the Orkneys and the barren anchorage of the Grand Fleet. Hashagen sighted a merchant ship, chased it and lost it; saw another and sank it; exchanged greetings with another boat, U61, on the surface homeward bound; sighted a sailing ship from Montreal headed for Aberdeen, and sank it; two days of bitter cold and storms and then 30 April, a brilliant sunny day. To the south, smoke—and two masts thin as needles.

The 'Master' of the enemy ship, Commander Lewis, recalled:

On April 30, 1917—the most disastrous week of the whole war for our shipping—I was in command of the Decoy Ship Q12, a sloop

---

*Coincidentally, the author lived in Blankenese opposite Blohm & Voss in around 1950, took part in amphibious training at Eckernförde when it was a British Army base, visited Helígoland after the (Hitler-built) U-Boat pens had been blown up and in 1970 dived the wreck of UB21 and recognised the torpedo for the danger that it was.

of some 1,500 tons, but in the course of her construction she had been altered in appearance to pass for a merchant ship. It was about 1.30 p.m. on a fine spring afternoon, we were steaming along some 200 miles off the west coast of Ireland.

A true merchant ship is normally much broader in the beam than a warship, and these exceptionally fine lines may have had something to do with what happened. To start with, seen end-on she would look not quite right.

Hashagen dived and headed towards this ship. Half an hour later he was close enough to see that she was painted black and steering a wild, zigzag course, as if wary of attack.

In the U-boat, they timed her. Alteration of course to 315°. Ten minutes later, an alteration of 330°. After another ten minutes, a further alteration to 345°. The Germans, still puzzled, tried to work out her mean course, so as to intersect hers. On her stern a rather tattered Red Ensign, the flag of the British Merchant Navy. That seemed odd to Hashagen; in his experience the British preferred to use neutral flags or markings. It all added up, indefinably, to caution.

Hashagen had begun his approach with the periscope three feet out of the water. Beside him the coxswain controlled the height of the lift on which his captain stood, to raise or lower the periscope on command.

'Run in the periscope. In—deeper still—a bit more—out a shade —in! In!'

The sea above was becoming very calm, a periscope would show a white feather of water as it ploughed along. But if it was raised for only a few seconds at a time, the momentary white wake could be taken for the breaking of a small wave.

'Higher—up a little more—down again—in!'

The enemy had introduced depth charges—they did not now have to rely on shellfire or ramming of a surfaced boat; they could kill her even when she was invisible to them, if they had a mark to aim their charges at, even though it was only at the estimated position of where her periscope had been last seen.

The black ship was altering course again. Set the stop watch. If he only keeps this course for his usual ten minutes, U62 at slowest speed will be in a firing position.

'Lower—down—up—right in.'

Apart from the brief periscope orders, everything goes deathly quiet.

Just the rattle of the hydroplanes being altered to maintain a constant depth.

As the watch hand ticked round, reached eight-and-a-half minutes from the enemy's last change of course, Hashagen ordered:

'Up!'

The black steamer's bows appeared in the left arc of the periscope and then passed the sighting wire. Blue-green water momentarily blotted it out. A wave. It became light again. The mast passed the sighting wire. There's the bridge!

'First tube, stand by.'

Another wave breaks over the periscope, vanishes. Now the steam's funnel comes into view.

'*Los* . . .'

The boat shivers slightly as the torpedo leaves the tube. It's going to be a hit, Hashagen feels it.

Lewis recorded the moments of suspense:

> I was on the bridge, when suddenly one of my seven look-outs reported: 'Periscope on the starboard bow, sir.' I saw it instantly, about 500 yards off, and gave the order to the helmsman to port his helm with a view to ramming or dropping a depth-charge on the U-boat. Before the ship answered his helm, however, the same look-out reported, 'Torpedo fired, sir,' and the track of the torpedo was plainly visible coming directly at us. It was an anxious moment. Would the torpedo go under us or would it strike us?

In U62 they counted the seconds. After only 20 seconds there was a 'heavy detonation'; and after 22 seconds (while the first explosion was still reverbrating in the water) came a second explosion 'decidedly more severe', which Hashagen assumed was a boiler explosion. So violently were these shocks felt in the U-boat that Hashagen ordered her taken down to ten fathoms to check in safety for damage.

For the Q-Ship the effect was fatal. Her disguise was penetrated, her motive power destroyed. She could not even call for help.

> The torpedo hit the ship fair amidships between the engine-room and the stokehold. A terrific explosion occurred, followed by another when the boilers exploded. The effect was disastrous; my biggest boat was thrown on to the deck, my wireless came down,

the disguise of my guns was exposed, and the ship was split in two, with a huge gap at the water-line on each side: she was practically in two bits, probably held together by one fractured beam. The Chief Engineer reported that everyone in the engine-room and stokehold had been killed.

Normally a Q-Ship had two crews—the real crew who remained out of sight in the machinery spaces below and the guns' crews who lay down in cover by their guns; the Captain had disguised periscopes from which he could, unseen, watch what the U-boat did when, hopefully, it had been tempted to the surface. Then there was the fake crew, the so-called 'Panic Party', including a rating dressed as the Master's wife, a sailor carrying a parrot in a cage, a negro who rushed up from below at the last moment and frantically shouted out to be saved. In all, a none-too-flattering (or even accurate) representation of the Merchant Navy; but great 'theatre', which had lured more than a dozen U-boat captains to their doom. But not this cautious prowler.

Hashagen crossed the bows of the Q-Ship with his periscope well out of the water as a gimmick to draw fire. The steamer was 'heavily buckled amidships' and there was no sign of the crew. She might have been deserted. But she wasn't. A gun concealed under the bridge opened up a 'heavy fire' on the periscope. Aha! thought Hashagen. He withdrew the periscope and, keeping ahead of the motionless vessel, opened the range.

Using the high-power lens, Hashagen confirmed what he had half-expected from the start.

On the stern there stands, very well masked, a heavy gun. The concealing flaps were splintered and pushed aside by the explosion of the torpedo. Yet I could only make out the gun after a long and careful examination. On either side, under the bridge, a 3-inch gun. Aft, two flaps in the ship's side have fallen outwards, behind which there are evidently torpedo tubes. A submarine decoy! Before the explosion there was, of course, nothing of all this to be seen.

Once the First Lieutenant and the Chief Engineer of the Q-Ship had told Commander Lewis that her end was only seconds away, he and a seaman hauled the iron safe containing the confidential books to the side and threw it overboard. Then they launched the three remaining boats and abandoned. Rowing and drifting, some distance from the ship, which was still afloat, they saw U62 surface about a mile away, saw the men come up through the conning tower, clear the guns away, and train both barrels apparently on them.

> We felt more than uncomfortable. In common with most people at that time, under the influence of war propaganda, we believed that the Germans would show us no mercy. At this rather trying moment my steward, a butler in private life, chose to say: 'I'm afraid I left your cabin in a terrible state, sir.' At that instant the U-boat fired, and then to our considerable relief we heard the shell pass overhead, saw the ship break in two, and go down vertically in two halves.

Hashagen described exactly this, and also that he saw a cloud of smoke and flame arise as the wreck went 'hissing into the depths'. He added:

> On the scene of the wreck there floated all sorts of things, among them bits of clothing, tables, chairs, charts, etc. In the lid of one of these ditty-boxes, under the usual picture of a pretty girl, we found what we sought—a postcard with the following address: 'Able Seaman Jackson, HMS Tulip (Q12)'. We now went up to the boats and examined with the greatest interest these fellows who had wished to end our lives. They were a somewhat evil-looking crowd, like a very down-at-heel troop of actors; but that, indeed was part of the big bluff! I decided to create a precedent and to take prisoner the leader of the band.

Commander Lewis's story tallies:

> The U-boat then came towards us and asked for the Captain, an honour I had no wish to claim, and certainly with no cap, collar, tie or coat, and a very dirty old pair of blue trousers, I looked more like a tramp than a Naval Commander.

However, Lewis raised his hand and was rowed alongside the submarine. A young officer, rather unnecessarily, told him that he was now a prisoner and Lewis was taken to Hashagen, who asked him if he had any weapons or papers. 'You will kill me now, Captain?' was

Lewis's first question according to Hashagen, to which, stunned, he blurted, 'No, not yet!' and then asked him, according to Lewis, to come along and have a drink. Which, being of a tactful nature, he did.

As an officer prisoner he was given a good bunk, lived in the officers' mess, was outfitted with a fur coat by the Staff Surgeon and a white ski-ing cap by Leutenant Illing, which greatly improved his appearance. The Staff Surgeon was growing a beard and, assuming that he had started when U62 left port, Lewis tried to work out how many days she had been at sea.

During his time in her, U62 sank some six steamers and six sailing ships, the former by torpedo, the latter by gunfire and then explosive charges after their crews had left. Torpedoing was mostly done at night. The boat cruised on the surface and being low in the water could speed past a merchant ship unseen to get ahead of her, then dive preparatory to the attack.

In daylight, those off watch could sit in the sun and take the fresh air, welcome after the confined hours in a narrow stinking tube. Gradually Lewis and Hashagen began to talk, but the only Service matter they discussed was the final stage of their duel. Lewis confirmed that when Hashagen loosed his torpedo, Q12 had full helm on and he fully intended to ram and then follow up with depth-charges. I had only been first by seconds, thought Hashagen.

One misty morning, when Lewis was on deck, a small British cruiser came out of the fog and he had to dive below with the Germans. He then had the unique experience of being depth-charged by a British ship. As his wife was working in the largest explosives factory in England, Lewis rather wondered, as the explosions came closer, if he was fated to be killed by one she had helped to make.

Nineteen days after sinking the Q-Ship, U62 reached Wilhelmshafen, having escaped being torpedoed by a British submarine on the way as well as depth-charged. Life in a U-boat was a high-risk business, too. The U-boat officers crammed his pockets with cigarettes for the journey to Karlsruhe and eventually Freiburg. When Lewis returned to England at the end of the war, he heard that his crew in their three boats had been picked up a day after Q12 was sunk.

Chapter Eighteen

ZEEBRUGGE AND C3

St George's Day, 23 April, 1918

April 1917 was the worst month (for Britain) in the U-boat war. A year later, the introduction of the age-old convoy system had sharply cut sinkings and figures showed that one third of British losses were incurred in the western part of the English Channel, caused by U-boats from their bases around Bruges in Flanders passing through the Straits of Dover in spite of the supposedly impenetrable 'Dover Barrage'.

'Room 40', monitoring and decoding the German wireless traffic, had early evidence that the 'Barrage' was no barrier; U-boats were passing through it at the rate of one a day. The officer commanding at Dover, Admiral Bacon, and his Chief of Staff, who was Evans of the Broke, read their evidence differently. When a U-boat struck a mine, there was an unmistakable upwelling of oil and often debris. But none of this had been seen. Therefore the U-boats had given up trying to penetrate the impenetrable barrage. There was a lone voice crying heresy. It belonged to Roger Keyes, back from the Dardanelles, and now Director of Plan S. Bacon was an extremely intelligent man, well-read and a thinker, even if sometimes extravagantly so, who was at all times utterly convinced that he was right. Any suggestion that U-boats could still get through was rubbish, and rubbish it remained until October 1917 when the wreck of UC44 was raised off Waterford in Southern Ireland.* Among the documents found in her was a navigational instruction:

* UC44 had fallen victim to Room 40, who had realised that the Germans could now read the code signal of success sent by the sweepers: 'No more mines remain!' Now UC44 was a regular visitor to Waterford and some clever chap suggested *not* sending the sweepers in to clear the next field laid by UC44 but instead sending out a (this time false) message: 'No more mines remain!' The only survivor from UC44 was Kapitan-leutnant Teben-Johans, who was eloquent on the sloppiness of the work carried out by the English sweepers, when he realised that it was his own mine he had hit.

Above: British destroyer firing a torpedo in the 1930s.
Photo: McKee collection

Left: Rare photograph taken from HMS *Prince of Wales*, showing the *Hood* minutes before the explosion that sank her.
Photo: Imperial War Museum, London

HMS *Valiant* at Gibraltar between the wars. A survivor of Jutland, she was rebuilt with trunked funnel and anti-torpedo 'blisters' before the Second World War.
Photo: McKee collection

An X-Craft, one of the midgets that did battle with the *Tirpitz* off Norway in 1943.
Photo: Royal Navy Submarine Museum, Gosport

The USS *Franklyn*, on fire and listing after an air attack off Japan in 1945.
Photo: US Naval Historical Center, Washington

Transfer of wounded from the USS *Bunker Hill* to the *Wilkes Barre* after a dive bombing attack off Okinawa, 1945.
Photo: US Naval Historical Center, Washington

Above: HMS *Amethyst*, whose captain, Kerens, broke through the blockade in the Yangtse river in 1949.
Photo: Imperial War Museum, London

Left: Simon, feline hero of the Yangtse incident. The only cat ever to have been awarded the Dickin Medal for bravery, the citation praised him for 'disposing of many rats though wounded by shell blast. Throughout the incident his behaviour was of the highest order.'
Photo: Imperial War Museum, London

It is best and safest to pass through the Straits of Dover on the way to the Atlantic seaways. Pass through at night and on the surface as far as possible through the area between Hoofden and Cherbourg, without being observed and without stopping. If forced to dive, go down to 40 metres and wait. Avoid being seen in the Channel . . . on the other hand those craft which in exceptional cases pass around Scotland are to let themselves be seen as freely as possible, in order to mislead the English.

The English had duly been misled. Their thinking had been logical: a submarine is built to go underwater; therefore the U-boats will go through the Straits underwater—right into the mine fields and explosive nets which we have laid. But the nets were suspended on sagging hawsers attached to buoys which were lit. Running on the surface the U-boats could pass right over the deep-laid mines and over the nets where they sagged deepest—between the buoys. And that is exactly what they had been doing, leaving no trace behind them—no explosions, no oil, no wreckage. And all, until now, taken as proof that the Dover Patrol was doing its job.

Keyes was summoned to the Admiralty and told, 'Roger, you've talked a hell of a lot about what ought to be done. Now go and do it.'

In the naval parlance of the time, Keyes had 'had wires (i.e. telegrams) about himself'. The messages were all the same: YOU ARE A SECOND NELSON. Of course, it is not at all a bad idea to model yourself on someone outstanding in your own line of business. Jellicoe had gone and been replaced by Beatty; Bacon had gone and been replaced by Keyes. Evans of the Broke went, said to be ill, Keyes now ordered what before he could only recommend: that more mines be laid, and the barrage be brightly illuminated at night and strongly patrolled. In 1918 fourteen U-boats were sunk trying to pass the Straits. Bacon had kept his small craft in harbour at night, foreseeing that they could be picked off by raiding German destroyers, and the Germans did in fact counter in just this way. On the night of 14–15 February they sank seven small British ships and severely damaged another seven. Two years after Jutland, British recognition and reporting procedures were as bad as ever; a British destroyer flotilla sighted the enemy but did not engage because of doubtful recognition.

Keyes revived and then revised plans previously prepared by Bacon and approved by Jellicoe for a fundamental removal of the trouble by striking at the U-boat bases on the coast of Flanders. This area had seen a great English victory over the French at the battle of Sluys in 1340. The Duke of Parma's invasion army had gathered in the canals here in 1588. But in 1918 what had been ports were now inland towns, connected to the sea only by canals. It was this difficult coast between France and Holland, with its shifting sandbanks and shallows, which protected the German submarine and destroyer flotillas, that now had to be assaulted.

The main base was the charming, canal-encircled old town of Bruges (Brugge), eight miles now from the sea. From Bruges canals led to two coastal ports, Zeebrugge in the north, nearest Holland, and Ostend (Oostende) nearer France. The plan selected (out of many) was to block the entrances of the canals at these two ports by sinking concrete-laden ships actually inside them. The German ships (up to 30 submarines and 35 destroyers, it was calculated) were out of reach at Bruges, so it was a case of trying to stop up their holes, the canal entrances at the two Belgian ports of Zeebrugge and Ostend.

Some use was made by Keyes in the final plan of ideas which had first been suggested by Admiral Bacon, particularly the diversionary attack on the mole at Zeebruggee, although he did not consider the suggestion that Coastal Motor Boats be sent in at high speed to torpedo the lock gates. The scheme which was adopted for Zeebrugge required three old cruisers to be sunk as blockships in that canal entrance—*Intrepid*, *Iphigenia* and *Thetis*; to cover their approach a diversionary attack upon the German guns and garrison on the mile-long mole was to be carried out by Royal Marines and seamen from the old cruiser *Vindictive* and the Mersey River ferries *Iris* and *Daffodil*; and to isolate the defenders of the mole from the shore a connecting viaduct (built to allow the tides to scour out the harbour naturally) was to be demolished by sending in two old submarines, their bows packed with explosives fused to explode after a short delay. The canal entrance at Ostend, which was not protected by a mole, was to be blocked directly by the *Brilliant* and *Sirius*.

It was a complicated 'set-piece' attack designed to achieve a near impossibility. The blockships were intended to be turned inside the canals so as to sink across them at right angles to their walls. Nowadays there are some specially designed ships which have this capability; but none were available in 1918. It was hoped that the presence of the wrecks in the canals, even if sunk at odd, slanting angles to the walls, would cause sandbanks to form around them, thus completing the blockage. The 'experts' consulted seemed sure that this would happen. Nowadays, with much, much greater experience of what happens to seabeds around wrecks it is clear that the opposite occurs—the currents actually scour out pits around the obstruction. The planners were also acting on an assumption common to the English—that the Germans are stupid, unimaginative and lacking in initiative. As an alarmed Polish general remarked, when presented with the bland, impossible Anglo-American plans for the Arnhem airborne operation in 1944, 'But the Germans, the Germans!'

The plans produced by Keyes were excellent in detail, enormously thorough, and the right men chosen for the tasks. But he was not confident. He was to write:

> My thoughts turned constantly to the assault on Santa Cruz in the Island of Tenerife in July 1797, when Nelson's impatient ardour impelled him to undertake a hazard, foredoomed by the state of the weather.

One begs to differ, knowing Santa Cruz. What Nelson had conspicuously failed to obtain was surprise first of all, and then chosen to try to put boats' crews ashore in totally unsuitable conditions. They were repulsed with heavy loss, unlike Blake's entirely successful enterprise in 1657. Keyes, however, did manage to obtain surprise, at least at Zeebrugge, in spite of two cancellations due to weather. Here, he was relying on instinct, on long knowledge of weather and sea conditions, rather than meticulous planning.

On 12 April not far short of 200 vessels set out, each with separate tasks, the RAF bombers turned up (another modern diversion), the monitors bombarded (as they often did, so that gave nothing away), 76 ships in one group and 60 in another were in sight of the air raid lighting up the Belgian coast as a distraction, when the onshore wind (ideal for their smokescreens) died away, and then changed direction, and blew offshore. It was a hard decision and Keyes could not be sure that he was right. By light signals (not by wireless) he flashed the recall and they all steamed clumsily back to the Swin, off the mouth of the Thames. They were clumsy because most were old, expendable ships while others, such as the demolition submarines, were being towed.

Some of them had certainly been detected, for four heavy shells had arrived 200 yards from Keyes in the *Warwick*. The Germans must have had some form of detection apparatus which was non-visual—perhaps sound-ranging gear. Once back in the Swin, Keyes, who was a shy man, had the embarrassing task of explaining his decision to the eager officers and men. By then a nasty gale was blowing, making clear that his decision had been fortunate. The next dark night with a favourable tide was only a few days away, so Keyes sent out another preparatorry signal, but when the ships in the Swin had got under way and were steaming for the Goodwins, the wind again rose to full gale and for the second time Keyes had to cancel.

Had the plan been compromised? How long could the 1,300 men be kept cooped up the ships? When was the next favourable dark weather period? All the questions to be familiar in the Second World War had to be met. Keyes, by telling outrageous lies, got approval from the First Sea Lord to make a third try, this time in moonlight conditions which he now swore were ideal. All he required was a high tide around midnight—in nine or ten days. He chose 22 April on grounds of weather and tides, not on the significance of the date (which few would have known anyway); but his wife did.

As he took a final walk with her on the night they were due to sail she remarked: 'Tomorrow is St George's Day . . . St George can be trusted to bring good fortune to England!'

Now he had his inspirational signal, to match Nelson's 'England expects . . .' (Nelson's first version said 'confides' but that had to be spelled out, whereas 'expects' was a single-flag hoist). Keyes sailed at 5 p.m. the next day, sending by semaphore his battle-signal: '*St George for England!*'

He really meant it, but it was not received entirely in the tone of high resolve with which it had been conceived. Captain Carpenter of the *Vindictive*, which was to storm the mole, signalled cheerfully back: '*May we give the dragon's tail a damn good twist!*' which, Keyes admitted, 'was very apt and to the point, but did not fit in with my mood at the moment.'

Two submarines had been selected to blow the viaduct connecting the Zeebrugge mole to the shore. This was to be done the moment the *Vindictive* crashed alongside the mole and Naval and Marine storming parties rushed ashore along the lowered drawbridges ('brows' in naval parlance) to knock out the gun batteries: so that the defenders of the gun positions could not then be reinforced from land. And all this merely as a diversion so that the enemy would not discover until too late that the key pieces of the assault were the blockships. Each submarine carried two dinghies, so that the crews (the smallest number possible) could get away after aiming the submarines at the viaduct, and let them finish their runs unmanned and unguided except for a gyro compass.

The two obsolescent boats chosen were C1 under Lieutenant A. C. Newbold and C3 under Lieutenant Richard Sandford. With the latter as second-in-command was Lieutenant John Howell-Price, Petty Officer Walter Harner as cox, Leading Seaman William Cleaver, and in the engine-room ERA Alan Roxburgh and Stoker Henry Bendall. Sandford, Bendall and Roxburgh gave brief accounts afterwards. The story they tell is the same, except that the remembered order in which they were wounded varies a little, rather naturally because several were hit twice, and it was all very noisy and chaotic. Both submarines were to be towed by destroyers and a steam picket boat was to watch over them and help rescue survivors, if any; this was commanded by the 27-year-old Richard Sandford's elder brother, Lt.-Cdr. Francis Sandford.

When the time came for C3 to slip her tow from the destroyer *Trident* there was no sign of C1 (which had parted her tow and so arrived too late to play any part) or of the escorting steam picket boat. However, she carried on, surfaced, under her own power. She was therefore late in arriving at Zeebrugge. The *Vindictive*, screened by smoke laid by Coastal Motor Boats, had arrived at one minute after midnight, to find a heavy swell making berthing alongside the mole difficult. Quite a little battle was going on there, gun flashes and small arms fire flickering in the night; and the wind once again changed round, so that it was blowing the smoke away offshore. A mile and a half of empty sea, lit by the glare of searchlights and gun flashes, lay between C3 and the mole-viaduct. She could not make the attack submerged, because the channel under the viaduct was too shallow; there was nothing for it but to run on slowly under her electric motors.

In the bow of C3 were packed many tons of a powerful explosive, amatol, seven tons of it according to Roxburgh. The area they had to cross on the surface was covered by a formidable gun battery sited on the shore end of the viaduct. Roxburgh recalled:

We made towards our destination under cover of a smoke screen, but as we were going along the mole this screen blew away from us instead of hiding us, owing to the wind changing, and so we came into full sight of the enemy at short range. And then he got busy. Star shells went up and searchlights turned full upon us. Big guns opened on us from the shore, so did pom-poms and rifles from the mole.

Sandford did not do as he was ordered—that is, set the submarine with the gyro compass to run in unmanned for the last few hundred yards; that was too chancy. He called everyone up on deck and made sure that C3 was headed directly for the piling which supported the viaduct (which carried rail and road communications onto the concrete mole farther out). Stoker Henry Bendall described it:

With her engines running smoothly the submarine glided into the shoal waters of Zeebrugge at midnight, the whole crew of six being on deck. The mole, looming up black in the darkness, and the viaduct joining it to the shore were clearly seen. It was a silent, nervy business. She was going full tilt when she hit the viaduct. It was a good jolt, but you can stand a lot when you hang on tight. We ran right into the middle of the viaduct and stuck there as intended. I do not think anybody said a word except: 'We're here all right!'

Sandford had in fact rammed C3 straight into the pilings right up to her conning tower, so that her amatol-laden nose was directly under the roadway above. And above them they could hear the German defenders. Curiously, they seemed to be laughing. It transpired later that they thought the submarine was trying to enter the harbour through the tiny gaps between the pilings of the viaduct and would wreck herself or be captured in the morning. Sandford himself said briefly:

There was no doubt about getting there. I set the fuse myself and I think the thing was done all right . . . We were lucky in being picked up by the picket boat afterwards. The firing from the shore was a bit severe at 200 yards, and only the fact that the sea was a bit rough and we were up and down a good deal saved us. The crew did their duty, every man. They were all volunteers and picked men.

This was shorthand for what actually happened. C3 had lost one motor-dinghy, so all six men had to pile into the sole remaining one.

There was an ominous clink-clang as they shoved it overboard into the water. The propeller of the dinghy had struck the submarine's casing and been knocked off. They were therefore reduced to rowing away, against a fast-flowing tide, 20 feet from German riflemen and machine-gunners stationed on the viaduct. And with their submarine due to disintegrate violently within minutes, which would certainly kill any-one in the water and might kill everyone anyway. But, as he said, 'the sea was a bit rough and we were up and down a good deal.' This may have put some of the Germans off their aim. Not all, however. Stoker Bendall remembered:

The lights were now on us and the machine-guns going from the shore. Before we had made 200 yards the submarine went up. There was a tremendous flash, bang, crash, and lots of concrete from the mole fell all around us in the water. It was lucky we were not struck. Coxswain Harner and I took the oars first, till I was knocked out. Then Cleaver grabbed the oar and carried on until the coxswain was hit. I was hit again, and Lieutenant Price, lifting me and Harner into the bows, took the oar, and was afterwards relieved by Roxburgh, when Lieutenant Sandford was hit.

This was in fact Sandford's second wound, in the thigh. The first bullet had hit him in the hand. ERA Roxburgh recalled:

Seeing us making off the Germans started firing at us at point blank range with rifles and pom-poms. Lieutenant Sandford was the first hit. He fell into my arms badly wounded. Then Bendall was shot down. Cleaver took his place at the oar, only to be shot down almost immediately, and I took his oar. Then the old submarine blew up with a terrific bang.

The picket boat commanded by Sandford's brother, which should have escorted the submarines in, had not taken kindly to being towed and had nearly capsized, so Francis Sandford cast off the tow and she proceeded literally under her own steam, the smallest vessel of the entire armada. He arrived only a few minutes late, in time to rescue them all, as Bendall remembered:

In the nick of time a picket boat found the skiff. We gave a shout of joy when we saw her. She took us on board and transferred us to another ship, HMS *Phoebe*.

The aim of the transfer was that the more severely wounded men from C3 could receive immediate medical attention. Francis Sandford remained off the mole to give assistance elsewhere before heading back to Dover alone. The 50-ft long picket boat had been holed and flooded forward and also sustained damage in the engine-room, but reached England with pumps working to capacity. All six men of C3 recovered from their wounds, but Richard Sandford was to die of pneumonia on 23 November, 1918, twelve days after the Armistice was signed. He was awarded the Victoria Cross and all the crew were decorated.

The overall casualties were given as 214 killed and 383 wounded; many great feats of gallantry were performed, but the number of decorations put in for by Keyes was a shock. It is a commander's duty to see his men suitably rewarded, but this was not the 'phoney war' of 1939–40; Britain alone had lost over a million killed with losses of one battalion in a morning exceeding the Zeebrugge total. Many must have felt also that bravery in a brief raid might well be easier than months of steady endurance under appalling conditions in the trenches with a constant drain of casualties. Also, the raid had failed, although it made good propaganda.

Room 40, monitoring the German wireless traffic, knew at once. The Zeebrugge channel was only partially blocked—small destroyers could get out; then, after 48 hours, dredging work allowed U-boats to get out; for a time only the larger types were compelled to use Ostend, where the failure had been complete. The all-important channel buoys had moved (or been removed) and so the two blockships *Brilliant* and *Sirius* stranded a mile east of the canal entrance. Determined to complete what he regarded as his great success at Zeebruge, Keyes sent in the *Vindictive* herself to block Ostend, but her captain was killed at the crucial moment and she grounded to one side of the entrance in shallow water. To rub in this further failure, the *Warwick*, which was Keyes' command ship for the operation, was mined and had to be towed back to Dover. Keyes was still determined to try again at Ostend, but finally the Admiralty cancelled a further operation either there or at Zeebrugge.

Like Admiral Bacon before him, and Bomber Command at one stage of the Second World War, Keyes refused to face unpalatable facts: that he had matched Nelson only in his bloody failure at Tenerife, not his overwhelming victory at Trafalgar. His claim of heroic success was widely welcomed by the press, and through them the public, depressed by the crisis on the Western Front brought about by transfer of German troops from the East freed by the collapse of Russia into Bolshevism. For what that was worth, the Zeebrugge story as trumpeted at the time gave a lift to morale, just as did the largely ineffective but dramatic Bomber Command raid on the Möhne and Eder dams at a low point of the 1939–45 war.

Keyes never did become another Nelson, although he was appointed to command the Mediterranean Fleet at Malta in 1925, and in 1940 was brought back by Churchill to take charge of amphibious warfare operations in which his son Geoffrey quickly became a Lieutenant-Colonel and won a posthumous VC after an abortive attempt to kill or capture Rommel.

However, the real lesson of Zeebrugge was learnt when a similar but more difficult raid was projected to prevent the battleship *Tirpitz* using the great dock at St Nazaire in France. Zeebrugge is on the sea and less than 80 miles from Dover. St Nazaire is five miles up the River Loire and 400 miles from the nearest major British naval base at Plymouth. In March 1942 the defenders also possessed radar and close-range automatic weapons not available in 1918. It was a far more difficult proposition. No attempt was made to sink blockships. Instead, the method used at Zeebrugge to bring down the viaduct by a submarine filled with explosives was used, suitably up-rated. The floating time-bomb in this case was the *Campbeltown*, an obsolete ex-USS destroyer which charged the lock-gates of the dock and a few hours later blew up under the German officers and technicians inspecting her. In *Victory at Sea*, written for the Admiralty by Lt.-Cdr. P. K. Kemp, the author commented:

And while Zeebrugge was a failure in that it did not stop the passage of U-boats for more than twenty-four hours, St Nazaire was a resounding success.

Chapter Nineteen

FAST BOATS AND RED BATTLESHIPS

The Skimmers at Kronstadt, August 1919

In the summer of 1919 there was a complicated war going inside Russia and on her borders; a small British naval force was operating in the Baltic from Finnish bases and the preoccupation of Admiral Walter Cowan was with the Red Fleet in Kronstadt, reputedly one of the best defended fortresses in the world. His force was not strong enough even to consider trying to take it. At this moment the Russian defences were nominally under the command of Commissar Gordienko, but the real director was Lev Davýdovich Bronstein, alias Trotsky, then a hero of the revolution but before long to become an unperson with an icepick in his skull at the orders of another old Bolshevik whose alias was Stalin.

Admiral Cowan was prepared to settle for two battleships and a submarine depot ship, lying in a basin at the Kronstadt naval base, as he well knew from his reconnaissance aircraft which overflew it and from the secret agents taken in there and taken out again by the 40-foot motor boat commanded by Lieutenant Augustus Agar. In that area the first week of August was the last week of summer; autumn and the ice were not far away. Put those three ships out of action temporarily and they would be no menace to Finland and the Baltic states until the ice melted the following year. And by then, who knew what would have happened?

The only time off he took was for an afternoon walk with an orderly who carried no rifle, merely a sheathed bayonet, because Cowan regarded carrying firearms in Finland as bad manners, this being a friendly country Britain was protecting. On this occasion he had a further companion in Lieutenant Agar who was not nominally under his command, because he took his orders from the intelligence chief known as 'C' in London. He had just put Agar in for the VC, because while motor-boating in the Baltic, the Lieutenant had happened to torpedo and sink the Bolshevik cruiser *Oleg*.

Cowan explained his plans for 'Operation RK', called after his friend Roger Keyes, whom he much admired. 'To give your enemy advance notice of your intentions, as we did at the Dardanelles, is to invite failure.' Keyes had obtained surprise with his blockships at Zeebrugge and complete surprise was what Cowan now intended to achieve at Kronstadt.

The plan involved sending in a force of Coastal Motor Boats, their noisy approach covered by the sound of aircraft which would carry a large number of small bombs and drop them at intervals to keep guns' crews in shelter. Commander C. C. Dobson would command the CMBs and Squadron-Leader Grahame Donald of the RAF would lead the aircraft. There were to be seven of the high-speed 'skimmers' supported by eight aircraft—one Sopwith Camel single-seat scout (or fighter); one Griffon; two Sopwith 1½ Strutters, a two-seat version of the Camel; and four Short seaplanes. Agar, in his smaller 40-foot motor boat, would lead initially, to give the newcomers (just out from England) confidence. Offshore, the attack force would be supported by and fall back on the cruisers and destroyers. The parent ship to the seven CMBs was a new HMS *Vindictive*, half an aircraft carrier, half a cruiser converted out of a monstrous conception of Fisher's. She was commanded by Captain Edgar Grace, son of the famous cricketer W. G. Grace.

Cowan did not believe in complicated detail orders such as had been necessary for the 'set piece' assault on Zeebrugge; he left it to the CMB leader and the RAF CO to arrange things between themselves. Cowan insisted merely that the raid should take place as early as possible to avoid the chances of leakage. Above all, he feared press leakage. He would not allow newspapermen with the fleet, giving *The Times* correspondent one interview based on a half-page of notes. Of course it is a newsman's duty to report the news and a commander's duty to stop him.

During the work-up period Donald established a base for his four seaplanes opposite the naval anchorage, so communication was easy, and extremely interesting for the signalmen with high-power telescopes on the bridge of the cruiser which acted as repeating ship for messages. The sandy beach by the seaplane base was used by Finnish villagers for nude mixed bathing, a local custom appalling to men from strait-laced

Pompey or Devonport or Chatham. But as the RAF seaplane crews soon joined the Finns without any apparent objection, the Naval signalmen had to endure the spectacle without complaint.

To reach their target the skimmers had to pass between the outlying forts, led by Agar, who normally took his agents in this way and then farther up the gulf to the outskirts of Petrogrod. As pilots they would use two smugglers, who on this occasion wanted extra pay (£25 each plus a double ration of rum) to cover the dangers of turning right into the naval base of Kronstadt on a long narrow island at the entrance of the gulf which led to Petrograd on the River Neva.

The plan was helped by a stroke of good luck with the weather; instead of summer calm a number of westerly gales piled up the level of the water in the eastern part of the Gulf of Finland to two or three feet above normal. The access routes for the CMBs were consequently increased.

Cowan always carried on him in a leather wallet a quotation from Nelson:

> In close actions at sea and hazardous operations on shore, something must always be left to chance . . . But in case signals can neither be seen nor perfectly understood, no captain can do wrong if he places his ship alongside one of the enemy.

This could no longer be applied literally, and in any case, as there were a number of tempting targets in the basins at Kronstadt, Cowan had to decide on their order of priority. He decided that the most important were the two battleships (which his force could not match); they were the *Andrei Pervozvanni*, commanded by Senior Commissar Raskolnikov, and the *Petropavlovsk*. The third most dangerous ship was the *Pamiat Azova*, a submarine depot ship which aerial photos showed as having two submarines alongside. After that was the *Rurik*, a former cruiser fitted as a minelayer and understood to be carrying 300 of them. Thus she was not a popular target. Ever since Russia's war with Japan in 1904–5, Russian mines had had the reputation of being the most deadly; from 1914 on, when put to the test, English mines were regarded as being the most ineffective. None of the CMB crews fancied touching off 300 Russian mines in one tremendous bang. The least priority was given to the dry dock in one corner of the basin. On the other hand, there appeared to be a guard destroyer, the *Gavriel*, anchored just outside; someone had better deal with her.

Agar, in his small 40-foot boat, would lead the way initially, following the route between the forts which he used when running agents into Red Russia. He would be followed by seven 55-foot CMBs, four of which carried two torpedoes, the others one only; they were slower than the forty-footers but carried more machine-guns and depth charges. They had arranged with the RAF to time their arrival so that the aeroplanes and seaplanes could cover their noisy approach and keep crews and gunners below decks. They would pass through the entrance to the main basin, which was 150 feet wide, in two groups because the space inside the basin was restricted and there were performance peculiaries of the CMBs to be taken account of. First of all, in order to launch torpedoes they had to be travelling at high speed; at slow speeds the torpedo just nose-dived to the bottom and blew up dangerously close. But at high speeds, although manoeuvrable, the boats had a wide turning circle; and space inside the basin was restricted. The 55-foot boats had two engines and two propellers, but no reversing gear; they couldn't turn by going ahead on one engine and astern on the other. The best they could do was to bang out the clutch on one engine to help the turn, then speed up again for the final dash to the target.

On 17 August two of the CMB officers, Dobson and Bremner, were given a final look in RAF aircraft at the ships they would be attacking that night. Then Admiral Cowan gave them a brief talk. 'No fireworks or pep-stuff . . . just plain, good common sense advice as to what to do and what he expected of them', according to Agar.

In the approach, Agar was followed by Lt. Napier in CMB24; the boat behind Napier had a badly tuned engine, very noisy and spitting flame. Napier's bow wave was high and distinctive. To starboard, half a mile away, three more skimmers were throwing up masses of spray from their bows, although they were all creaming along easily at only 20 knots, hoping not to be detected by the forts. But when the Russians woke up, they opened fire with light guns and machine-guns, without switching on their searchlights. The boats increased speed and raced away in a wide circle towards the main channel to Petrograd.

Then, having evaded the fire of the forts, they turned to starboard to get into Kronstadt dockyard. The three boats they had seen closer inshore to starboard had been led by their smuggler-pilot through a channel in the shallows not used before, and owing to the increased three feet or so of depth caused by the gale, did not run aground; also, it proved to be a short cut. These three were CMB79 (Bremner) whose target was the depot ship *Pamiat Azova*, CMB31 (Dobson) who was to attack the battleship *Andrei Pervozvanni* and CMB88 (Dayrell-Reed) with the other battleship *Petropavlovsk* as his objective. Bremner's boat carried net cutters and gun cotton charges to blow any boom that might be across the entrance, but they were not needed.

Bremner went straight through into the basin and with his single torpedo hit the submarine depot ship *Pamiat Azova*. Agar, waiting outside, heard the roar of the explosion amid the droning of the aircraft masking the attack, and saw the red flashes of their bomb bursts. Complete surprise had been obtained and confusion caused by the mix of aircraft engines above and speedboat engines on the water.

Bremner then peeled off and sped towards his waiting billet by a hospital ship near the two battleships. That left the basin clear for difficult manoeuvres by the two following boats. Dobson in CMB31 had to make a sharp turn, slowing to do so, then speed up to launch his two torpedoes at the *Andrei Pervozvanni*. He was on course at exactly the right moment, and both torpedoes hit the battleship. Then he too peeled off to join Bremner at the waiting billet, leaving the basin clear for CMB88, commanded by Dayrell-Reed and his second-in-command, Gordon Steele.

The Russian searchlights were now on, sweeping the water with a blinding glare, and the Russian machine-guns with what Agar thought of as 'horrible typewriter sounds' were firing at anything that moved. Into this came 'Mossy' Reed in CMB88, compelled to make an even tighter turn before straightening for the high speed dash at the *Petropavlovsk*, moored close to the first battleship.

His head could be seen sticking over the canvas screen which shielded the wheel and the torpedo-firing controls, as he began the turn to attack. Then it fell forward, and the boat continued to turn instead of straightening for the fast run up to the target. Gordon Steele, who was shouldering a Lewis light machine-gun, seeing that 'Mossy' Reed had been shot through the head, jumped to take over the wheel. Getting the boat back under control, he resumed the run to the target, firing both torpedoes at the last moment. One struck under the forward turret, the other hit a heavy cable securing the battleship to the wharf.

Steele then went to the waiting billet by the hospital ship and two of the three boats went out of the basin at high speed. The Russians were now ready for them, but the CMBs made masking smoke and were supported by the airmen who dived onto the forts and gun positions, firing tracer bullets. 'Mossy' Reed died shortly after Steele had transferred him to Admiral Cowan's flagship. These three boats had received only minor damage.

Having, as instructed, kept out of the way of the attacking CMBs, Agar closed the entrance of a smaller basin known as the military harbour, which held destroyers and light craft, and fired his torpedo through the entrance into the middle of them. There was a satisfactory explosion. Agar then returned to his watching station off the main basin, out of the way of approaching or returning CMBs, and from there saw the hits on the three most important Russian ships. Meanwhile CMB24 (Napier) had attempted to torpedo the patrol destroyer *Gavriel* but missed; either the torpedo ran deep or was deflected. In reply, a shell either from the *Gavriel* or from the shore, hit CMB24 and split her in two. As she sank, her Welsh mechanic was heard to comment, 'That's sugared it.' From the water, her survivors saw the first two CMBs come out at high speed, their tracer bullets streaking like meteors at the *Gavriel* which had been trying to machine-gun the men floating in the water. Two hours later they were picked up by white-clothed Russian sailors in a grey rowing boat.

The third boat, CMB79 under Bremner, followed the first two out and as she did so collided with the first boat of the second wave, CMB62 under Lt.-Cdr. J. Brade, who had apparently been blinded by searchlights, almost cutting No.79 in half. But by keeping his engine going, Brade was able to drive both boats clear of the entrance to the basin, where Bremner scuttled No.79 and transferred his crew to Brade's CMB. A shell from the *Gavriel* put Brade out of action, after he had fired his two torpedoes at the destroyer—these two also missed. Brade was killed, Bremner badly wounded, and both boats were lost.

The two boats which were to follow Brade failed entirely. Howard's boat broke down with engine trouble and Bodley's was hit and had its torpedo-firing gear shot away. Agar's boat was the last to leave, and seeing her alone, Fl.-Lt. Fletcher of the RAF turned back to strafe the channel forts with tracer bullets.

In all, four of the skimmers were lost—CMBs 24, 62, 67 and 79—but all the aircraft returned safely. In return, they had put out of action two battleships and a submarine depot ship, their most important targets. All three were photographed from the air, lying heeled over in shallow water. The *Gavriel*, which had escaped three torpedoes, fell victim two months later to a British mine (a later, effective model) laid by the CMBs in the main Petrograd channel. Both Dobson and Steele were awarded the VC.

'Mossy' Reed was buried in Finland with full honours, as were the dead recovered by the Russians, this due mainly to Senior Commissar Gordienko, who had formerly been a Petty Officer in the Tsar's Royal Yacht.

Admiral Cowan spoke to everyone who had taken part, at sea and in the air, saying that their action had meant the end of any Russian threat by sea to Finland and the freedom of the Baltic states. But not for long, alas, as history was to show.

Chapter Twenty

DESTROYERS' WAR

Norway, April–June 1940

Both the British and the Germans began early in the Second World War to contemplate invading Norway, not out of any dislike of the Norwegians but because of the importance of the iron ore traffic to Germany from the ports of Northern Norway. The Germans got there first, with improvised efficiency. The British and French got there late, with improvised muddle.

The British Navy in particular now had good cause to know that 'Winston's back', for the First Lord of the Admiralty, in the words of a noted British historian, Michael Howard, 'interfered, usually disastrously, with every detail of the Norwegian campaign'. In spite of this, a victory was won at the iron ore port of Narvik, but too late to be of use.

Winston Churchill, mindful of what he thought of as the lesson of the Dardanelles more than twenty years before—that the Admirals were too cautious and would do nothing if not prodded—was at this moment firm in his recent victory over Hitler's U-boats. The Admiralty had produced figures of U-boats sunk which, as usual, were somewhat optimistic, but these figures did not satisfy the First Lord of the Admiralty; he wanted more. So he added some of his own, which were announced. And so the man on the Clapham omnibus was happy that the Navy was in good hands, while the over-cautious officer, whose claims were somewhat near the truth, was sacked and sent to sea. Churchill minuted briskly:

> The conclusion to which this officer comes is that all the attacks, except the actual 15 of which we have remnants, have failed. This conclusion leads me to think that it might be a good thing if Captain Talbot went to sea as soon as possible.

However, the U-boats (which had not been sunk) made very little difference to the Norwegian campaign, because the German Admiralty had been negligent in testing new weapons.

Churchill had never actually understood the 1914–18 Navy, let alone the 1939–40 fleet which was quite different. There had been considerable technical changes and there was a good deal of theory to be tested, and not by the British alone. The only practical experience either side had gained was by intervening, or pretending not to intervene, in the Spanish Civil War. Norway was to provide a sterner test, where ships had to be sunk in fact, not just in communiqués. Necessarily, no one could be expected to get it all exactly right first time. The two big questions were: what effect would air power have on warships? And would 'asdic' (detection by sonar) really make the U-boat menace a thing of the past?

The British Navy, as we now know, much under-estimated the effect of air power, not only in respect of battleships—which they did not believe could be sunk by bombers—but also in the threat they might present to more vulnerable although admittedly more agile warships. Norway did not entirely settle this matter. The final proof was to be provided by Winston Churchill himself, who, promoted to national leadership, in 1941 sent two capital ships to the Far East in the hope that they would prove a 'deterrent' to the warlike aims of Japan. The Japanese sank both the new *Prince of Wales* and the old *Repulse* in short order, for the loss of three aircraft and 18 men.

The British Navy, as we now know also, much over-estimated the effect of sonar on their anti-submarine capabilities. The U-boat still presented a considerable threat—except in the early stages of the war. The Germans had fitted their torpedoes as well as their mines with magnetic 'pistols' (or detonators) designed to explode in the vicinity of a large metal object. It was not necessary to score a direct hit. The mines proved to be a menace immediately but the detonators for the torpedoes were often faulty, thus drawing the submarines' teeth; but the technicians blamed the bad aim (so they said) of the U-boat commanders and not the results of their own technical and scientific work. As, by definition, scientists, especially German scientists, cannot make mistakes, while notoriously submarine commanders can get their calculations wrong, the truth was an inordinately long time being established, fortunately for the British Navy.

There was one other factor in the background to the opening stages of the war. Germany had been thoroughly disarmed after the 1914–18 war. Only a few ancient vessels remained of the Kaiser's navy. Consequently, Hitler had had to build a new one. The bulk of the new German Navy consisted of modern ships. In pursuit of an early policy of Peace-with-Britain, recently discarded, Hitler had accepted severe limitations to his U-boat arm. German submarines were good, but there were not many of them and their torpedoes often proved defective. The British Navy, although much stronger in numbers, possessed many obsolete ships, some built prior to 1914. This was the result of the infamous 'Ten-year rule', begun by Lloyd George in 1919, when it was sensible enough to plan on the basis of 'no war in the next ten years'. But in 1928 Winston Churchill made this rule automatic, instead of being regularly reviewed; and so the British armed forces continued to be run down until the rule was abandoned in 1932, ironically by a government headed by a pacifist, Ramsay MacDonald.

In 1940 it was easier for Germany to invade a neutral country than it was for Britain and France. The Allies had earmarked a force, apparently intended to assist the Finns in their fight against Soviet invasion, which might give them a toehold in Scandinavia via Narvik, but Finnish resistance collapsed in March. Instead, the British War Cabinet decided to mine Norwegian territorial waters and thus force the iron-ore ships out into international waters; but they first disbanded the bulk of the land forces earmarked for their invasion.

The dates finally chosen were 8 and 9 April. The 8th was the British date for their mining of Norwegian waters (illegal) with some troops standing by just in case the Germans reacted. The 9th was the German date for the simultaneous invasion of Denmark by land and of Norway by sea and air (even more illegal). Virtually the whole of the German Navy and a fair proportion of the Luftwaffe were to take part. No one had recent experience of large-scale amphibious warfare, the last experiment having been at Gallipoli, which had convinced military leaders that it was impractical against prepared defences. The two operations meshed with each other.

The British Commander-in-Chief, Admiral Forbes, began to believe, as reports came in, that he was facing a full-scale German attack on Norway; but back in London at the Admiralty it was assumed that this was only some operation designed to pass the *Scharnhorst* and *Gneisnau* out into the Atlantic as raiders. The Admiralty also decided to reinforce Forbes who was in the battleship *Rodney*, and to this end disembarked the troops already on board four cruisers and then sent them out with no capability to join in land operations.

This is not the place to relate the whole Norwegian campaign. The two German forces we are concerned with were those destined for Trondheim, about one-third of the way up the Norwegian coast, and for the far north iron-ore port of Narvik in the Arctic. The Narvik force consisted of ten destroyers carrying some 2,000 soldiers, covered by the *Scharnhorst* and *Gneisnau*; the Trondheim force was embarked in four destroyers, covered by the heavy cruiser *Hipper*. Had the Admiralty adhered to their original plan, the British troops embarked in the four cruisers could have forestalled the German landings at Narvik, but as they were now sitting on their kit on the quayside at Rosyth, the British fleet could do little.

The Admiralty had cancelled the southern mine-laying operation but let the force destined for Bodo, just south of Narvik, proceed. The weather was dreadful with bad visibility and heavy seas, but the four mine-laying destroyers completed their task, supported by the battle-cruiser *Renown* and eight destroyers, and then patrolled the minefield they had laid, less a single ship, the destroyer *Glowworm* which had lost a man overboard two days before, and having gone back to recover him and in the dreadful weather, been unable to catch up and rejoin. She never did rejoin. Her last word was a sighting report of enemy destroyers which faded out. Only after the war, did the Admiralty learn her fate.

British destroyers tended to be rather smaller than German and were armed with 4.7s instead of 5-inch. The *Glowworm* displaced 1,350 tons and was commanded by Lt.-Cdr. Gerard Broadmead Roope. Having found and rescued the seaman swept overboard, she was steaming north through seas so mountainous that spray burst over her bridge. These forced Roope to slow to ten knots during the night; at daybreak the mist curtain parted to reveal the first of two German destroyers, one of which was the *Berndt von Arnim*, 1,625 tons. The Germans were wide awake and got off the first shot—a white column of water leaped up 400 yards away.

Glowworm put on speed into the heavy sea and immediately began to 'ship it green'; not just spray but solid ocean roaring over her forward deck and half-burying in icy water the sailors manning 'A' gun and hurling vast sheets of spray high over the bridge. The director control tower, 50 feet up, was flooded, the guns' crews were half the time

half-submerged and two men were swept completely overboard. This
time, there was no going back. Their German opponents were suffering
in the same way and scored no hits. As the *Glowworm* turned, her
navigator was hurled against the chart table and had an arm broken.
There was a burst of black smoke from the forecastle of the leading
German, then the yellow glow of fire—possibly from ready-use
ammunition around the gun.

Their two opponents then altered course away from the British
destroyer and vanished into a rain squall; Roope followed them in
chase. As they drove into the clear on the far side, heaving and
plunging, deluged with water, the starboard lookout shouted:

'Bridge! Enemy in sight! Cruiser!'

They had found the *Hipper* with her eight 8-inch guns and five inches
of side armour, over 650 feet long.

With desperate urgency, Roope passed a string of orders:

'Port 20! Steer 060! Engine-room—make smoke!' And to Lieutenant
Robert Ramsay, 'Stand by all tubes!'

The range on the bridge-repeater was recording 5,000 yards, but still
the cruiser had not fired, although her muzzles were trained on the
destroyer with its thin, unarmoured hull. Then the yellow flashes
leaped out and the 8-inch 'bricks' came hurtling towards them.

No one makes cold, clinical, exact observations at such a time.
Ramsay noted that the blood that opened up from the torn face of the
navigator clotted at once in the cold and would not run down. He saw
the sub-lieutenant bent over the 'make smoke' gong to the engine room,
when a thick fragment of shell casing struck his chest and hurled him
backwards. There was the memory of his own finger stabbing at the
firing buttons as the destroyer turned so that the broadside tubes came
on, and the whoosh! as each torpedo leaped away into the sea; the
tangle of shredded plating and twisted brass, the sulphurous stench of
explosives; the tension after each ripple of yellow flashes from the 8-inch
guns of the armoured giant. Roope turning round to remark: 'Wind's
all right for our smoke.'

Then they plunged into the stench of their own smoke-screen. Time
to look around. Only Roope and himself were still alive on the
bridge. Roope ordered the mess cleared away, including the dead,
then said:

'Stand by with the after tubes. I'm coming round—'

He was interrupted by the arrival of another 8-inch shell. It blew open the armoured director-control tower above the bridge and the wreckage fell across the siren wires leading from the bridge to the funnel. With a roar of steam the siren began to give a continuous whooping wail, eerie and earsplitting, as if the *Glowworm* was giving out her death cry, which in fact she was.

The badly hurt destroyer plunged back through her own smoke and steamed into the open, naked, directly at her enemy. Another shell exploded in the transmitting station, killing most of the men there; and yet another burst in the first-aid station which had been set up in the captain's after cabin; the wounded men lying there were either killed or wounded again, their helpers cut down.

Roope called down the wheel-house voice-pipe:

'Full ahead, together!'

To Ramsay he sounded exultant as he said: 'Stand by to ram!'

The ship was shuddering, not merely from the heavy shells which kept hitting but from burying her bows into each green and foaming sea which rose at her.

The armoured side of the *Hipper* loomed like a steel wall. She rose on a wave and hurled herself at it.

The bow crumpled like a box of matches squeezed in the hand; it gave the impression that the bridge was sliding forwards rather than the bows crumpling up. Roope reversed his engines, and that may have been a mistake, because it took the destroyer far enough away from the *Hipper* for the German guns to bear, at point-blank range, as the *Glowworm* heeled over. From the shattered, sinking destroyer, a single gun fired one last shot; then her starboard heel increased so much that it was impossible to reload. Roope ordered abandon ship.

Some of the wounded were got into the sea with lifebelts on, amid the chaos of German gunfire and the whoo-whooo' of the demented siren, until the water throttled its cry. The *Glowworm* rolled right over, men running down the side as she went, eventually to stand on her bottom plates as the foam-streaked waves burst upon them as on a half-tide rock. Of her 140-man crew, 110 men went down with her, including Gerard Roope.

Among the thirty survivors was Lieutenant Ramsay, now the senior officer. The *Hipper*'s boats picked them up, although two died later in captivity, and as senior survivor Ramsay was brought before the German captain who told him that his torpedoes had missed by only a few metres but that the impact of the *Glowworm*'s bows had caused sufficient damage to require dockyard repairs. It was only after the war, when the 28 survivors returned home, that the full story was known. Roope was awarded the VC, Ramsay the DSO, and three ratings the Conspicious Gallantry medal.

The *Glowworm* had gone down on 8 April, during the minelaying operations by the British and while the German destroyers with the invasion troops aboard, screened by their heavy ships, were moving north ready to assault at dawn on the 9th. All of this in wintry weather with rain squalls and flurries of snow. And with the British Admiralty intent upon their own plans and expecting, not a full-scale German invasion but at most a feeble reaction to their own aggressive strategy.

Admiral Whitworth in the old battlecruiser *Renown* had at first steamed south to help *Glowworm*, but second thoughts counselled that the objective of the German force was most likely Narvik (which it was), so he turned north to cut them off. His destroyer group were already near the Vest Fjord covering the minefield. Admiral Forbes, the Commander-in-chief, detached the battlecruiser *Repulse*, the cruiser *Penelope* and four destroyers to aid *Glowworm*. The Admiralty then ordered Admiral Whitworth's destroyer, which was still in the Narvik area to join the *Renown*. This intervention from London ensured that the ten German destroyers bound for Narvik found the way unguarded, and put their troops ashore. They took the town without any opposition at sea or on shore.

Admiral Whitworth in *Renown* sighted the *Scharnhorst* and *Gneisnau* early on 9 April; they were returning from their task of seeing the ten destroyers safely into Narvik. The British destroyers could not keep up in the heavy seas then running, but the *Renown* pressed on and scored a number of hits on the *Gneisnau*. The German vessels could perhaps be described as light battleships rather than battlecruisers; they were modern replacements for the two cruisers lost at the Falklands battle in 1914, and could probably have dealt with the *Renown*. Instead, they used their superior speed to run away. Hitler was always as nervous as a bridegroom about his big warships, continually advising caution in their use; and this may perhaps explain the German admiral's conduct.

Whitworth then received another order from the Admiralty: to proceed to Vest Fjord and make sure that no enemy ships entered and went up to Narvik. There were now of course ten German destroyers loitering off Narvik and the town was in German hands. Also on that evening of 9 April, the Commander-in-Chief, Admiral Forbes, ordered some destroyers to be sent up to Narvik 'to make certain that no enemy troops land'.

The result was that five British destroyers under Captain Warburton-Lee entered the long Fjord at dawn on 10 April and surprised some of the ten German destroyers—it was snowing heavily. By gun and torpedo they sank two of the Germans and damaged three others, also some German merchant ships. They lost the *Hunter* sunk and the *Hardy* run aground. That was the first battle of Narvik.

The second battle took place on 13 April. Admiral Whitworth transferred from the battlecruiser *Renown* to the old battleship *Warspite*, which had come to reinforce him, and accompanied by nine destroyers went in with overwhelming force to mop up the remaining Germans. The greatest risk was to take a big ship into confined reef-strewn waters in bad weather. Now it was the turn of the Germans to make a brave stand; but inevitably they lost their remaining eight destroyers plus a U-boat lurking in a side fjord, which was found and sunk by an aircraft launched from the *Warspite*.

Narvik was eventually captured, six weeks later, by which time it was too late; the Germans had most of Norway and had opened a new offensive in the West and were over-running Holland, Belgium and France with astounding ease. Evacuation was ordered, which was successfully carried out by the Navy, but it is recorded that on the day that the battalion which had first landed at Harstad was embarked for home, their motor transport arrived from England; and had to be pushed into the sea, unused.

The Germans planned to disrupt the various evacuations, in particular by a raid into the Harstad area by the *Scharnhorst, Gneisnau, Hipper* and four destroyers. On 8 June they intercepted a small convoy consisting of a homeward-bound tanker, an empty transport, a hospital ship and a trawler as escort. They sank them all, except the hospital ship, which was allowed to proceed. Air reconnaissance gave them another sighting report—two carriers. Admiral Marschall sent the *Hipper* and the four destroyers into the safety of Trondheim, and took his two fast battleships farther north. On the afternoon of 8 June smoke was sighted from the *Scharnhorst* and they were soon in sight of the slab-sided silhouette of an aircraft carrier, like a giant barn afloat.

It was the *Glorious*, 22,500 tons, escorted by two destroyers, *Acasta* and *Ardent*. Her captain was d'Oyley-Hughes, who as a lieutenant in E11, had helped harry the Turks in the Marmara back in 1915. Unlike the United States Navy, the British did not require carrier captains to be airmen. Perhaps that is the explanation of why the *Glorious* was caught unready. She had aboard torpedo-carrying Swordfish biplanes and a squadron of high-speed Hurricane fighters evacuated with their pilots from Norway. Apparently d'Oyley-Hughes believed that he had to fear only submarine attack and his high speed should cope with that; he had the aircraft to patrol the North Sea for miles around, but none of his aircraft were ready even to launch.

The two destroyers, her only defence now, raced to lay a smokescreen between the German battleships and the carrier; but the 11-inch shells of the enemy, exploding among the aircraft and petrol stores in the hangars, turned the *Glorious* into an inferno. The *Ardent*, under Lt.-Cdr. J. F. Barker, closed the battleships at speed, turned broadside to them and fired a full salvo of torpedoes. Two minutes later, riven by the fire of the German heavy guns, the *Ardent* sank.

The *Acasta*, under Cdr. C. E. Glasfurd, made use of the *Ardent*'s smokescreen to continue the battle, alone. The *Ardent* had already gone and by this time the *Glorious* also had disappeared. When she emerged from the smoke, she was hit repeatedly, but before she could sink, turned and fired her torpedoes. One hit the *Scharnhorst* aft, damaging a propeller shaft and flooding an engine-room and a magazine. Then she sank. The two battleships abandoned their raid and so missed a much more important convoy—carrying troops, evacuating.

The Norwegian campaign, although an example of muddle and high-level interference, did have one vital result. It cost the Germans, sunk or out of action, a great part of their modern destroyer force, and some of their cruisers and light cruisers. Lack of these was later to make the hesitantly proposed invasion of Britain, Operation Sealion, largely a propaganda exercise.

The campaign also structured the lesson: the importance of superior air cover during difficult amphibious operations, a lesson still applicable to the Falklands in 1982. Oddly, in late 1943, at Churchill's insistence, the lesson was early disregarded—with predictable results. At a time when Germany was obviously losing the war and on the defensive, Winston Churchill prodded his Service chiefs into a mini-Dardanelles in the Italian-held islands of the Dodecanese off Turkey. The parallel with Gallipoli was very close. The nearest German air bases were 70 and 150 miles away; the nearest Allied air bases 350 miles distant. But these were the sort of statistics that Churchill tended to ignore. His American allies gave only brief, minute, reluctant help. For them, it was wasting lives and resources on a sideshow which could not be decisive.

Against the tide of the war generally, the Germans won—and in less than a week. The new Gallipoli cost the British forces four cruisers damaged (one beyond repair), six destroyers sunk and four damaged, two submarines sunk, ten coastal vessels and minesweepers sunk, 115 RAF aircraft lost, and 4,800 soldiers killed, wounded, missing or prisoner.

Chapter Twenty-One

THE AMCS

Rawalpindi and *Scharnhorst,* 1939; *Jervis Bay* and *Scheer,* 1940

The Armed Merchant Cruiser craze started in the Great War of 1914–18. Both Britain and Germany added to their warship list by putting comparatively small guns (5–6-inch) into comparatively large ships (liners of 20,000 tons or so). They were fast, had good endurance, would not sink quickly if hit simply because they were large, and could be converted from peacetime use, for which they were now redundant, by strengthening their decks at the points where guns were to be placed. Some were converted actually on the building slips in peacetime in collaboration with their future owners, who were given a subsidy to sweeten the process.

Consequently, submarine commanders in both world wars, having sunk what were in fact passenger liners carrying passengers, could plausibly claim that they had mistaken the ship for a passenger liner armed with guns and on war patrol.

In the winter of 1939 I can remember one such lying at South Railway Jetty by Portsmouth Dockyard while, so the 'buzz' said, the work of conversion was carried out. But in neither of the two world wars did such ships continue in service long. This is why.

Britain's war with Germany began in September 1939. The Germans had built many of their warships as commerce raiders and the first one to be caught was the *Graf Spee*, named after the victor of Coronel, the hero of the Falklands. She was a curious hybrid of 10,000 tons, which the British press called a 'pocket battleship'. To aid her when she was intercepted by a British cruiser squadron, the German Admiralty sent out the *Scharnhorst* and *Gneisnau*, 26,000 tons with a speed of close to 30 knots, armed with nine 11-inch guns and a 12–13-inch armour belt amidships. Other nations' battleships were large and armed with

14-inch to (in the case of the Japanese) 18-inch guns, but this pair made excellent raiders.

In their December breakout into the Atlantic between the Orkneys and Iceland they encountered not a convoy but a single liner on solitary patrol, the armed merchant cruiser *Rawalpindi*, commanded by Captain E. C. Kennedy. Against the two heavy German ships she stood no chance at all. All she could do was give the alarm, and on sighting the first German ship, the *Scharnhorst*, she reported her as a single pocket battleship, the *Deutschland*.

The captain of the *Scharnhorst* did not open fire at once. Five times he signalled: heave to and abandon ship.

Captain Kennedy's reply was to lob a salvo of 6-inch shells at the *Gneisnau* and hit her amidships. The Germans then promptly sank her. The big 6-inch gun cruiser *Newcastle* picked up the *Rawalpindi*'s sighting report but was too late to interfere.

The next heroic sacrifice was that of the *Jervis Bay* a year later, in November 1940. She was a 14,160-ton passenger/cargo liner named after a bay in New South Wales, and was commanded by an Irishman, Captain E. S. F. Fegen. She was the sole escort for a convoy from Halifax which numbered 38 ships, including the 16,698-ton *Rangitiki*, a sister ship to the ill-fated *Rawalpindi* but armed defensively, and the 11,181-ton tanker *San Demetrio* which was to become briefly famous: a film, 'San Demetrio London', was to present her story to a wider audience.

The German commander-in-chief, Admiral Raeder, began a campaign of commerce raiding towards the end of 1940. The first ship he sent out was the pocket battleship *Admiral Scheer* under Captain Theodor Krancke, with six 11-inch guns on a heavy cruiser displacement of around 10,000 tons. She was similar to the lost *Graf Spee* but with one major difference—her formerly unmistakable silhouette had been altered to resemble that of the *Scharnhorst* and *Gneisnau* and other heavy units, including those, such as the *Bismarck*, still building. This policy meant that every big German ship had the same silhouette, whether it was a battleship, a battlecruiser, a pocket battleship or a heavy cruiser. This would pose recognition problems for enemy reconnaissance aircraft and encourage reporting mistakes, even by experts. Normally RAF aircrew knew as much about ship recognition as sailors knew about aircraft recognition—that is, NIL.

The crew of the *Jervis Bay* was the usual mixture of regular Naval officers, recalled Reservists, Merchant Navy men in the RNR, RNVR officers (possibly ex-yachtsmen) and 'hostile' (for 'Hostilities only') ratings. Their ages were often much above that of the average service-man of all nations at the start of a war—teens to early twenties. One who served in such ships called them 'converted death traps'. They were only second-line ships after all, ordered to do a first-rate job.

The *Scheer* carried an Arado seaplane on a catapult which reported the convoy approaching 88 miles distant. The time was 12.40. Half the day's daylight was gone, but Krancke decided to attack at once rather than wait for dawn next day. The first he saw of the convoy was its smoke, then four ships, then six ships, then more. It was now 16.30 (i.e. 4.30 p.m.). Lieutenant Petersen, in peacetime a merchant sailor with Hapag, could see no warship with them, although one vessel had an unusual deck structure for a cargo ship. He thought she was an armed merchant cruiser, an opinion which seemed to be confirmed when she turned out from her convoy towards the *Scheer*. Then she began to signal to the German. That concluded the debate on identification—the signalling lamp was much larger and more powerful than any cargo ship would have. She had to be an armed auxiliary.

In the *Jervis Bay* a similar debate had been going on. The ships were still separated by many miles.

One experienced Petty Officer said the traditional famous last words, 'One of ours,' adding, 'a battler. *Ramillies* class.'

'R class battlewagon,' said someone else.

Through his gunlayer's telescope another seaman ticked off the recognition points: 'Single funnel, with a cowl . . . looks like *Resolution*.'

A Scots seaman who had served in the *Resolution* said, 'It's not the *Reso*. It's another class.'

As indeed it was. Triple winking points of yellow light from both fore and after turrets of the stranger confirmed that he was right.

In the *Jervis Bay*'s wireless office, the operator began to tap out the sighting report, interrupted by the rumble of the *Scheer*'s salvo arriving between the columns of ships in the convoy. Fegen ordered full ahead, maximum revs. As the armed liner turned out of the line, he signalled to his convoy: '*Prepare to scatter*.' Dropping smoke floats to screen them, Fegen put his ship between the *Scheer* and the ships he had to protect. Liners are immense, wall-sided ships, marvellous targets with plating almost paper-thin.

In the *Scheer*, deafened and rocked by the noise and blast of their own heavy guns, they meticulously timed the battle. The *Jervis Bay* lasted an incredible 22 minutes 22 seconds under the blows of 11-inch shells, delaying the raider and saving most of the merchantmen which also joined in the battle by making smoke and firing with their small defensive guns.

The wireless room was knocked out, the steering went haywire. Men fell, others staggered about wounded. Fegen had one leg blown off, the other mutilated. Most of the guns fell silent, except that at the stern. Fegen crawled to that gun, to direct its fire, sheltering behind lifeboats from the shell fragments that whined away from the violent explosions and clanged against the superstructure.

From the *Scheer* they saw the *Jervis Bay* begin to burn, trailing black smoke which further hid the convoy. They noted how the fire of her guns, so prompt at first, now began to fall away until finally only a single gun, that at the stern, was still in action. She fell away from her course and came to a stop, settling in the water, burning fiercely from the bridge to aft of the funnel. There was 30 feet of water in the engine-room when men began to abandon ship.

The *Scheer* passed on, trying to pick off the fattest targets amid the fleeing, scattered ships. The oil tanker *San Demetrio* was burning and abandoned; but later, some of her crew reboarded her and got the tanker's fires out, eventually reaching England. By then, it was long after dark, with the raider compelled to seek further prey with her searchlights.

The *Trewellard, Fresno City, Kenbane Head, Beaverford* and *Maiden* sank that day or in the night; the *Vingaland* fell victim next day to the bombs of a Focke-Wulf Condor. The rest of the Halifax convoy had escaped, thanks to Fegen's sacrifice of himself and his ship and most of his crew. A posthumous VC was their reward as well as his.

Chapter Twenty-Two

BATTLESHIP *BISMARCK*

Raider Brought to Bay, May 1941

In the Second World War there was of course no thought of the small German Navy trying to bring on a battleship fight with the numerically superior but stretched British fleet. A combination of surface raiding and U-boat attacks appeared the most profitable. The surface raiding fleet did consist of the German equivalent to the armed merchant cruiser, except that the guns and torpedoes were hidden, plus the new fast battleships and cruisers. The example of the *Emden* pointed to how effective this might be; but there was also the example of what the German warships had done, including the battlecruisers after Jutland, in attacking British convoys to Norway. Now the Norwegian coastline, right up into the Arctic Circle, was under German control and offered bases to the raiders ideally situated for a breakout into the Atlantic whenever weather conditions of fog or storm made such an attempt attractive.

Meanwhile, the chances for single raiders—or even a pair, for they could not risk heavy damage far from base—had been much reduced. The British were now escorting their many convoys with battleships —admittedly, old, slow battleships—instead of puny-armed ex-liners. Admiral Raeder decided that the answer was to send out a fleet of warships, including his heaviest. Just completed were the big battleship, *Bismarck*, 42,500 tons, with eight 15-inch guns, capable of a speed in excess of 30 knots, and the big 8-inch gun cruiser *Prinz Eugen*. They were in the Baltic. The smaller fast battleships *Scharnhorst* and *Gneisnau* were at Brest on the Brittany coast of France. To put those four into the Atlantic as a squadron would nearly paralyse the complicated system of convoys upon which Britain relied for food and raw materials.

Unfortunately for Raeder's plans, the *Scharnhorst* proved to require lengthy refitting at Brest where the *Gneisnau* was moored in the harbour. On 6 April a Canadian pilot of Coastal Command, F/O Kenneth Campbell, roared in low over the mole and was shot down almost at once; but his torpedo hit the *Gneisnau*, putting her out of service for half a year. That left only *Bismarck* and *Prinz Eugen* to carry out a raid on merchant shipping in which the battleship would seek action against the convoy escorts while the smaller ships dealt with the cargo vessels. Up to now, raiders had been forbidden to engage real warships if these appeared, but to break off action and look for another convoy. This made sense in terms of war effectiveness, and was in line with the Führer's thinking—and Hitler was a profound psychologist as far as his own people were concerned; he even had a pocket battleship called the *Deutschland* renamed as the *Lützow*, on the grounds that the sinking of a ship called 'Germany' would cause enemy hilarity and depress the German people.

He also took battleships at face value—mightily impressive embodiments of national power. To lose one would lower national morale. In this view he was not alone. The British public, primed by the press, regarded their battleships in just this way. Their loss in battle could have an effect devastating out of all proportion. Churchill understood this as well as Hitler did—a big battleship was a valuable political prop.

For Raeder, worse was to come. The *Prinz Eugen* was damaged in the Baltic by a magnetic mine; her repairs further delayed the operation. It might have been best to cancel for the moment, but Raeder knew that Hitler was about to invade Russia, which might cause him to ban all naval adventures. As it was, the Führer visited the two raiders at Gdynia before they sailed on the enterprise in May. May was a little late for the breakout—the long winter darkness in the latitude of Iceland and Greenland was beginning to give way to the longer days of approaching summer, when 'night' is really a grey sky rather than true dark.

The two ships left Gdynia (now Gdansk) on 18 May, commanded by Admiral Lütjens who would have preferred to wait until the *Scharnhorst* and *Gneisnau* could take part, but was over-ruled. Already in position on their route were five tankers, two supply ships and two reconnaissance ships, an embryonic 'fleet train'.

At sea, during the time of their breakout, were eleven British convoys in the threatened area, six inward bound, five outward. From first to

last, the number of warships involved in trying to find and destroy the
two raiders were: eight battleships and battlecruisers, two aircraft
carriers, four 8-inch gun cruisers, seven smaller cruisers, twenty-one
destroyers, six submarines and many shore-based aircraft. Fuel was to
be a vital factor for the British too, and they needed a fleet train equally;
but this way of thinking was alien to them, whereas the Americans,
operating in the boundless Pacific, took such a support force for
granted.

Of primary importance was information: from spies, from radio
intercepts, from code-breaking, from interpretation and evaluation of
the results. For the Germans too information on the enemy's moves and
their own counter-moves to deny him information was equally vital.
The British tried to keep a watch on the *Bismarck* while the Germans
flew photo-recce over Scapa Flow. To deny information about the entry
of the two raiders into the North Sea, the Germans stopped all
merchant ship movement in the Kattegat and Skaggerak. There should
be no witnesses of the raiders' passage past Sweden and Norway.

As the two warships passed through the silent waters between
Denmark and Sweden, a ship was sighted to the eastward, against the
green coast of Sweden, steering a parallel course to the Germans. It was
the Swedish cruiser *Gotland*, the warship of a neutral nation. She stayed
with them for several hours, then broke off. Admiral Lütjens radioed
that his presence had been betrayed. And indeed it had, although not
immediately. The *Gotland*'s sighting report was seen by a number of
people in Sweden, including Major Törnberg, chief of staff to the head
of the Swedish Secret Service. He was pro-Norwegian and pro-British
and told the Norwegian military attaché, Colonel Roscher Lund, and
also his British counterpart, Captain Henry Denham. At nine o'clock
that night Denham sent a signal to the Director of Naval Intelligence,
which, when de-coded, read:

Kattegat today 20th May. At 1500 two large warships escorted by
three destroyers, five escort vessels, ten or twelve aircraft passed
Marstrand course north-west. B.3.

'B.3' was the grading Denham awarded his informants: B, on a
grading of A to E, indicated his assessment of his source as 'good'; '3' his
assessment of its accuracy as 'possible'. The DNI shortly after received
a signal from a Norwegian spy network led by Viggo Axelssen, which

confirmed Denham's report. The news was passed by telephone, much more secure than radio, direct to Admiral Tovey's flagship *King George V* lying in Scapa Flow.

Scapa, even in spring, was a desolate, barren place. It was claimed that the saddest journey in the world was on the leave train back from London, the most joyous the train going south. Opposite, on the island of Hoy, was the battleship *Iron Duke*, Jellicoels flagship at Jutland, bombed and run ashore early on in this war. There were about five buildings and five trees on Hoy; there was an Admiralty scheme to station Wrens at Scapa, vigorously opposed by the wives of the sailors and soldiers stationed there. The only naked bodies sunbathing on the beaches were seals. On a route march, you could see them and also the First World War battlecruiser *Derfflinger* bottom up in a 'geo' during her salvage.

The commander of the Home Fleet at Scapa during the Second World War, Admiral Tovey, had at Jutland been the captain of the destroyer *Onslow* which had helped sink the *Wiesbaden* more than twenty years before. But he shared with Jellicoe one problem—the short range of his ships, the new need for oil fuel instead of the old need for coal. He had to know when to sail to achieve an interception; to search without accurate information about the quarry would be simply to beat the air and risk running out of fuel.

The Germans had already given him pointers—their recce flights over Scapa and also over the Denmark Strait between Iceland and Greenland, one of the obvious routes for raiders to break out into the Atlantic. That Strait was already being patrolled by two cruisers—the *Norfolk*, with early none-too-useful radar, and the *Suffolk*, with a much improved radar capability. Their job would be to shadow, not fight.

Like the *Prinz Eugen* and other German heavy cruisers they were forbidden to fight a battleship, which was simply suicide with no chance of success. The Germans too had radar at an early stage; later it was to be eclipsed by Allied developments. Lütjens was not well served for this operation by the German intelligence services, either now or later, although Admiral Canaris, head of the Abwehr, the German counter-intelligence service, signalled to him that British agents had already reported the German squadron's outward movements. But he had guessed that.

Admiral Tovey at Scapa would be ill-advised to go out on a rumour or a guesstimate; he preferred to await definite evidence of the quarry's movements before giving the order to sail his ships. With him at Scapa he had the old battlecruiser *Hood*, at 42,000 tons the largest warship in the British Navy, but with recommended extra protection for her magazines not yet carried out; the new battleship *Prince of Wales*, whose turrets were giving trouble and had the builder's men in civilian clothes on board and working at them. This force of two big ships with destroyer escort would sail under Admiral Holland. Tovey himself was in the British fleet flagship *King George V*, sister ship to the newer *Prince of Wales*; the aircraft carrier *Victorious*, new and not yet worked up, which was due to escort an important convoy to the Middle East; and waiting in the Clyde to meet her was the old battlecruiser *Repulse*, which he could also draw on in emergency. There were also various old battleships, much slower than their German opponents, escorting some of the convoys now at sea.

Norfolk and *Suffolk* were out watching the Denmark Strait; two newer cruisers, the *Manchester* and the *Birmingham*, plus five trawlers, watching the gap between Iceland and the Faroes. There was a smaller gap to be watched also, between the Faroes and the old Viking kingdoms of Shetland and Orkney just north of Scotland. Tovey ordered air recce of the Norwegian fjords to track the quarry in its progress north.

Two Spitfires of Coastal Command's photographic unit took off —one for Oslo, the capital of Norway, and the other for the Bergen fjords. It was the latter, piloted by F/O Suckling, which brought back to Lerwick in the Shetlands photographs which positively identified the quarry. *Prinz Eugen* had gone in to top up with fuel; *Bismarck* had not, perhaps relying on one of the tankers lying along the route of their breakout.

Then the weather closed in. An air strike ordered against the German ships took place after they had left again, the bombers dropping their loads blind. Tovey decided to sail *Hood* and *Prince of Wales* with six destroyers to the south-west of Iceland so as to be able to cover two escape routes—that between Iceland and Greenland and that between Iceland and the Faroes. Two big ships and six destroyers against one big ship and one heavy cruiser. But Tovey wanted more evidence before sailing himself, as his force was the last centrally placed reserve. The weather was too bad for Coastal Command aircraft to check the hazardous coast of Norway, which often rises steeply from the sea. In bad weather it would be all too easy to find Norway the hard way, literally, and dead airmen tell no tales. Tovey turned to the code-breakers of Bletchley Park who had recently had windfalls, as a result of naval operations, in capturing enemy code documents and even a complete 'Enigma' coding machine; but they were not yet able to help.

On 22 May Captain Fancourt of the RN Air Station at Hatson in the Orkneys decided to attempt with a naval aircraft what the RAF had been unable to do. It was not a matter of machines but of men. In his office, pushing a pen, was Commander Rotherham, whose flying experience dated back to prehistoric days when one might have to navigate by noting the direction and details of waves seen from almost wave-top height. This ability rather than slick modern gadgets was appropriate to the present navigating problem. An old American twin-motor bomber, relegated to target-towing, was selected for the job.

It was not a case of just pouring oneself into an aircraft and roaring off in a cloud of glory. One had to pick, on the high-sided Norwegian coast with its many fjords all seeming similar in low cloud, some hopefully identifiable landmark and then lay off a track towards it with an error in a known direction, say to the right. So when you arrived at the coast, you knew you had to turn left and not right to find the landmark. This is to simplify, for course and track are generally not the same, they depend upon the wind, which can and probably will vary when in flight. So the Maryland had to fly dangerously low at times and then pull up and vanish into cloud, losing sight of the sea; and to make the next check on the track made good, the aircraft had to be taken down again—all too easy to see the sea too late or, when the coast looms darkly in the vapour, fail to turn in time. From these brief glimpses of the waves Commander Rotherham had to estimate wind speed and direction and if necessary make alterations to the course flown.

It all went exactly right—so easy to say—and the fjords were thoroughly examined and Bergen overflown with a good deal of protest from the Germans. Luckily it was only flak, the weather was too bad for fighters. But in case he was shot down in the next few minutes, Rotherham wrote a message to be sent by the radio operator to Coastal Command; but he could not raise them and so transmitted on the target-towing squadron wavelength. Into their routine exercise and training messages came this urgent operational signal of the utmost importance to Tovey, to the Admiralty and to the Prime Minister. Nil report. No sign of *Bismarck* and *Prinz Eugen* anywhere near Bergen.

Tovey then originated a stream of messages: the carrier *Victorious*, with four cruisers and six destroyers to be ready by 10.15 p.m. to follow him out of Scapa; the battlecruiser *Repulse* to sail from the Clyde and meet him next morning north of the Hebrides; the cruiser *Suffolk* with her better radar to join the *Norfolk* in patrolling the Denmark Strait (one fuelled while the other stayed on station); the cruiser *Arethusa* to join the *Birmingham* and *Manchester* patrolling the Iceland-Faroes passage.

When the news reached London, Churchill appealed to the American President for help, in case the British Navy failed.

Hitler was not informed. Only when the breakout had succeeded did Raeder report to the Führer; this was wise, for even as it was Hitler became profoundly worried—the ships might be damaged by torpedoes—there could be unfavourable reactions in America—he suggested recalling the raiders. Raeder answered that the most difficult part of the operation was now over, and Hitler reluctantly agreed that it could proceed. One supposes that he may not have appreciated the importance of a success; Hitler was after all intent then on the adventure of his lifetime—the attack on Bolshevik Russia; and of course he had just launched the airborne attack designed to take Crete from the British, following on his capture of Jugoslavia and Greece, involving yet another British evacuation in face of the power of the Wehrmacht.

The Luftwaffe was naturally covering Scapa when weather allowed, but they did not notice the departure of the *Hood* and *Prince of Wales*, being misled by a single real battleship plus two dummy ships. Similarly, the German wireless interception service reported no increase of traffic, nor did any decoded message suggest that any part of Tovey's fleet had sailed or that the British had any idea where the raiders were. A further piece of information given to Lütjens was quite false, that Force 'H' had sailed for Crete. This squadron under Admiral Somerville consisted of the battlecruiser *Renown*, the carrier *Ark Royal*, the cruiser *Sheffield* and destroyers; all with battle-experienced crews; they were still at Gibraltar, well placed to intervene.

Another piece of information, which turned out to be correct, was from one of the met men on board, Dr Externbrink, who forecast fog for the present, clearing later when they were in the Denmark Straits. Lütjens decided not to spend time refuelling from a waiting tanker but to press on at higher speed to try to clear the Straits before the mist lifted.

Most of the way, the raiders went through shrouded, as forecast, then a narrow curtain of visibility opened up, with the fog lying heavily to the south, where Iceland lay, but giving clear views of the Arctic icepack towards Greenland. The route was further narrowed not only by the ice but by a notified British minefield. The crews of the German ships, most of them young, were many of them seeing for the first time the land of seals and the polar bear; they would not have been human if some had not thought, 'Mother, if only you could see me now!' On the bridge of the *Prinz Eugen* Captain Brinkmann, training his binoculars on the fog bank to port with the patrolling British cruisers in mind, commented, 'If they're anywhere in these parts, they're in there.'

As indeed they were, popping cautiously out of the fog for a sight of their quarry, ready to duck back if it appeared; they could not afford damage to their radar and wireless gear, otherwise they became useless. *Suffolk*, with a revolving scanner, had radar coverage in all directions except astern, and with a range of 13 miles. Captain Ellis took a keen interest in the new gadgetry and how it worked. His bridge was more comfortable than that of *Norfolk* which was open and unheated on unnecessarily Nelsonic lines; but in common with many others in this war and earlier conflicts, his duties kept him very short of sleep. Many ships and aircraft were looking for the raiders which had not been reported for more than two days, in which time they could have gone a thousand miles. Able Seaman Newell, the starboard after lookout, shouted:

'Ship bearing Green One Four Oh!'

And then amended that to:

'*Two* ships bearing Green One Four Oh!'

What he had seen was the towering black shape of the *Bismarck* emerging from a mist patch seven miles distant, followed by the smaller but similar silhouette of the *Prinz Eugen*. Ellis ordered hard-a-port and full speed ahead to duck into the fog bank while another officer pressed the alarm bell. While the crew drew on boots, grabbed coats and lifejackets and pounded away to their action stations, the *Suffolk* was sending her sighting report to Admiral Tovey who did not receive it (the aerials were iced up and not working properly). However, *Norfolk* was nearer and she acted on the information, but misjudged and came out of the fog to find *Bismarck* heading directly for the cruiser and only six miles away.

The Germans had failed to notice *Suffolk* during the two or three minutes of her appearance before she got back into the fog, but *Norfolk* was greeted at once by twinkling yellow flashes and the roaring, express-train sound of approaching shells and the 200-foot high water-spouts leaping from the sea around her. Each shell weighed a ton, including the one that did not explode but bounced off the surface of the water and bounded over the cruiser's bridge. Five salvoes erupted before she merged into the fog off Iceland. It was her sighting report which was received by bases and ships—by Tovey in *King George V*, relieved to find his dispositions correct; by Churchill at the Admiralty; by the battleship *Rodney* 800 miles away; by Sir James Somerville at Gibraltar; by Vice-Admiral Holland in the *Hood* 300 miles away, accompanied by the *Prince of Wales*; and by the *Bismarck* and *Prinz Eugen*. The *Suffolk* followed them astern, keeping her distance with her 13-mile radar and *Norfolk* with her fixed aerials relied on *Suffolk*.

Admiral Holland was already steering an interception course when he received the sighting report; he worked out a plan for an almost head-on encounter, with the enemy silhouetted against the light, the *Bismarck* leading. The blast of *Bismarck*'s guns had put her forward radar out of action; therefore Admiral Lütjens ordered *Prinz Eugen* to overtake and assume the lead. Then *Suffolk*'s radar lost the *Bismarck* temporarily, and Lütjens made an alteration of course. The result was that the two British capital ships intercepted the Germans at a slight angle, so that only their forward turrets could bear; and that halved their fire-power advantage, so that they were now approximately equal.

But it seems also that the *Hood* opened fire on *Prinz Eugen*, believing she was the *Bismarck*, but failed to hit her; so it must have been the *Prince of Wales* which scored hits on the *Bismarck*. Also Admiral Holland, apparently following standard instructions, was keeping his consort on a close, tight rein, giving the *Prince of Wales* no room to vary her speed or course to confuse the enemy's aim. In the *Suffolk*, there was elation: two British heavy ships against one German. There could be no doubt about the result.

In the German squadron there was confusion as to the identity of the British ships; in view of the reports from air recce of Scapa Flow, the big ships had been still there until recently; these two must be cruisers, hence no need to order the *Prinz Eugen* to withdraw (cruisers being forbidden to engage battleships).

The British fired first. To an officer in the *Prinz Eugen* the flashes seemed 'great fiery rings like suns'. Battleship guns, not cruiser's. Both German ships replied, concentrating on the *Hood*, to the horrified relief of the watchers in the *Prince of Wales*. Shell splashes appeared on both sides of the *Hood*—a straddle. A fire began to glow amidships on the boatdeck where the ammunition for the 4-inch AA guns was stored. Admiral Holland then ordered a turn to port by both ships so as to bring their after turrets into action as well. The *Bismarck* fired again on the *Hood*. Another white forest of shell splashes rose up. One shell at least made no splash.

A huge ball of flame boiled up amidships to four times the height of her mainmast, followed by a swelling cloud of dark yellow smoke. And out of the smoke emerged objects—part of a 15-inch gun turret, the mainmast, the main derrick, and some of the battlecruiser's own shells bursting like fireworks in puffs of white smoke above her.

Fourteen hundred men had gone, leaving three survivors only to be picked up. *Bismarck* had disposed of the *Hood*, the largest warship in the world, with five or six salvoes. She then directed her fire at the *Prince of Wales*, and with another dozen salvoes or so, drove her to break off action. *Hood* had not hit anything, not even the *Prinze Eugen*. The old German gunnery superiority of the First World War was still apparent, as was the tendency of British battlecruisers to blow up.

Few of those present actually saw what happened, then or later, because they were below decks. The executive officer of the *Prinz Eugen*, hearing the announcement that *Hood* had blown up, did not believe it. 'Some poor fellow up there has gone off his head.' In the plotting office below the bridge in the *Prince of Wales*, it was impossible to tell the difference between the shock of their own guns firing and the shock of hits from the *Bismarck*. Only when blood began trickling out of the voicepipe did they realise that there was anything wrong. A 15-inch shell had killed everyone on the bridge except the captain, the navigating officer (though he was wounded) and the chief yeoman of signals. She was hit four times by the *Bismarck*, three times by the *Prinz Eugen*. And although she got several straddles on the German battleship, only a few of her guns were actually firing. As the civilian workmen cleared one jam in a turret, another developed. As she turned away, making smoke, Y turret jammed, making the four guns in it useless.

It would have been ridiculous to carry on like this, and risk losing a battleship for no real gain. But between *Prince of Wales* turning away and the time when Admiral Holland had led her and the *Hood* into battle against a theoretically inferior German squadron, only 21 minutes had elapsed. The *Hood* had gone because of failures in British design (she was laid down in 1916) which, although realised later, had never been remedied because there seemed to be no time to do it, she was so busy cruising the Empire and 'showing the flag'. The turret trouble with the *Prince of Wales* has been referred to as 'teething', but it seems to have been more than that. Unlike the Germans and Japanese who had soon begun to build bigger than the naval treaties allowed, the British had 'played the game' and in so doing had tried to put a gallon into a pint pot. Four guns into each turret instead of two or three, for instance, instead of a bigger ship with adequate space for the machinery.

With the death of Vice-Admiral Holland in the *Hood*, Rear-Admiral Wake-Walker in the *Norfolk* was the senior officer; with the *Prince of Wales* under his command the task of shadowing became easier, there was less chance of the *Bismarck* fatally ambushing one of the cruisers. What he could not know was how much damage, if any, had been inflicted on the enemy. A cloud of smoke had been seen to come from the battleship, but that might be merely a hit shaking up the dirt and soot inside the funnel.

The *Prinz Eugen* had a souvenir from the *Hood*, a large, jagged shell splinter found at the base of the funnel. One shell from the *Prince of Wales* had hit the captain's motorboat on the upper deck of the *Bismarck* and destroyed it by impact, without exploding. A second shell had gone into the hull amidships and put two boilers out of action, scalding five men. A third shell had struck at about waterline level on the port side, gone clean through and out the starboard side, without exploding. But in its passing it had penetrated two oil tanks initiating a two-way flow—of water into the oil and of oil into the sea. It had also damaged the suction valves, cutting the amount of fuel available by 1,000 tons. These were prime factors influencing Lütjens's decision to abandon the raiding cruise and go to a major dockyard in France, St Nazaire.

Some of the facts were known in the *Suffolk* soon after the action and within 90 minutes she had signalled that the *Bismarck* had reduced speed to 22 knots and was leaving an oil-wake behind her. This message was not received by the *Norfolk*. A Sunderland flying boat had sighted and been fired at by the *Bismarck* and had reported ambiguously 'losing oil', which was read in the *Norfolk* as referring to the flying boat rather than the battleship. However, on their return to Iceland the crew of the Sunderland made clear what they meant and this news was broadcast to all British forces.

The Admiralty were constructing a wide net around the scene. They called up the old battleships, widely dispersed, which were guarding convoys: two of the 'R' class, *Revenge* and *Ramillies*, slightly smaller, inferior versions of the *Queen Elizabeths*; the post-war battleship *Rodney* with nine 16-inch guns; various cruisers, many destroyers, a submarine, and, most importantly, Force 'H' from Gibraltar—with the carrier *Ark Royal* and the old battlecruiser *Renown*. It has been suggested that the loss of the *Hood* caused widespread shock, but I was living near Portsmouth, where she was well known, and noted in my diary simply: 'Heard about the *Hood*. We've got plenty of capital ships, so it's not very important.' It was only on 27 May, when the news of the Navy's losses off Crete came in, that both Servicemen and civilians reacted angrily. That was realistic.

From the British point of view—ignorant of the actual situation in the *Bismarck*—the enemy could have a number of options: abandon the breakout and go back north to Norway: abandon the breakout and go south to a French base; or break out onto the Atlantic convoy routes and cause havoc. Admiral Tovey decided not to favour any of these options but maintain a central course, and watch what happened.

In Germany, the view was taken that the man on the spot—in this scene Lütjens—knew best (a view diametrically opposite to British practice); but that all help should be given to the *Bismarck*. Admiral Dönitz offered all available U-boats to set a trap for the battleship's pursuers. At this time the U-boat had not been mastered—far from it, Britain was losing that vital part of the war. The Luftwaffe was ordered to co-operate and preparations were made to receive the *Bismarck* at the Normandy dock in St Nazaire and protect her with balloons and flak. And, of course, Britain was still under German air attack by night. Crete was almost lost.

But at least the position, if not the intentions, of the German ships was known. Admiral Tovey's force was at that moment the nearest: the new battleship *King George V*, the old battlecruiser *Repulse* (even worse protected than the *Hood*), the new carrier *Victorious* and its outdated warplanes flown for the most part by boys without battle experience, and five cruisers. The *Bismarck* (unknown to everyone she had parted company with the now much faster *Prinz Eugen*) was about 120 miles away, the extreme flying limit of the torpedo bombers carried by the *Victorious*. These were nine Swordfish, often called 'Stringbags' because of their maze of struts and wires, led by Eugene Esmonde. Optimists said they could do 95 mph. Authors careless of historical accuracy have compared them to the Wright Brothers' early biplanes. This is quite untrue; on the contrary they resembled the oldfashioned and lumbering biplanes of which von Richthofen took such great toll in around 1916–17. In a rising sea and darkness they had to take off from a pitching flight deck with their heavy loads, navigate over water towards a rapidly moving target, and return to a base which had moved in the meantime.

The first ship they found was the US Coastguard cutter *Modoc* (a neutral, more or less), whose crew had had their Atlantic monotony broken by a sight of the great *Bismarck* hurrying south. Then out of the clouds came these ancient crates—two wings and fixed undercarriages!—like some flying circus of the 1920s; and then, in hot pursuit of the German battleship came two cruisers and another battleship. This battleship trained its guns on the *Modoc* while some of the German flak directed at the Swordfish went past and nearly hit the American vessel.

Oddly, none of the Swordfish were shot down. One of the experienced pilots, noting the position of the flak bursts ahead, surmised that no German could possibly imagine in this day and age that any aircraft could fly as slowly as a 'Stringbag' and were allowing too much deflection. Ironically, when it came time for the *Prince of Wales* and the *Repulse* to meet Japanese Navy torpedo bombers in December of the same year, the British gunners, having practised against British aircraft and not believing that the Japs could have anything better, missed astern, firing at the air where the Japanese had been.

However, in spite of the difficulties, one Swordfish scored a hit. But the torpedo ran on the surface instead of 30 feet down and so struck the armour belt, causing only superficial damage and casualties. And despite the darkness and the rising sea, all the planes landed safely back on the *Victorious*.

The three close pursuers of the *Bismarck*, the two cruisers *Suffolk* and *Norfolk*, and the wounded *Prince of Wales* with the twisted steel and bloodied flesh on her bridge still being cleared away, were in an odd formation and being harried by the Admiralty. 'Admiralty' at this time meant Admiral Pound, with Winston Churchill impatiently overruling him. Pound by now was old and sick and frequently in pain which caused him loss of sleep; Churchill must have been worried by the way the war was going and for his own authority in the House of Commons, and was anyway always in the habit of prodding his Generals and Admirals.

Late that afternoon of 24 May, the 'Admiralty' had sent a signal to Admiral Wake-Walker asking what he intended to do about the *Prince of Wales* 're-engaging'. The request was not as polite as it sounds: it was an accusation of, at best, slackness, at worst, cowardice. It was not appreciated. Tovey too took in this signal and determined that if it was made again, he would break wireless silence to back Wake-Walker's conduct. But the damage had been done.

Wake-Walker had abandoned the search pattern for a closer grouping more suitable for attack, at the same time zig-zagging to avoid possible U-boat torpedoes, although this meant that the *Suffolk*'s radar on one leg would briefly lost contact with the quarry; but should pick it up again when course was altered back. That is, of course, if the *Bismarck* herself maintained her present course and did not alter.

Captain Ellis in the *Suffolk* was spending his fourth night without sleep apart from catnaps. The radar operators, staring at the screens for the sweep hand to light up momentarily as the radio waves struck an object and were reflected back, were tired beyond belief, eyes gritty with staring. Around 3.30 in the morning of 25 May the sweep hand failed to spark on any contact. That had happened before and they had always found again; but not this time. The cruiser increased speed to shorten the range, but still the sweep hand failed to light up on the target. At 5 a.m. Ellis had to signal:

'Have lost contact with enemy.'

We know now that the *Bismarck* had changed course from roughly south-west to approximately south-east, making for Brest initially rather than St Nazaire owing to shortage of fuel. So even air reconnaissance failed to find her. Tovey's decision was to cover the way west, where the *Bismarck* could do immense damage to the convoys; if she turned north it would be to go home, or if to France, it would also be in a sense going home.

Then an apparently inexplicable thing happened. British direction finding stations listening on the German battleship frequency reported messages at 6.54 a.m. and again at 7.48 a.m. It was Lütjens reporting to Germany on the efficiency of British radar, the sinking of the *Hood*, his own worsened fuel situation as a result of damage—long signals. The D/F stations had plenty of time to get cross bearings. Clearly, the

German Admiral believed that the British cruisers were still in radar contact, and knew also that he was leaving a broad trail of oil behind him. It has been suggested that because the *Bismarck*'s 'passive' radar was still picking up the probing waves of the *Suffolk*, Lütjens assumed that the *Suffolk* could also detect the *Bismarck* with her 'active' set. Neither side knew too much about the other's radar, but 'passive' had a much longer range than 'active', so this may be the complete explanation. But tiredness and strain may have had something to do with it also.

No really satisfactory explanation, agreed by all witnesses, has been reached for what now occurred on the British side. Admittedly, the bearings from D/F were not good, in the technical sense that the angles made were not sharp enough for high accuracy; but even so they were wrongly plotted in Admiral Tovey's flagship, so she and her consorts chased away out into the Atlantic while the *Bismarck* carried on in the opposite direction, getting farther and farther away, nearer and nearer to France.

At the Admiralty, opinion hardened throughout the day that the German was making for the Biscay coast, not into the Atlantic; and Tovey then reversed his course, but now well behind in the chase. However, during the day he also took in a message to the battleship *Rodney* from the Admiralty, telling her to move towards the Iceland-Faroes gap in conjunction with himself; it has been suggested that this false and contradictory signal was made at the insistence of Winston Churchill. Another signal, on the U-boat frequency, received at such strength as to suggest it was sent by a battleship, showed the originator to be on the track of the *Bismarck* heading for France. But the originator was in fact a U-boat.

There were other intercepted messages which, although correct, played no part in what happened because they were received and decoded too late to be anything but 'history'. One was from a French naval officer in touch with a Resistance group reporting preparations in Brest to receive the *Bismarck*; most of the delay occurred because of the time taken to get the message to a secret transmitter. Another source was a high-ranking Luftwaffe officer in Athens, whose son was in the battleship. He, using diplomatic privileges, asked Berlin for her destination, and Berlin replied that it was Brest.

Although *Bismarck* seemed to have evaded her immediate pursuers, Admiral Lütjens was not confident that he could avoid the entire

British fleet for another thousand miles; in an address to the crew, he warned them of this. At the same time somewhat despondent planners at the British Admiralty were working out the air searches for the next day, 26 May. The Atlantic was a big place and visibility was not always good. When these plans reached Coastal Command, Air Marshal Sir Frederick Bowhill made an amendment. He had spent 22 years of his life at sea, in both Royal and Merchant Navies, had even been round the Horn under sail. The track proposed by the Admiralty, as *Bismarck*'s likeliest, did not impress him, except that it was the most direct. It had of course been approved by the two most senior Admirals, Pound and Phillips, but Bowhill would not have done it this way had he been in the *Bismarck*. Firstly, the track ran far too close to British airfields; secondly, it involved a landfall in darkness on a rocky and dangerous coast. Had he been in Lütjens's shoes, he would have headed first for Spain. To cover the area he thought most likely, he proposed an additional patrol.

The flying boat which undertook this duty was Catalina Z from 209 Squadron of RAF Coastal Command, with a British pilot and an American second pilot, Ensign Leonard Smith, whose job was to teach the British about the American Catalina and learn from the British something of operational flying. Smith was at the controls when the sighting was made at 1030 on the morning of 26 May—a distant black shape which resolved itself into a hostile battleship; very hostile, as her upperworks spat sheets of flame and puffs of smoke blossomed like black mushrooms around the Catalina.

The pilot, F/O Dennis Briggs, got off the sighting report which was read in Berlin just as easily as in London. Her position was just under 700 miles from Brest, still beyond the range of fighter cover. In the British Admiralty it could be seen how close some ships had come to finding her the previous day. But at that moment *King George V* was 135 miles to the north, the *Rodney* 125 miles to the north-east. However, Admiral Somerville's Force 'H' was not only closer, at 100 miles, she was also between the *Bismarck* and Brest. His flagship, the old battle-cruiser *Renown*, was even less formidable than the *Hood* had proved to be; the *Sheffield* was only a cruiser; but the *Ark Royal*'s air groups were veterans of the Mediterranean war. They might be able to stop the *Bismarck* or slow her down.

There had been closer contacts still, known to the Germans but not the British. From high up in the battleship, a lookout had seen the masts of what was in fact a destroyer force led by Rear-Admiral Vian passing by along the horizon, and Herbert Wohlfarth in U556 had sighted Somerville's Force 'H' and might have torpedoed both the carrier and the battlecruiser—only he had just expended his last on a scrawny little merchantman. That single last torpedo might have changed everything.

Now there was a gale blowing, the flight deck of the carrier plunging into the waves as if she was a destroyer, and when she rolled it was sometimes to 30 degrees. In the afternoon the torpedo Swordfish began coming up in the lifts; in their takeoffs several seemed to touch their wheels in the spray, but all got away safely. Somerville had sent the cruiser *Sheffield* on ahead to find and shadow the *Bismarck*, but his message to that effect reached the *Ark Royal* too late to be decoded in time to warn the pilots. Only when they were airborne was an urgent, uncoded message sent: 'Look out for *Sheffield*.'

In Tovey's flagship *King George V*, the reports from Somerville regarding the Swordfish strike had set the staff wondering how the old biplanes would get on in this weather. The long pursuit, with its cliff-hanging climaxes, had drained emotion, but everyone was keyed up, unable to settle. Then, the fighting top of a battleship was sighted in the murk. It was the *Rodney* with her nine 16-inch guns to complement the ten 14-inch of the *King George V*. In spite of attempts by the 'Admiralty' over the last thirty hours to steer her all over the ocean, she had made contact and the odds were now two to one in British favour. Her engines were in a sad state, long overdue for dockyard attention and she could not make even 22 knots. That suited Tovey as he needed to conserve fuel. He signalled the Admiralty that if *Bismarck*'s speed had not been lowered by midnight, he would have to break off the chase, although the *Rodney* would not reach that state until next morning.

Ten minutes later the news they were all waiting for came in from Admiral Somerville:

> '*Estimate no hits.*'

That was it, then. Everyone went silent.

Somerville did not then choose to amplify with details of the torpedo attack by the Swordfish. It was not the right moment to report that the ship attacked had been, not the *Bismarck*, but his own cruiser the *Sheffield*, busy shadowing her. Thinking *Bismarck*, and not knowing about *Sheffield*, the pilots had seen the *Bismarck* and carried out a standard converging attack so that, whichever way the target ship turned, she would run into a torpedo. But the captain of *Sheffield* had spotted the attack pattern too and, aided by the premature explosion of five or more of the torpedoes, had succeeded in dodging the remainder dropped.

This was not the time for recriminations. Somerville sent the Swordfish out again and, warned by the premature explosion of the torpedoes armed with magnetic pistols, armed them this time with torpedoes which would explode only on contact.

Five hours to midnight. In Tovey's flagship there was little hope of a second strike being successful (they still did not know that the target had been *Sheffield*). In the *Bismarck* during the day hopes, low after the air sighting, had risen as nothing had happened. By dawn they would be in sight of escape from peril. Their lost fuel was telling; but for that they could by now, steaming at much higher speed, have been within range of Luftwaffe cover.

The second strike took off under a low ceiling of 600 feet and into frequent rainstorms above angry seas. The battleship was hidden in the murk and no co-ordinated attack by all aircraft together on converging courses was possible; instead they staggered on in groups of two and three.

In *King George V* the buzzer from the wireless office signalled the arrival of another message:

'From the leader of the striking force. Estimate no hits.'

In the *Rodney* the same message was received and her captain broadcast an announcement to that effect, adding:

'We have lost our last chance of slowing down the enemy and bringing him to action.'

They assumed in both ships that the standard all-together-now attack had been tried—and had failed.

Then came a message from the *Sheffield*:

'*Enemy's course 340 degrees.*'

There were some bitter comments. This course was directly towards them instead of directly away; clearly someone had made the easiest error of all—to mistake the reciprocal course for the actual course. Poor chap.

Then came the next message, this time from a Swordfish:

'Enemy steering due north.' The Brittany ports were south-east. But of course, *Bismarck* must have turned away from a torpedo and would soon resume course to the south-east.

But she didn't. The next message was from the *Sheffield* again. *Bismarck*'s course was now north, following a further Swordfish report of north-north-west. The raider was going round in circles!

Only after careful interrogation of the aircrew did Captain Maund of the *Ark Royal* signal:

> '*Estimate one hit amidships. Possible second hit on starboard quarter.*'

This cautious statement, for there were other, less definite claims, seems to have been correct; and it was the second torpedo near the stern which had been critical—it had jammed the rudder 15 degrees to port. *Bismarck*'s engines were undamaged, her armament was still fully effective, but by no combination of engine orders could the battleship be made to go towards Brest. Cautiously, but with great moral courage, Tovey decided to wait for dawn and not risk a confused night action.

What happened then was more like an execution than war, with the *Bismarck* unable to manoeuvre. It has been compared to the last stages of a bullfight. *King George V* and *Rodney* moved in together, the latter not hampered by being tied to the former's apron strings as had happened with *Hood*. The German fire, accurate enough at first, fell off and then died away under the bombardment; the forward turrets were knocked out, then those aft. Fires could be see burning inside through holes in the hull. The British cruisers joined in also with their 8-inch guns. But still the *Bismarck*'s ensigns flew and still she did not sink.

Admiral Tovey is supposed to have made a gesture of exasperation, miming that he was about to throw his binoculars at her. He would have to go home from lack of fuel. As he left he signalled: 'Any ship with torpedoes to close *Bismarck* and torpedo her.' The cruiser *Dorsetshire* moved in, put two torpedoes into one side, one torpedo into the other. The Swordfish were available but were not required. The wrecked battleship, low in the water and burning, leaned over until the sea ran into the funnel and slowly turned bottom up. Tovey remembered the fight with the *Wiesbaden* at Jutland when he wrote his despatch:

> '*She put up a most gallant fight against impossible odds, worthy of the old days of the Imperial German Navy.*'

Tovey was less enamoured of the Admiralty and Winston Churchill in particular, who had sent him an extraordinary message:

'*Bismarck* must be sunk at all costs and if to do this it is necessary for *King George V* to remain on the scene, then she must do so, even if it subsequently means towing *King George V.*'

In the flagship this signal at first caused laughter, then anger as the implications sank in. U-boats must be hurrying to the scene, even if they had not already begun to arrive (which they had); a battleship immobilised or under tow would be a dream target. There would be no need for the Luftwaffe. The British flagship along with her Admiral and crew would go the same way as the *Bismarck*, and for no good reason. 'It was the stupidest and most ill-considered signal ever made,' said Tovey. Admittedly, when it was made Churchill did not know that the *Bismarck*, although not yet down, was out of the war; even so, it is unpleasantly reminiscent of Sir Richard Grenville's wild attempt to scuttle the *Revenge* with all her sick and wounded still aboard.

The *Bismarck* went down just after having received three torpedoes from the *Dorsetshire*, but also after her own scuttling charges had been activated. The British picked up 102 survivors before having to cease rescue operations because of possible U-boat activity—one man in the water by the *Dorsetshire* had lost both arms but hung on to a rope with his teeth, and a midshipman, Joe Brooks, went down to save him but failed. U74 picked up three more survivors on a raft; the weather ship *Sachsenwald* picked up two more; the Spanish cruiser *Canarias* found only dead men drifting with the wreckage.

Out of more than 2,000 men, only 107 survived. Most, many wounded, went down with her still alive, such as the crew of a gun turret whose hatch had jammed, who could be heard shouting to get out. Others were trapped by wreckage or flames, others again simply sat and waited for the end. The Admiral and the Captain went down with the ship. But many hundreds of men who had got into the sea simply disappeared when the British had to cease rescue attempts.

The *Prinz Eugen* got home to a French base. Tovey's *King George V* got back with hardly any fuel left. The Luftwaffe missed him, but found some of the destroyers crawling home low on fuel and sank one.

The complexity of the operation and the search area covered could only be compared to Nelson's chase of Villeneuve during the Trafalgar campaign, although the tempo was faster and the Admirals were directed from afar.

In June 1989 the wreck of *Bismarck* was discovered lying on the slope of a seamount three miles down. This was on the eleventh day of a high-tech search carried out by a team led by Robert D. Ballard of the Woods Hole Oceanographic Institution. They had previously found the liner *Titanic* in 12,500 feet; *Bismarck* was deeper at 15,617 feet. They recorded the wreck in more than 1,000 still photographs and many video films. Unlike the *Titanic*, the *Bismarck*'s hull was surprisingly intact, with no sign of implosion, and this made Dr Ballard suspect that the battleship had indeed been scuttled.

Chapter Twenty-Three

ITALIANS UNDERWATER

Malta, July 1941: Alexandria, December 1941

Italian experiments in attacking enemy harbours by stealth and ingenious daring, rather than brute force backed by elaborate planning, dated back to the First World War. Various techniques, from swimmers towing explosive charges to motorboats with caterpillar tracks to enable them to climb over defensive obstacles, were thought up and experimented with. Their most spectacular success was in sinking the Austrian battleship *Viribus Unitis* at Pola in the Adriatic on 1 November, 1918, ten days before the Armistice.

The idea lay dormant until the run-up of tension leading to the Second World War, of which an early marker was Mussolini's invasion of Abyssinia, followed by the imposition of sanctions by the League of Nations, and a potential confrontation between the Italian Navy and the British Mediterranean Fleet based on Alexandria in Egypt, the island of Malta in the middle of the Mediterranean, and the rock fortress of Gibraltar, looking out over the Atlantic. To the British, these bases were essential links in the spine of Empire; to the Italians the island of Malta, with a partly Italian population and situated just south of Sicily, could now be looked on as a threat.

The idea behind the creation of the special unit, given the cover-name of 10th Light Flotilla (La Decima Flottiglia MAS), was to strike vital blows at the British Navy in all its Mediterranean bases at the outset of war and so cripple it immediately. Such schemes almost never come to fruition because of too optimistic a vision on one side and excessive conservatism on the other, with financial considerations in the middle. The Japanese attack on Pearl Harbor in December 1941 is a notable exception (although the midget-submarine assault which was part of the Japanese plan proved a total failure).

The Italians did develop the necessary range of weapons and equipment, however. There were three basic types of vehicle, each of which would have to be transported most of the distance from any Italian base to within a few miles of the chosen target. The first was the Explosive Motor Boat capable of around 30 knots. This was piloted by one man and propelled by an outboard motor which also steered it and could be lifted so as to allow the boat to go over a boom defence. The boat was very lightly built and carried a 300-kg explosive charge in the bows which would detach on impact and sink towards the bottom, exploding by a pressure fuse. To avoid being killed by it, the pilot released a float, flung himself backwards off the speeding boat just before the impact, and got onto the float. Brave man! The biggest success achieved with this method of attack was in Suda Bay on the island of Crete, then a temporary British naval base. The heavy cruiser, *York* and some merchant ships were sunk.

The second vehicle can be regarded either as an outsize torpedo or as a very small submarine, about 22 feet long, far too small to be piloted even by midgets. The two-man crew actually rode on it, astride, one behind the other, on seats and behind a shield: the drag must have been immense, and the Italians described them crudely as 'pigs'. Of course, the 'pig' pilots wore the new frogman-type diving gear— lightweight suits, oxygen-rebreathing sets which did not give off bubbles but had a severe depth restriction, and, on occasion, fins (or flippers). These two-man torpedoes could be carried to very near the target port by a conventional submarine fitted with big canisters on deck which acted as 'hangars' for the torpedoes.

The third vehicle which could be employed was a conventional man, in suit, mask, swim-fins and oxygen-rebreather, carrying or towing to the targets small explosive charges. In British popular postwar parlance, these were called 'frogmen'. In similar British naval equipment there was a depth limitation of 30 feet; but the Italians could and did go deeper (even in peacetime, just to hunt fish). As the oxygen was re-circulated and breathed again, this type of set gave longer duration than the civilian-type aqualung using compressed air.

The three methods did not go well together, largely because of the different speeds averaged. Thirty-plus knots for the Explosive Motor Boats, three knots for piloted 'pigs', and perhaps one knot for the 'frogmen'.

In many ways the Mediterranean was ideal for the slow-speed

underwater vehicles: the water was warm, there was little tide and few currents, visibility was usually of champagne quality (which worked both ways, for it made submarines easily detectable from the air, even as deep as 150 feet).

Italy entered the war on 10 June, 1940, by which time the Germans unaided had beaten the Allies in Europe and expelled the last British forces from the continent. In that year the 10th Light Flotilla attempted to attack Alexandria twice and lost both the submarines transporting the 'pigs'—in August the *Iride* was sunk by a bomber, in September the *Gondar* was sunk by ships. In October Gibraltar was attacked by 'pigs' without success. In March 1941 the Explosive Motor Boats had their great victory in Suda Bay, Crete; in May the 'pigs' failed again at Gibraltar; and in July came the suicidal assault on Grand Harbour, Malta. Only after that were there impressive successes at Gibraltar and Alexandria.

The assault on Malta involved a mixed unit using both fast Explosive Motor Boats and slow 'pigs'. Malta had been more or less neutralised at this time by air power, so the potential targets offered were few, and it still remained a uniquely defensible fortress. In the sixteenth century it had defied a Turkish invasion force and afterwards had been further fortified. Grand Harbour was covered by solid stone walls rising almost sheer above the water on both sides, with modern artillery instead of culverin and cannon; and the sea was watched by radar day and night.

The Gibraltar failures had meant the loss or abandonment of 'pigs' and 'frogmen's gear; the Suda Bay success had revealed the method and an intact example of the means. Surprise had been lost, since all the attacking methods were known by the British. A certain amount of frustration must have been felt by the Italians who had begun with such grandiose plans and high hopes foiled, as they saw it, by lack of vision by their own authorities. This, however, is the almost inevitable fate of pioneers. Contributing further to the final rash decision must have been the failure, for technical reasons due to the fundamentally frail means employed, of successive attempts to approach Grand Harbour; while an element of the tragedy was undoubtedly the sentence of professional death passed by the unit's doctor on Major Teseo Tesei, one of the two co-inventors and pioneers of the unit which had always regarded Malta as its prime objective. A diver and pilot of one of the 'pigs', Tesei had recently been declared 'unfit for diving for six months, owing to serious cardiac weakness'. In spite of this he made underwater inspections of the torpedoed battleship *Conte de Cavour*. But the medical verdict must have signalled to him the approaching end of the life he loved.

He campaigned to be used against Malta and less than a week before the final attack wrote to a friend that he would shortly 'attain the highest of all honours, that of giving my life for the King and the honour of the Flag. As you know this is the supreme desire of a soldier and the most sublime joy . . .' But he could not do this alone; as pilot of a 'pig' he had a companion, Petty Officer Pedretti. Poor Pedretti!

According to Prince J. Valerio Borghese, a submarine commander and leader of the underwater division of the 10th Light Flotilla, the only information the Italians had about Malta at this time was from aerial reconnaissance. Most of the Maltese are probably Phoenician, but there were many Italians and some Normans. Of course, Malta was not a British colony; the island had been occupied by the French during Napoleon's reign, and in consequence the Maltese had welcomed the British as liberators. The result for Italy in 1941 was that nothing was known for sure about the defence of the two main naval harbours which flanked the fortified town of Valletta, Grand Harbour on one side and Marsamuscetto (Marsamxett in Maltese) on the other, where the smaller warships, destroyers and submarines were berthed.

It was planned to devote a 'pig' to each of the harbours, to blow a way through any boom. The headland between the two harbour entrances was crowned by Fort St Elmo which, as originally built, had for a month in May and June 1565 held off a vastly superior force of Turks; the defending Knights numbered many Frenchmen, Italians and Spaniards. The defence to the death, literally, of Fort St Elmo is one of the classics of siege warfare. The Knights (although some wavered) seem to have been of like mind to Major Tesei. And in the same place, separated merely by some four centuries of time.

It was assumed by the Italians in 1941 that the entrance to Grand Harbour at least must be impassable. But the entrance, not too unlike that of Zeebrugge, was narrowed by a mole which was connected to the mainland at St Elmo by a bridge. Tesei was to destroy the nets which blocked the passage under the bridge, normally used by very small craft only. Through this gap, once blown by Tesei's warhead, the small Explosive Motor Boats would tear at 30 knots to wreak havoc in Grand Harbour and the creeks which led off it.

As a small boy during the tenure of Admiral Keyes in the late 1920s, I knew this area. There were on sale in Malta at this time tins of biscuits fashioned in the shape of motor torpedo boats, and my brother and I used to float them on the saltwater pools among the rocks under the jutting prow of Fort St Elmo. We were well aware, after years of living in Valletta, of the heroic defence of St Elmo by the Knights long ago. The appalling event which was to take place almost under our feet in a war still remote would have been inconceivable at that time.

The commander of the 10th Light, Moccagatta, led the attack in person. The old plan, which had so often proved troublesome, of towing the frail Explosive Boats, was changed. A former destroyer, the *Diana*, was to carry them on board to within a short distance of Malta; and she would tow a special motor boat called an MTL which would cast off and carry the 'pigs' to their correct launch point. The pilots' heads being only just above the water, identifying the right landfall would be hard for them. One of Moccagatta's senior officers, Lt.-Cdr. Giobbe, expressed uneasiness about the operation to Moccagatta, who said he felt confident.

The little fleet left Augusta in Sicily at sunset on 25 July. When the *Diana* was some 20 miles from Malta she launched the nine Explosive Boats which were to penetrate Grand Harbour. One sank immediately. The remaining eight boats, marshalled by Giobbe, set off in line ahead for Malta escorted by two large rescue motor boats. The MTL carrying the two 'pigs' was cast off and also headed for Malta. The Italian air force was supposed to fly diversionary attacks to cover the noise of engines at sea.

Giobbe's feeling of unease was justified. The approach of the force showed on British radar and the close-range defences were alert, with the efficiency of war-experienced men, mostly Maltese. Their weapons included machine-guns, rapid-firing Bofors guns and 6-pounders. No one was likely to loose off in a fit of fear or wild enthusiasm; they would wait for the order.

A single Italian aeroplane arrived over Malta at 2.45 in the morning of 26 July; and shortly afterwards the MTL launched the two 'pigs' just off the mole bridge by St Elmo. The manned torpedo piloted by Costa had engine trouble and time was lost while Tesei tried to help him. As Costa left to make his approach to Marsamuscetto Harbour, he remarked that they were now an hour late. Tesei told him: 'At 4.30 the net has to blow up and it will blow up. If I am late, I shall fire the charge straight away.'

Giobbe in his big rescue boat led the eight Explosive Boats at dead slow speed to within sight of the bridge in the mole. And there they waited, their target silhouetted against the night sky. And the British waited too. At 4.20 two Italian aeroplanes arrived, ten minutes before the defences were to be breached. At 4.30 the thump of an underwater explosion was heard. And that was all.

Giobbe did not know, and was never to know, of that last conversation between Costa and Tesei. In his mind must have been the thought that Tesei might be underwater, retiring. Then he made up his mind. He gave orders to the Explosive Boats driven by Frassetto and Carabelli. If the net under the bridge was still intact, then they should blow a way through with their boats; the other six boats would wait on the result.

The two attackers set off at high speed in a sudden burst of spray, bows rising out of the water. Frassetto baled out 80 metres from the net hanging down under the bridge, and climbed onto his escape raft; but heard no explosion. Behind him Carabelli roaring past, bound for the net. He did not bale out, but there was a roar as the explosive charge went off—and the bridge collapsed, blocking the way through far more effectively than any net.

The British searchlights came on, brilliantly illuminating the remaining six boats as they sped towards the broken span of the bridge, their pilots not realising that their way in was blocked. And with the searchlights' glare came a hail of cross-fire hammering away at the six frail targets, which were brought to a stop almost immediately. 'A few seconds were enough for all movement on the water to cease,' ran a British report.

The striking force was wiped out entirely; all the Explosive Boats were destroyed; Tesei and Pedretti's 'pig' was destroyed with its own charge, Costa was captured and his 'pig' lost. On their return the supporting motor boats were attacked by Hurricane fighters which encountered Italian Macchi fighters. One motor boat was sunk, one captured; the MFL was lost also. Two Macchis and one Hurricane were shot down. The 10th Light had lost 15 men dead and 18 captured.

In the water off Fort St Elmo the British found the remains of a frogman's breathing mask with bits of flesh and tufts of hair attached. Major Tesei, who was determined to succeed at all costs? Or Petty Officer Pedretti who could only follow?

The naval surgeon who had reported Tesei 'unfit for diving for six months' was also among the dead, as were Moccagatta and Giobbe, the leaders.

Only eleven Italians returned alive from the shattered assault force. In an abandoned motor boat captured by the British was someone's lucky mascot, a white furry dog with a red bow. A British typist adopted him and 'Bruno-Bianco' was her mascot from now on.

One might have thought that such outright disaster must have resulted in the disbandment of the remnants, but this was not so. The Italians persevered. In September 1941 they went back to Gibraltar a third time, with the big warships in the inner harbour their priority target. But the British defenders were alert now to underwater attack. Still, the 'pigs' sank four merchant ships including some tankers; total for a night's work by a handful of men riding cheap weapons—30,000 tons.

In December a prime target appeared—Britain's last remaining battleships in the Mediterranean. In November German U-boats in the Mediterranean had sunk two important ships—the famous aircraft carrier *Ark Royal* and the old battleship *Barham*. That left only two battleships, both of the same 1912 class, the *Queen Elizabeth* and the *Valiant*, whereas the Italian battlefleet now numbered five, three modernised ships of First War vintage and two new and powerful units, the *Vittorio Veneto* and the *Littorio*. The only two ships which could oppose these five, the old *Queen Elizabeth* and *Valiant*, were now safe behind elaborate defences in Alexandria Harbour.

Two unsuccessful attempts had been made on Alexandria the previous year, in August and September 1940. This would be the third. The nucleus of the small fleet required in 1940 was the small submarine *Iride* (Iris) of around 600 tons plus the MTB *Calipso* to carry the 'pigs' from the main base at La Spezia in northern Italy to an advanced base on the North African coast in the Gulf of Bomba just west of Tobruk, where a tanker and some other Italian vessels were anchored. This unusual concentration attracted the notice of the British air reconnaissance; also the Italians lingered there because the submarine had not been tested when carrying the 'pigs' and that test was to be carried out on the Libyan coast, which was on the enemy's doorstep. As the *Iride* was leaving for deeper water to carry out the test, three low-flying British aircraft appeared. The central one dropped a torpedo, his companions flew down the side of the submarine, machine-gunning, before attacking the other targets there.

The torpedo struck the bows of the *Iride*, which sank at once. Only fourteen men came to the surface from where the wreck lay. All the underwater diving gear was in her, but the pilots of the 'pigs' got down without breathing apparatus, as she lay in only 15 metres, and secured a marker buoy. When new diving gear was brought from Tobruk it was found that there were nine men trapped alive in the after part of the wreck, which had been blown in two, and that their escape hatch had jammed. It took the divers 20 hours to clear the hatch; they found jammed under it the corpses of two petty officers who had tried to get out and failed. The remaining seven men were cajoled to flood their compartment and then swim underwater and in semi-darkness to the hatch, go through that small gap, and make for the surface of the sea some 30 feet above. Some had to be threatened before they would do it. All seven finally reached the surface, one with a great shout of relief at seeing the sun again, but two poor chaps, following their natural instincts, kept their mouths closed while underwater and did not breathe out on the ascent; and they died.

That was the end of the August attempt, but the Italians tried again the following month. Two small modern submarines, the *Gondar* and the *Scire*, were converted as underwater transports for the 'pigs', with hangars on deck to accommodate them, thus doing away with the necessity for a separate surface vessel. The *Gondar* was chosen for the second attempt in September 1940 but was ordered to turn back at the last minute because the British fleet had left Alexandria. On her return the submarine was detected and depth-charged for twelve hours. All tanks had to be blown in a last attempt to reach the surface and let the crew get out, where two British destroyers, a corvette and a Sunderland flying boat were waiting for them.

The third attempt on Alexandria did not occur until more than a year later, in December 1941, when success would be even more vital to the Axis powers. The *Scire*, under Prince J. Valerio Borghese, was chosen to transport the 'pigs' and much more careful training and planning preceded the attack. An interesting evaluation of the volunteers for this hazardous duty was employed. Personal motives were probed and personal circumstances examined. For instance, financial trouble was regarded as a valid reason for refusing a volunteer, as was being crossed in love, or involvement in family quarrels. This was shrewd. While any of these events might act as spurs to gallant conduct in ordinary sailors and soldiers, an underwater operator requires above all to be calm and peaceful in his mind. Anything emotionally jarring is highly dangerous.

Borghese also stressed the ability to keep secrets, and not necessarily just the obvious ones but of every detail concerned with the work. 'It is easier,' he wrote, 'to get an Italian to lay down his life than to make the sacrifice of holding his tongue.' He noted the 'compulsive urge' among Italians 'to show that they are well informed and to boast'. The Prince does his countrymen an injustice. Many males, of whatever nation, and not a few females also, feel this same urge for self-importance. It may be argued that for divers, who operate alone, this feeling is a necessary ingredient for success; it is the open expression of it which is dangerous in wartime. Secrecy was indeed vital to all these stealthy operations of the Italians, and it was the first test all the volunteers had to pass.

From already accepted and trained volunteers an appeal was made in this case for those who would be prepared to take part in an important operation from which the chances of a return were problematical. Those accepted were requested to settle their affairs as at best they could expect only imprisonment for an unknown period of years. Six men were chosen to man three 'pigs', with one reserve team.

This time the advanced base was not on the coast of North Africa where the land battles raged back and forth at great speed, but on the quiet Greek island of Leros in the Dodecanese group then belonging to Italy. The coast of Turkey was not far away and the British did have a 'secret' harbour there, so vigilance could not be relaxed. The local naval commander came over from Rhodes, demanding that an exercise be laid on for him (which would of course have been noted by the Greeks and by them to the Allies) but Borghese had authority to refuse, which he did.

His own part was vital. He had to penetrate the minefields guarding Alexandria and make a night landfall on a low coast lacking in prominent landmarks. Really precise navigation was required.

On the night of 18 December it was dark and calm, perfect conditions; the *Scire* arrived at exactly the right place after navigating blind; the three 'pigs' were launched. Manned by de la Penne and Bianchi, Marceglia and Schergat, Martellotta and Marino, they disappeared into the night. For the next two nights the submarine *Zaffiro* was to lie ten miles off Rosetta in the Nile delta in case any of the pilots managed to escape, find a boat, and come out to them. But no one came. Air reconnaissance later confirmed two battleships damaged.

When Italy changed sides in 1943, the six missing men emerged from British POW camps. They had entered the harbour at about the same time as some British destroyers, had suffered slight shocks but no serious effects from the small explosive charges being dropped into the water as a routine defence measure.

Marceglia reported that everything had gone exactly to plan. They had found the battleship *Queen Elizabeth* and fastened the charge by means of a line slung between the bilge keels on either side of the hull. He had not been particularly thrilled, he was very tired and beginning to get chilled. They saw men on the deck of the battleship but were not themselves seen. They went ashore, ditching the 'pig' and their diving gear. Pretending to be French sailors (part of the surrendered French fleet was at Alexandria), they got as far as Rosetta where the Egyptian police were not fooled.

Martellotta's target had been a tanker, but the first ship he found was a cruiser; reluctantly, he obeyed orders and left her, found the tanker, set his charge and released the incendiaries supposed to ignite the oil in due course. Cold and breathing pure oxygen was having an effect: he had a headache, his lips could longer keep the mouthpiece in, and he had to vomit, so he surfaced. The incendiaries were distributed, then they went ashore but did not get past the Egyptian control post. They were still being interrogated when, one after another, they heard three explosions in the harbour.

De la Penne reported that things had gone a little bit wrong from the start, when his thin diving suit was torn. When you go into the sea without a fully protective suit, you begin to die; it may first seem 'bracing' or 'invigorating' but in fact it is the beginning of medical death. The warmth flows out of your body into the water. Courageous men become cowardly, energetic men become lethargic; the will to live slackens. Judge, then, what de la Penne did in these circumstances. Sighting a large mass which was the *Valiant* he went through the net barrier on the surface because he recognised the onset of cold and knew its effects. He touched the hull for a moment, then the 'pig' went out of control towards the bottom at 17 metres. De la Penne dived after it and found that his companion, Bianchi, was missing. The 'pig' had landed some distance away, so he tried to start the motor so as to drive it back to the *Valiant*.

The motor would not start. He investigated, found that a steel wire had fouled the propeller. The 22-foot long 'pig' could now be moved nearer only if he dragged it physically through the water. But which way? He tried using his compass. It was useless. Physical effort was causing his mask to fog and his frantic movements were raising dense masses of upwelling muck from the bottom, so that he was lost inside a dark cloud of his own making. At any moment he expected the British to become aware of what was happening, drop explosive charges and ruin the operation. Panting, sweating, he dragged at the stubborn, awkward 'pig', guided now in his direction not by vision but by the sound of a pump inside the battleship which was his target. After forty minutes' extreme exertion, underwater and in the dark, he bumped against the steel hull. He set the time fuses and surfaced, wrenched off his mask and breathed pure air instead of compressed oxygen.

Someone called out to him, a searchlight came on, a machine-gun opened up. He swam back to the battleship's mooring buoy and found there, clinging to it, his missing companion, Bianchi, who had fainted underwater but had made the surface and had hidden by the buoy to avoid giving the alarm.

The *Valiant* could of course be saved simply by moving her, for the charge was lying under the hull, not slung from it as had been intended. While waiting to be picked up, the two Italians could clearly hear the British talking; assuming that the operation had been bungled by two panic-stricken Italians, they were being facetious. De la Penne told Bianchi that they might soon change their minds about Italians.

A British motorboat took them ashore for interrogation, where a British officer, making wild gestures with a revolver, told them in best Germanic style that he would soon find ways of making them talk—a clear indication that he was averse to violence.

The threat proving unsuccessful, another method was tried. The two Italians were taken aboard the battleship and brought before her commanding officer, Captain Morgan. He asked where the charge was and when they did not reply sent them below to a place very near where the charge would presently go off. Their armed escort offered rum and cigarettes and kindness, but this did not work either. However, from the name on their capbands, the Italians could see that they were in the bowels of the *Valiant*.

When his watch told him that it was almost time, de la Penne asked to speak to the Captain, and on being escorted on deck told him that nothing could stop an imminent explosion and that he could still get his men to safety. Morgan again asked where the charge was and as de la

Penne was silent, had him sent down below again. The explosion put out the lights and visibly shook the hull. Then it began to list to port.

De la Penne got on deck again in time to see the results of the explosion underneath the *Queen Elizabeth*. Neither of the battleships actually sank, the harbour was too shallow for that, they simply sat on the bottom with their waterlines unnaturally high. Effectively, they were out of the war.

In the same month, under the bombs and torpedoes of the Japanese naval air arm, the *Prince of Wales* and *Repulse* went to their death under Tom Phillips, an admiral who believed almost to the last minute that bombers could not sink battleships. In Africa, the Germans beat the British Army and drove it back to the gates of Cairo. Malta was at its last gasp. At this nadir of the war for Britain, the Italian fleet had total superiority in capital ships and with the Germans might have invaded and taken Malta, with incalculable consequences.

But Malta held, barely supplied; and must have made an invasion at the best very costly, at the least a humiliating failure for the Axis. Gold medals, Italy's highest award, were announced for the attackers now behind barbed wire; but when it came to the presentation to Luigi de la Penne, to be made in 1945 by the Crown Prince of Italy, one of the spectators stepped forward to present the medal instead. He was Admiral Sir Charles Morgan, formerly captain of the *Valiant*, and an old acquaintance under very different circumstances of Luigi de la Penne.

Chapter Twenty-Four

X-CRAFT: THE MIDGETS V. THE *TIRPITZ*

Norway, September 1943

Adolf Hitler and Winston Churchill were agreed on just one thing: Norway. Hitler thought Churchill would invade Norway, Churchill thought Norway should be invaded. In Scotland a mountain formation was raised and trained—the 52 (Lowland) Infantry Division, so-called because it was raised from the Lowlands rather than the Highlands of Scotland. Ironically, when it was at last committed it was in Holland, much of which is below sea level, and you can't get much lower than that.

From Scotland to Narvik is more than a thousand miles, well beyond the reach of air cover but well within the range of the local Luftwaffe. Somebody must have pointed this out to the Prime Minister, reminding him also of what had happened in 1940. The much desired/feared invasion never took place. Norway was occupied peacefully at the end of the war in Europe. But there were good reasons to hit specific targets in Norway, especially during the ill-starred attempts to run war material to Russia even during days of long daylight. These convoys were unsound militarily but thought expedient to keep Stalin in the war, although at the time Hitler left him little choice. They were ravaged by U-boats from underneath, by the Heinkels and Junkers from above, and by the occasional surface raider. The most menacing of these was the battleship *Tirpitz*, sister ship to the *Bismarck*. The British had to retain two battleships in home waters in case she came out and fell on a convoy, or just backed up the smaller raiders, as had already occurred at Spitzbergen. The Norwegian fjords presented an interesting variant to the basic problem of how to attack major enemy units in defended bases.

The Italian initiative had been soon copied. The British 'pig' was now in existence and the Italians were soon in possession of examples. Based on the earliest Italian model, with no improvements, judged Borghese; and as for the suits the unfortunate divers were forced to wear, the poor design must be responsible for the their heavy losses, he thought. In any case, this type of underwater attack was anything but appropriate to fjords running deeply between high mountains into the heart of Norway a thousand miles away, and in exceedingly cold, if clear, waters. Divers in a Mediterranean type suit would soon be paralytic if immersed inside the Arctic Circle.

The idea of the midget submarine with a small crew totally enclosed within the hull (unlike the 'pig') had been developed by the Japanese; but these rather pathetic two-man vehicles had so fair failed notably in the Pacific. At Hamble, between Portsmouth and Southampton, the British developed a larger, sturdier, longer-range type of midget which resembled the very first submarines ever introduced into the Royal Navy, based as it happens on an anti-British Irish-American design, the Holland boat of 1898.

The X-craft were four-seater submarines which did not carry torpedoes; instead they had two one-ton charges strapped on either side, to be left as calling cards underneath the battleship, fused as appropriate. They were 51 feet long with a beam of eight-and-a-half feet and a height of ten feet. They could dive to 300 feet and at a cruising speed of four knots could cover 1,500 miles (theoretically); after 1,500 miles the crew in that restricted space would be in no condition to make an attack. If he was a small man the commanding officer could just about stand upright at the highest point by the periscope; no one else could. The first lieutenant was seated behind him and operated the engine controls, the diving hydroplanes, the pumping system for making the boat heavier or lighter, and the auxiliary machinery. The ERA sat forward on the starboard side and controlled the steering wheel; the gyro-compass repeater was here under his eye. There was a fourth man, usually a rating rather than an officer, who carried out navigation and did the diving if required. If the boat was caught in nets, his job was to put on a heavy diving suit clearly based on the old nineteenth century dress used with a copper helmet and weighted boots, get into a special chamber which could be flooded up, then open the hatch and get out into the chill water, which in the British Navy is known as the 'oggin.

The target ships were based in Altenfjord, a deep inlet of the North Cape of Norway, athwart the convoy route from the west to Murmansk in the USSR. The three ships normally based there were the *Tirpitz*, Germany's latest and last great battleship, the *Scharnhorst*, a light fast battleship usually described as a battlecruiser, and the heavy armoured cruiser *Lützow* (ex-*Deutschsland*), often referred to as a pocket battleship.

The displacement of the *Tirpitz* is given variously, as anything from 42,000 tons to 56,000 tons. Anyway she was a big, formidable ship with an overall length of 828 feet, a broad beam of 119 feet, manned by 2,340 men and capable of 31 knots. Her side armour was 15 inches and there was an armoured deck, about the level of the waterline, which covered the vitals with an eight-inch thick layer of armour plate. This carapace did not extend to the bows or the stern which, if holed, could not sink the ship.

The attack on the three ships, when air reconnaissance reported them all in their anchorages, was to be carried out by six of the midgets—X5, X6, X7, X8, X9 and X10. The method of delivery to the area of Altenfjord was a tow by normal-size submarines, a T-class boat of around 1,500 tons and five of the S-class of around 1,000 tons. During this one thousand-mile journey the midgets would be manned by the reserve crews, who would be replaced by fresh, operational crews when close to the fjords. The Italians also, although in less severe conditions, had met this problem with the crews of their 'pigs', who were sent away to a mountain resort to get fit and then brought in by train, ship or aeroplane at the last moment possible, so as to ensure that they were in tip-top condition for their arduous as well as dangerous task.

Security strict enough to please Prince Valerio Borghese was maintained at the X-craft base in Loch Cairnbawn in Scotland as the day for the operation neared; obviously, the naval authorities did not share his belief that it was only Italian sailors who were talkative. Leave was stopped, no ship was allowed to depart. Late in the evening of 11 September, the six submarines towing six midgets left for the far north of Norway. The midgets were submerged most of the time, but the big towing submarines came to the surface during the night; the operational crews of the X-craft shared in the fresh air. The passage crews of the midgets were allowed to surface only a few times a day and then for only 15 minutes at a time. The atmosphere inside the tiny boats must have been almost unendurable, and without the stimulus of impending action. Three times, while submerged, tows broke; and the fact was not always immediately realised in the big submarines.

X9 lost her tow and disappeared; and was never seen again. X8 lost her tow and was forced to jettison her charges, one of which caused considerable damage although a good distance away. X10 got as far as Norway but fire developed, as well as compass trouble; to go on in that state might have jeopardised the chances of the others, so X10 turned back. Her target had been the *Scharnhorst*, which had sailed for firing practice, so nothing was lost. The three submarines which reached the fjord complex and went inside all had the *Tirpitz* as their assigned target and all reached her where she was tucked away in Kaa fjord, an offshoot of the main Altenfjord, behind lines of nets. These three were X5 (Lt. Henry Henty-Creer), X6 (Lt. Donald Cameron) and X7 (Lt. Godfrey Place).

They arrived off the Norwegian coast on 20 September, one night early, and transferred the crews. Up to this time the main excitement had been the parting of tows, the loss of X9, the damaging explosion when X8's saddle charges had to be jettisoned, the occasion when X6, surfaced, snagged a stray German horned mine and Place kicked it away with his foot (not recommended mine disposal practice), and the sighting of a surfaced U-boat which the big submarines were forbidden to attack. Then, at the last, X10 caught fire. They had travelled 1,200 miles, with only six more miles to go. In the dark morning of 22 September the three remaining boats set out to negotiate the heavy duty nets which at several places spanned the main fjord, guarded and covered by guns, and then get through or under the further lines of nets closely surrounding the *Tirpitz* herself.

At 0500 the deck log of the battleship shows the following entries:

Called all hands.
Set normal anti-aircraft and anti-sabotage watch ashore and afloat.
Boat-gate in anti-torpedo nets opened for boat and tug traffic.
Hydrophone listening office closed down.

Just another monotonous day for thousands of men far from home in a foreign country amid a sparse and hostile population. Of course this was better than the Russian front—anything was better than the Russian front—but in France now, it was said that Germans lived like gods. All those delicious women with their men away in prison camps or at forced labour . . .

For two hours or so normal daily routine continued in this outpost of the Reich set down inside the Polar Circle. Then at seven minutes past seven in the morning, a lookout reported seeing a big fish in the water—'a black submarine-like object'. Perhaps a porpoise? Donald Cameron's X6 had got through all the nets but due to a faulty compass had run aground on a sandbank. He got off but almost at once broke surface again thirty yards from the battleship, and this time the alarm went in earnest; he was too close in for any of the guns to bear, only small arms could engage X6.

Steam was ordered for the *Tirpitz* to leave her mooring in case mines had been laid beneath her, then they were countermanded when another midget submarine was sighted. This was X7 (Godfrey Place). So there was more than one submarine! There might be others unseen out there; best for *Tirpitz* to remain within her defences but veer on her cables away from the charges. After a delay, yet another submarine appeared just outside the protective ring of nets. This must have been X5 (Henty-Creer).

What had struck Donald Cameron was the incongruity at the start of the attack, waiting inside an enemy harbour with the earphones on, listening to the BBC, listening also to the noise of the German harbour craft moving about on guard for the big battleship. Sound carries a long way under water, not just engine noise but the cavitation effect of the screws. His difficulties had been mainly small mechanical defects not yet ironed out. His periscope flooded, one of the saddle charges flooded, which gave them a thirteen degree list and trimming trouble. He got through the outer defences 'by good luck', and then the inner screen of nets around the *Tirpitz* because they had been opened half an hour before to allow boat traffic in and out. Periscope out of action, he floundered around blind inside the nets, grounded, attacked on the surface, dropping the charges alongside the *Tirpitz* and scuttling the X6 on top of them. There was a one-hour fuse delay. He was being interrogated when they went off.

Place, on the other hand, in X7, did have trouble with the nets, which held and delayed him, and finally, although he got through the inner defence nets and laid his charges under the battleship, he could not find his way out again. He had reckoned on them being only 50 feet deep, leaving a gap between the steel curtains and the seabed at 120 feet; but there didn't seem to be a gap. Getting caught several times and blowing tanks to get out, began to exhaust their air. Finally Place crossed the net defences on the surface, provoked to see that *Tirpitz* was still there in spite of the explosions which has just blown X7 out of the net.

They went down again and sat on the bottom in 120 feet and thought about what to do. Depth charges were being dropped, so they decided not to risk a buoyant ascent with the DSEA (Davis Escape Apparatus) but to go to the surface and surrender by waving a white sweater. Place opened the fore hatch and duly waved the sweater and the Germans obligingly stopped firing. Then the barely buoyant X7 drifted against a German battle practice target, Place stepped onto that just as the bows of X7 with the opened hatch dipped below the water, and the midget sank from sight into 120 feet. There was no way the three remaining men could get the craft to the surface again, so they had to flood up quickly, breathing from the DSEA sets. It was not realised at that time how lethal pure oxygen could be at great depths. Only one man reached the surface, and he was almost unconscious.

Place was picked up by a motorboat and felt highly ridiculous walking on to the quarterdeck of the German flagship, normally a setting for immaculate uniforms and high ceremonial, 'in vest, pants, sea-boot stockings and army boots size twelve'. Now it was his turn to be interrogated, a British submarine saboteur by a German officer, as contrasted with the British officer's interrogation of an Italian under-water saboteur at Alexandria nearly two years before. In this case the German did not waste words, he just said that Place would be shot if he didn't say where he had laid his mines. Place replied that he was an English officer and demanded the courtesy to which his rank entitled him. Godfrey Place survived the threat sufficiently to collect in due course his VC from Buckingham Palace.

Donald Cameron also got the VC and he, like de la Penne before him, did not talk but kept looking at his watch while the minutes ticked away. Then even the great *Tirpitz* rose five feet in the air as the charges exploded. After that, only a long spell in a German dockyard would make the battleship fully operational again. Instead, she was patched up as far as possible and kept in Norwegian ports so as to appear to threaten British convoys, although in fact not fit to do so. Finally, she was sunk by the RAF in September 1944 when her fate hardly mattered one way or the other.

The fate of Henty-Creer's X5 has not been conclusively established. He was certainly seen by the Germans who sank him, but whether or not he had first managed to lay his charges is not known. In the 1970s amateur diving expeditions led by Peter Cornish found parts of an X-craft and a number of sunken German ships, but the mystery of X5 remains. The relatives of those who must have died in her would like to think that she had laid her charges and that her crew did not die in vain.

Chapter Twenty-Five

HERO SHIPS—SUICIDE PILOTS

Franklyn—Iwo Jima, March 1945; *Bunker Hill*—Okinawa,
May 1945

The US Navy considers the *Franklyn* and the *Bunker Hill*, both big
aircraft carriers, to be their two worst-damaged ships to survive and get
back after a battle. Carriers are extremely vulnerable, just big floating
bombs, stacked with petrol and ammunition inside very light hulls.
Both these carriers were 27,100 tons, 872 feet long with 93-foot beam;
carried 3,448 men and could make around 33 knots. The *Bunker Hill*
was commissioned in May 1943, the *Franklyn* in January 1944.

Some of the toughest ships are oil tankers, because they are built
internally to the same plan as a bee's honeycomb, to prevent the oil
sloshing about uncontrollably, which it would do if the hull were not so
intricately sub-divided. The risk of fire is indeed great, if the tanks are
full, but much more menacing if they are not, because then the vapour
inside turns the hull, literally, into a bomb. These are some of the
reasons why fully-loaded tankers, holed and burning, have even so
completed their journeys; the other reason is the determination of their
masters and crews, and, of course, luck.

Well-known contenders for the 'tankers that got through in spite of'
trophy would be the *San Demetrio* of London, 11,181 tons, which, as
recorded in Chapter 21, was abandoned on fire during the December
1940 attack on the convoy guarded by the *Jervis Bay*, was reboarded by
some of the crew, the fires put out and damage repaired, and sailed
home; and the *Ohio*, 9,263 tons, built to high specifications at Chester,
Pennsylvania, for Texaco and survived the most horrific of the critical
Malta convoys in August 1942 with a British captain and crew.
Admittedly she finished up dead in the water, her back almost broken,
and had to be towed the final distance. She was the only tanker of that
convoy to get through, and without her and the other four ships which

were all that reached the beleaguered island, Malta would have had to surrender. One ship of that convoy which did not get through was the *Waimarama*, carrying aviation spirit and ammunition; 80 out of her crew of 107 were killed, a salutary reminder that the civilian crews of merchant ships also serve.

However, because of their enormous crews and built-in vulnerability, the story of the two big US Navy carriers, and the immense toll of lives lost or shattered, which in spite of that survived and got home, is probably unique. At the same time it serves to hint at the necessarily untold aspect of the Japanese '*Shimpu*' units, better known as the Kamikaze or 'divine wind' after the typhoon which in the thirteenth century shattered the invading fleet of the Emperor Kublai Khan. Most were not religious or patriotic fanatics anxious to die for their country, but young university students who did not believe in an after-life but felt an obligation to defend their own people when Japan was threatened by overwhelming odds.

Of course, there is a distinct difference between going to certain death and, on the other hand, like some of their enemies, going to almost certain death. On one day one US infantry company fighting ashore on Okinawa had at the end only three unwounded men left out of 89 who had attacked in the morning. And on the first day of the invasion, one infantryman whose unit had met little opposition on the beach commented, 'I've already lived longer than I thought I would.'

A major factor in the shattering successes of the Kamikaze assaults was the fact that the big US carriers, unlike the British, did not have armoured flight decks; this allowed a US carrier to carry more planes than a British one but made it more vulnerable. In the spring of 1945 a British task force, which included two battleships and four big fleet carriers, was operating in the Pacific off Okinawa, employing a copy of the American fleet train organisation. All four carriers were hit by suicide planes, one of them twice, but were put out of action for a matter of hours only.

War experiences depend a lot on where you are, what you can see, what you are doing, what happens to you personally, and whether you have a family at home to worry about. What you can see is usually far from being the whole of the action and very often the ears tell you much more than your eyes, once they have become educated. There isn't any great computer in the sky to which afterwards young war buffs can plug in and get a really authentic picture. Alas.

So, for contrast, let us see what happened to the *Franklyn* through the eyes of her commanding officer, Captain Leslie E. Gehres, a professional with ultimate responsibility for his ship and some of his officers; and for the *Bunker Hill* a 22-year-old country boy from Michigan, acting as loader on a 20 mm gun.

At 0708 hours on 19 March the *Franklyn* was part of Vice-Admiral Marc Mitscher's Task Force 58, about 90 miles off the Japanese island of Kyushu, and since dawn had been launching strikes against the airfields there. Forty-five aircraft had taken off for the first mission of the day, while 31 more were massed on the flight deck ready for take-off, armed with bombs and rockets. Among those stationed on the carrier's bridge were the Captain, Leslie Gehres, the navigator, Cdr. Stephen Jurika, and the officer of the deck, Lt. Tappen. The assistant air officer, Lt.-Cdr. David Berger, was below on the flight deck by the island.

Captain Gehres was simply blown off his feet, without audible or visual warning. On his feet again, recovering from the shock, he saw a sheet of flame forward on the flight deck, spreading aft; and then a great gout of flame and black smoke came out of the forward well, which enveloped the bridge. He ordered the ship turned to starboard and speed slowed to two-thirds, as that would, aided by the wind, keep the fire from spreading aft among the 31 aircraft grouped there, fully fuelled and armed.

Lt.-Cdr. David Berger was concussed and disorientated by the blast wave; then he saw a huge tongue of red flame shoot out from the hangar deck by the elevator on the port side, followed by a great gush of heavy, acrid smoke which seemed to envelop the whole ship and pinned him to the side of the island structure, until he thought he must suffocate. By moving up and forward along the line of 40 mm gun sponsons, he was still unable to get clear of the smoke, and the lack of oxygen made it clear that he had the choice of: stay and suffocate or jump overboard. But at that moment the Captain's order to turn the ship took the smoke away and Berger was able to take part in jettisoning the ready-use AA ammunition and fighting the fires which were now consuming the ship and its flammable contents.

The navigator, Stephen Jurika, saw the bombs, not one but two and, he judged, of 250 kg size (about 550 lbs). They simply flashed into his field of vision. He did not see the plane which dropped them, merely its shadow sweeping across the island structure. The 5-inch AA guns trained round to follow the attacker on its way aft, pouring out shells.

One American aircraft had just roared forward in its take-off, while the rest were parked aft waiting to come out of their places for launching.

The first bomb went into the flight deck parallel to the bridge almost on the tail of the plane which was taking off. The second bomb—the captain did not then know that there had been two bombs, not just one—landed aft among the planes waiting to taking off, fully fuelled, fully armed. Some of them were tossed into the air and sideways by the blast, their whirling propellers cutting into other aircraft. Dense smoke pouring over the flight deck then hid much of the scene from Jurika's view.

> The explosions which followed were soul-shaking. The ship shud-
> dered, rocked under the impacts and emerged from periods of
> vibration only to be rocked by other heavy blasts. Fifty-caliber
> ammunition in the planes on deck set up a staccato chattering and
> the air was well punctuated with streaks of tracer. Twenty- and 40
> millimeter ammunition went next as the gallery mounts caught
> fire. *Tiny Tims* (large 11¾-inch rockets) from the Corsairs parked
> aft on the flight deck took off with an eerie whooshing sound. I saw
> two pass us on the bridge off to starboard, strike the sea and
> ricochet for several hundred yards. Others took off up the flight
> deck.

The attacker, which had dived down out of low cloud, had not been detected by the ship's radar; its bombs had been semi-armour piercing with about 25-seconds' delay to enable them to penetrate deep into the ship before exploding. All this could be worked out afterwards. At the time virtually nothing was known to the captain and others on the bridge, for the first result of the first heavy explosion was to ruin communications, except for a single sound-powered line from the conn to the aft steering position, and from there via a similar line to the main engine control. Orders were given to flood the main magazines but there was no indication of whether or not this had been achieved. In fact, the waterlines leading to the sprinklers for the after magazines were ruptured, but that too was not known until much later.

Captain Gehres was therefore compelled to command in the dark to begin with, and a great deal depended on the individual initiative of officers and men in a vast ship with a population equal to that of a small town. Training in fire-fighting had been an important part of damage control training in the US Navy; but the damage control Centre was inaccessible and power for most of the fire pumps had been lost. Men had to make do with two diesel-operated pumps, hand held apparatus and breathing sets. From the bridge nothing could be seen aft of the island for the billowing smoke from fires. As the radios had also been put out of action, signals could only be exchanged with neighbouring ships by old-fashioned semaphore. The *Sante Fe*, close on the starboard quarter, semaphored:

'Are your magazines flooded?'

Captain Gehres could only semaphore back: *'Am not sure, but believe so.'*

The smoke hid from view the devastation wrought among the planes positioned aft for take-off. These consisted of five bombers, fourteen torpedo bombers and twelve fighters. Then, according to Cdr. Jurika,

At 0952 the most terrific blast of the morning resulted from a five-inch ready-service magazine being set afire. The ship felt as though it were a rat being shaken by an angry cat. Whole aircraft engines with propellers attached and debris of all description were flung high into the air and descended on the general area like hail on a reef. One engine and prop struck the navigating bridge a glancing blow about three feet from my head, and for a couple of moments I will admit to ducking under the overhang of the masthead light. By now the list had increased to eight degrees to starboard, and continued increasing at approximately one degree every 10 minutes.

From time to time a number of ships helped with the fire-fighting and the cruiser *Santa Fe* came alongside like a liberty boat to the jetty and began to take wounded aboard. The valuable air crews were evacuated this way, plus non-essential personnel and a couple of admirals. The burning carrier was now slow in the water and drifting towards Japan about fifty miles away, and therefore Admiral Mitscher had to find another ship from which to exercise command of the whole Task Force; he was accompanied by Admiral Davison who had been aboard as an observer. The destroyers *Hickox* and *Miller* came up to the stern of the *Franklyn*, which was burning fiercely above them, and took off men trapped there by the flames and smoke and also men who had jumped overboard and were in the water.

It must have been about this time that Admiral Mitscher advised that the order 'Prepare to abandon ship' should be given. There were many men huddled forward away from the fires and it was possible a main magazine might blow, but Captain Gehres thought there was still a chance. He asked Cdr. Jurika whether he thought these men should be evacuated to safety; and Jurika replied not yet. When the question was put to Lt. Tappen, the young officer of the deck, he shook his head emphatically.

Those who have recalled the scenes aboard in print have written that they were 'indescribable', perhaps to spare the feelings of the relatives of the dead. To start with, the aircraft ready to take off were manned; many must have died amid the fires and explosions. The two bombs had gone deep into the ship, cutting down the men at work on the planes in the hangars, trapping other men behind twisted steel and walls of fire and smoke. And with each explosion of aviation fuel, of bombs, torpedoes and rockets, many more men were torn apart or incinerated.

The task force was still under attack and the towering smoke plumes of the *Franklyn* made her an obvious target. At 1254 a 'Judy' (a single-engined reconnaissance plane) made a fast glide-bombing run from the starboard side under heavy AA fire, the bomb whistling into the water 200 yards away and erupting with a roar. The noise which accompanies any battle cannot for technical reasons be recorded and even if it could, the sounds would blow the transmitters. Consequently television and film viewers, and radio listeners too, receive only a mild, censored version of what it was really like to be there.

At about 2 p.m. on the same day, 19 March, the listing, smoking carrier was taken in tow by the cruiser *Pittsburgh*, hauled around to a southerly course and eventually worked up to a speed of three knots —about the pace of a man walking easily. By now the major explosions had ceased, although there were smaller sounds from the 40 mm and 20 mm ammunition for light AA guns known in Britain by the names of the makers, Bofors and Oerlikon. To fight the fires forward there were only the two diesel-powered pumps; the fires aft were fought by some of the accompanying destroyers.

At first the machinery rooms down below were too hot for men to enter, but during the night one fire room cooled sufficiently for three boilers to be lit. This aided the tow and produced a speed of six knots. Steering was difficult because the heavy list of the carrier altered the shape of her underwater profile; she tended to drag the stern of the *Pittsburgh* around. Counter-flooding operations to reduce the list did not go well, because the Damage Control Center was inaccessible and the hydraulic controls of the valves were out of commission; men had to put on breathing sets to get at the valves. From being heeled to starboard the ship heeled to port and lay over at ten degrees.

On the morning of 20 March another boiler was brought into operation and by noon speed had been worked up to 14 knots. The towline could be cast off and the *Franklyn* began to work up to 15 knots. A few stubborn fires still burned, but one gyro compass was working, some of the light AA guns were back in commission and a telephone line rigged to the guns from the bridge. That night, flares and firing could be seen on the horizon astern where the Japanese were presumably looking for the carrier to complete her destruction.

From dawn onwards on 21 March the men aboard still fit for duty had the indescribable task of finding and removing for burial the bodies—hundreds and hundreds of them—lying in the tangled, twisted interior of the carrier. Her official complement was 3,448 men, of whom 724 had been killed and 265 wounded. Still aboard at this time were 106 officers and some 500 men, of whom 100 of the officers and 300 of the men were fit for duty. The remainder had already been evacuated to other ships or picked up by them in the water.

At 11.51 a.m. a 'Betty' (a two-engined bomber) made a fast low run-in on the starboard side but was 'splashed' with a violent explosion by the patrolling American fighters. Occasional fires still flared up but a portable radar had now been set up on the bridge and one radio receiver was in commission; transmission however was confined to a single walkie-talkie. By the morning of 22 March the list had been reduced to six degrees to port, speed was 19 knots, and the *Franklyn* joined Task Force 58 again, which was on its way to refuel at Ulithi. During the run to Ulithi, where she arrived and anchored on 24 March, the work of extricating and identifying over 400 bodies, many badly charred or mangled, was continued. At noon she took her place astern of the other group carriers *Wasp* and *Enterprise*, just like any other warship coming in to refuel.

It seems that the worst day for the survivors still aboard the *Franklyn* had been the 20th, with constant threats of further air attacks, lack of

sleep and of hot food—or any food at all—and the normal depression
and let-down that follows on a period of white-hot activity and excitement or, as the case may be, terror. Watching a war film in a warm
room on a satisfied stomach and after a full night's restful slumber is
one thing; actual war is another. Lt.-Cdr. David Berger wrote:

> . . . all this caused the nerves of the crew to be very much jangled.
> We were all very jittery from lack of sleep and what had happened
> the previous day and all these various alerts of bogeys being
> around and the noise of the ship's guns, such as they were, firing
> and those of the guns of the force did a great deal to unstabilize
> further the emotions of the people who were aboard the ship.

In short, even those who stayed and did their duty were not
supermen of legend but ordinary mortals.

*   *   *

The *Franklyn* was the worst-damaged American ship to return from the
battle, with nearly 800 casualties. The next worst-damaged was a
similar carrier, the *Bunker Hill*, which suffered 353 killed, 43 missing
and 264 wounded from a Kamikaze attack off Okinawa on 11 May
1945. Although both ships were listed as 27,000 tons displacement,
with full war load they must have been a good deal more than that.

Bunker Hill was named after a famous battle of the War of Independence, which, contrary to general belief, the British won but with
massive, unnecessary casualties because a general could not be
bothered to think it out; instead he attacked head on, the easy way for
the general, the murderous way for the men who have to assault with all
the advantage given to the enemy's side. Among her battle honours in
1945, the *Bunker Hill* could claim 'Bloody Tarawa', an All-American
version of the same military philosophy, with a 'dodging tide' on a
shallow reef as the deadly obstacle.

That was two years before. The tide of war now was flooding towards
Japan herself, although her soldiers still fought stubbornly. The first of
April, 1945, was D-day for Okinawa, with the Kamikaze menace at its
height. American airmen now were much more experienced than the
Japanese; the deadly veterans of the early Pearl Harbor days were
mostly dead. On 7 April the Japanese made a powerful sally at the

American invasion fleet lying off the island; this was spearheaded by the literally 'giant' battleship *Yamato*, 64,170 tons, armed with nine 18-inch guns. She and her sister ship the *Mushashi* were the largest battleships ever built, but the age of the battleship had passed, although factions in the British, American and Japanese Navies still believed in the big gun, and hoped to prove it with another, better-conducted Jutland. They never got the chance. Neither of the giants ever got close enough to fight another battleship; both succumbed to air-launched torpedoes and bombs. *Bunker Hill*'s aircraft claimed six torpedo hits on the *Yamato*, among the many which helped put the giant down. With her went a cruiser and four destroyers.

But the Japanese could still hit back at the vulnerable carriers and the 'picket line' of destroyers flung out around them to give warning. Some 1,400 Kamikazes and an equal number of ordinary planes fell on the invasion fleets. On 11 May a 'Zeke' (a Mitsubishi single-seater fighter) broke out of cloud and dived onto the *Bunker Hill*'s flight deck. On its tail almost came what was probably a 'Judy' which dropped a 500lb bomb which struck the flight deck to port of the island, the bomber itself also crashing onto the carrier. Vice-Admiral Marc Mitscher, formerly of the *Franklyn*, was aboard the *Bunker Hill*, too, and for one lowly seaman gunner this made the prospects even more frightening; he felt like being at the centre of a big bull's eye!

Seaman 2nd Class William Rowe was 22 years old. He had been deferred earlier in the war because he had a family to support, but in 1944 he was called up. The man in the queue ahead of him was advised not to join the navy because 'they were catching hell out there in the Pacific'. Rowe wanted the navy because he figured the life would be better—a decent place to sleep instead of some dirty hole in the ground, real food instead of C-rations. He had a point there.

Home was in Painesville, Michigan, a town of 3,500 people in the middle of the copper belt. The ship he joined carried almost exactly that number of people and looked from the quay when he first saw it like a giant apartment block. He had worked hard in the copper mines but the US Navy worked him harder—'to the bone'. Those on the flight deck were 150 feet above the water, many of those working down below were 30 feet below the waves. The ship was 'a little city, with its own library, canteen, and chapels'. Rowe had met few Americans outside his home town, and found many of the men he now met reserved, except for sailors from Kentucky and Tennessee, who were friendly.

In the Pacific they were based on Ulithi in the Caroline Islands, 450 miles east of the Philippines. Mail from home was a most important item. 'You would see the most horrible expressions on the faces of those men who didn't get any while everyone else was reading theirs.'

Rowe's first experience of major combat was off Iwo Jima in February 1945. The drilling machines in the copper mines had been noisy, but this was something else again! The pilots who came back reported that the Japs were so well dug in, their bombs were having little effect. Rowe never suffered from seasickness, although the carrier was on the edge of a typhoon which broke up and sank some of the American destroyers. Still, the edge of her flight deck actually dipped into the water, which must have been something to see.

On the day that did the damage, 11 May, 1945, the carrier was 400 miles from Japan, within range of enemy airfields, while on her flight deck, ready for a strike against Okinawa, were 30 planes fuelled and armed, while another 48 were being prepared to come up. The day before, the *Bunker Hill* had taken on board two million gallons of fuel and oil.

At 10.45 that morning, the gun crews were at 'Easy'; they could read or write letters, remaining at their action stations. Without warning a Japanese fighter dived out of the clouds. The bomb went through the flight deck, through the carrier's side, and exploded out over the water, while the suicide plane roared aft towards the aircraft grouped ready for take-off. There was an explosion of flame as the Japanese pilot incinerated himself together with the American airmen.

Thirty seconds later another Japanese appeared, a dive-bomber coming at the Americans almost vertically with a rising, screaming roar. Tracer shells from the AA guns were pouring into him but he came on apparently unscratched. 'Hit him! Hit him!' yelled Rowe. The steady, deadly approach was terrifying. The Japanese plane struck the carrier amidships about forty feet from Rowe and flipped over, ploughing into the superstructure with a bang that shook the ship. The wooden flight deck burst into flames.

The engine of the dive-bomber smashed into the flag office and killed 14 of Admiral Mitscher's staff. Thirty pilots waiting in a room below, ready kitted up, were suffocated by the deadly fumes as they tried to escape; their charred corpses were found heaped in the passageway. Temperatures in engine and boiler rooms reached 130 degrees. Captain George Seitz, her commander, turned the *Bunker Hill* across the wind, to take the flames and smoke away from the ship; then he manoeuvred so that the carrier's list would help pour ammunition, petrol and oil across the deck and into the sea.

The gun mounting where Rowe was became hemmed in by the fires; and about 15 minutes after the ship was hit, an air officer ordered everyone there to go overboard to avoid being fried alive. That was all very well, but the gun mount was 80 feet above the water and Rowe was afraid of heights. He was also afraid of being suffocated by smoke or fried by the fires, so he scrambled over the mount to get away from that, and, afraid to jump, hung to the side of the burning carrier. Finally, he let go.

He was without his lifejacket but still had his helmet on, and the impact with the sea knocked it back hard. Also, the carrier was still going ahead, so Rowe found himself speedily swept astern by the ship's wake, tumbled over and poured under by the mighty torrent produced by the giant ship's screws. Rowe tried to claw his way to the surface, but found it difficult, so that momentarily he thought he would never be able to breath again. When he did, he was still being submerged by the wake, and looked for a lifejacket to keep his head up.

He saw a floating lifejacket nearby and grabbed it, sharing with a man who had been injured, and two other men. For two hours they were bobbing about in the Pacific, looking after the injured sailor, watching the *Bunker Hill* moving away and pouring out a great column of black smoke to the skies, the destroyers circling around in her wake and the planes flying above and waggling their wings when they found groups of survivors. Were some of those planes Japanese? they wondered. Rowe's incongruous worry was about the depth they were in. Of course, you could drown as easily in ten feet as you could in 10,000 feet, but the thought of an immensity of ocean below worried him.

Eventually a destroyer came up, lowered a scrambling net down her side, and they all climbed aboard. Next day they were taken back to the *Bunker Hill* and Rowe was shocked by the spectacle of the flight deck. Line after line of corpses were laid out. He was assigned to the clean-up crew and helped put 73 more bodies into canvas shrouds for burial. Many were charred beyond recognition; dental charts had to be used for identification. One poor thing had been a personal friend. From noon to sunset burials went on; in groups of ten or twenty at a time the dead went over the side. Down below the decks were deep in water and Rowe was always afraid that he might step on a submerged corpse.

After the war, for a short time, he had nightmares about that. In his dreams, he was digging for worms, struck a piece of wood—and then a body. After a time, these dreams stopped.

While they were still in Seattle, for the carrier to be repaired—she required a completely new flight deck—the news came that the war was over. They had been reprieved, they would survive. 'If anyone tells you they weren't scared, they're lying,' Rowe once said. But what he remembered also was the bond they had had, the feeling of being part of one big team.

Time magazine rated the *Bunker Hill* as 'next to the *Franklyn* the most cruelly ravaged US ship ever to reach port under her own power'. No doubt others might differ. There were the picket destroyers, for instance. In a period of 80 minutes the *Laffey* was attacked twenty-two times; six suicide planes crashed into her, and four bombs. More than a third of her crew were killed or wounded. But she got back and was returned to service. There is a story that one of the destroyers out on picket duty put up a big sign and an arrow, saying, 'CARRIERS THAT WAY'. It would have been true, for carriers were indeed the 'bull's eye' for an ambitious Japanese.

Chapter Twenty-Six

DOWN THE YANGTSE

Amethyst—1949

HMS *Amethyst* was an anti-submarine sloop built for convoy escort duties in 1942–3. Later, she would have been classed as a frigate. The qualities for which she was designed were long range at fair but not fast speeds, good sea-keeping qualities, and the necessary anti-submarine and anti-aircraft armament. In 1945 she shared in the destruction of U482 and on her own sank U1208. She was not built to withstand shell fire. Her vital statistics were: displacement—1,350 tons; length—just under 300 feet; beam—38½ feet; draught—8 feet 9 inches; complement—192.

In April 1949 she was to relieve the British guardship HMS *Consort* at Nanking, the capital of Nationalist China, where she acted as a visible expression of British power, a radio communications centre for the British embassy there, and an armed refuge in times of trouble. The *Amethyst* sailed on 19 April from Shanghai near the mouth of the Yangtse, for Nanking, 180 miles upstream. The Nationalist government of Chiang Kai-shek had given her a safe-conduct through the war zone.

A critical moment in the civil war was approaching; the rebel forces of the Chinese People's Liberation Army had closed up to the north bank of the Yangtse along much of its length. The Nationalist forces held the southern bank. The rebels, for they did not yet claim to be a government, were about to attempt a bold operation—the crossing of a fast, wide tidal river under fire. Aware of the risks, the Chinese Communist leader, Mao Tse-Tung, had given the Nationalists in Nanking an ultimatum, which included a demand for an unopposed crossing of the river. A few hours before its expiry on 20 April, the Nationalists rejected it. Soon after dawn on the 20th, the *Amethyst*, with large Union Jacks draped down both sides, entered the stretch where the two rival Chinese armies confronted each other and an assault crossing by the Red forces was imminent.

Perhaps a recent parallel might be the crossing of the Rhine in Spring 1945. If a foreign warship, belonging to a power formally neutral but known to be inclined to Germany, had steamed up river into the field of fire of the hundreds of batteries positioned to cover the crossing, the result might have been the same. The first Red Chinese batteries dropped a few shells not too near the *Amethyst*, then, apparently taking in the significance of the Union Jack displayed boldly on her starboard side, ceased fire. The next group of guns had a different commander.

So far, what had happened could be classed as an unfortunate misunderstanding. But when a shell screamed high over the ship, and the captain, Lt.-Cdr. B. M. Skinner, ordered revs for full speed, and this was followed by a succession of hits, one of which struck the wheelhouse and wounded the coxswain, an international incident had begun. Another seaman took the wheel, but the sloop, now at full speed, had turned off course. Skinner ordered fire to be returned, but almost at once two more shells struck the bridge, wiping out by wounds or death everyone there. Then the gunnery control was knocked out, then the sick bay. With Skinner mortally wounded, the engines were ordered astern but too late. The *Amethyst* bumped the mud of Lo-ch'eng (Rose Island) and became a stationary target.

The lighter Bofors and Oerlikon guns had been damaged and only 'X' turret aft could bear. Thirty rounds were fired in local control, before more hits disabled the mounting. Just one message was got off in plain language:

Am under heavy fire. Am aground. Large number of casualties.

The message was received by HMS *Consort* in Nanking and the Ambassador, Sir Ralph Stevenson, was informed; his attempts to arrange a ceasefire failed. Shelling continued and then small arms fire also, although the sloop hung out a flag of truce. At the same time, preparations were made to repel boarders, for towing, and for abandoning. Many of the wounded were sent ashore and with the aid of Nationalist soldiers evacuated safely over the river bank, which was mined in anticipation of the Communist assault.

The destroyer *Consort*, coming from Nanking, passed the *Amethyst* at 29 knots, ten British flags flying and all guns firing; then turned to try and take the sloop in tow. But she could not suppress the Communist fire for long enough and suffered severely herself, hit 56 times with ten men killed and 20 wounded. *Amethyst* had been hit 50 times and had suffered 22 killed and 29 wounded. As the destroyer was already low on provisions she carried on down the Yangtse to Shanghai.

Communist fire ceased and by lightening the ship and manoeuvring the engines, *Amethyst* was got off the mud during the night. She found a secure haven in which to see to the wounded but any attempt to move brought a warning shell from the shore. Gunfire was heard from down river, which proved to be the sound of an attempted breakthrough by the heavy cruiser *London* (with an Admiral aboard) and the sloop *Black Swan*. The cruiser had 15 killed and 37 wounded, the sloop seven wounded, and both ships were forced to turn back. The old dictum, only occasionally and in special circumstances disproved, that warships cannot successfully engage shore batteries, plainly still applied; there are limitations to sea power.

Air power was more successful. A single Sunderland flying boat landed that afternoon, and was able to put an RAF doctor and his medical supplies ashore via a sampan before Communist shellfire compelled the pilot to take off again. The doctor examined the seriously wounded still left in the sloop and ordered their evacuation through the Nationalist lines; they eventually reached Shanghai and the American hospital ship *Repose*, but the captain of the *Amethyst* died before he reached there.

The *Amethyst* was moved several times and eventually reached Chiao Shan, where she got a new captain. Lt.-Cdr. John Kerans, the assistant naval attaché at Nanking, had already been involved in the evacuation overland of some of the crew. He was 33 and knew this part of China from before the war when he had served in the guard ship at Nanking. He first had the dead buried in the river, weighted with 4-inch shells; then considered the worst case—how to scuttle the ship and march the crew back to Shanghai along the banks of the Grand Canal. Next morning, 23 April, the sloop moved down river in an attempt to find a safer berth, which was difficult because that afternoon they had a ringside seat for the crossing of the Yangtse by Mao's army. They were in what is known in Europe as the 'Forward Area' of two armies.

The beleaguered community now numbered 69 officers and men of the Royal Navy, one RAF doctor, one NAAFI canteen manager, eight

Chinese stewards, plus Peggy the dog and Simon the cat, both to be heavily involved during the summer with anti-rat operations.

On 26 April they met the local Red Chinese battery commander, Major Kung, who maintained that it was the *Amethyst* which had first opened fire and that in total the British warships had caused 252 Chinese casualties. He promised that he would not open fire again provided the sloop did not move and agreed to provide them with a sampan, 'manned' by three Chinese women, as a means of ship-to-shore communication, since the British ship's boats had been destroyed by shellfire. They also had talks with the local garrison commander, Captain Tai-ko Liang.

It may be that the higher leadership had not had time to think out how best to deal with the problem; after all, they were primarily concerned with the capture of Nanking, the enemy's capital. But in the last week of May there was evidence of a change. Colonel Kang Mao-chao, the Political Commissar of the 3rd Artillery Regiment, Chinkiang Front, was appointed official negotiator, with Kerans as the British representative. The *Amethyst* would not be allowed to go down river unless it was admitted that:

> The *Amethyst* was guilty of invading China and infringing Chinese sovereignty.
> That the British were wholly to blame.
> That the British should pay compensation for the damage they had done and the losses they had caused.

Eleven conferences were held to argue these matters, lasting from one to four hours; all very civil, refreshments being provided, the lure of promised supplies of food and fuel being offered in the hope of an admission of British guilt. No doubt they saw themselves as the coming rulers of China, no doubt they did resent the arrogant intrusion of foreign warships on to a Chinese battlefield. Also, they were victorious in war; and that lends a peculiar arrogance of its own.

Kerans, because his code books had been destroyed, had to take delicately worded instructions from his superiors, who were in a quandary. Of course, the Yangtse was an international highway and they had Chinese permission to use it—but it was the permission of the Nationalist government of Chiang-Kai-shek. But, just as clearly, the British were being held to ransom by the Red Chinese and negotiations were being spun out so as to obtain a political objective. The process, hardly recognised at the time, has since become all too familiar when hostages, some of them already dead, are offered in exchange for this or that concession to this or that revolutionary group.

From spring to the stifling summer on the Yangtse the sloop was besieged, but not unreasonably so; the Chinese maintained that they were disputing with the British government, not its servants. Local traders were allowed to visit the ship and barter food for flour and sugar; drums of oil fuel were supplied, to keep the power going; even mail was allowed—after a time. The damage to the ship was repaired as much as possible and the superstructure altered by this. With local traders being brought to and fro by the sampan girls, everything had to appear normal and, if not normal, then easily explainable. Kerans had received permission to try to break out: ostensibly he and his superiors were discussing the avoidance of typhoons; and indeed Typhoon Gloria inundated the valley on 24 July. Some of the Chinese batteries were flooded out although most had been moved forward with the advancing Red Army. Colonel Kang Mao-chao had gone to Nanking, the Nationalists' fallen capital. There was just enough fuel left to make the passage down river to Shanghai.

The Yangtse has many shallows and shifting sandbanks; the sloop drew nearly nine feet; and naturally it was not possible to obtain a pilot. The summer floods from the mountains of Tibet were a favourable factor; 15 feet of excess water meant a faster flowing river, a quicker passage to Shanghai and greater depth over the hazardous shallows. There was also a boom across the river at Chiang-yin. On 30 July Kerans decided to chance it and told the crew. He would go that night and to avoid passing Communist heavy guns near the mouth of the Yangtse at dawn, the *Amethyst* would have to leave an hour before moonset at 11 p.m.; but for most of the journey she would be shrouded in darkness. Any bright metal on the hull was dulled with black paint; canvas screens altered her silhouette; the anchor cable was muffled with greased wadding.

At 10 p.m. the greased and muffled cable slipped silently into the river and the *Amethyst* came alive. A merchant ship, the *Kiang Ling Liberation*, was going down stream, and Kerans eased the British sloop into her wake. At 10.25 a flare went up and the merchant ship ahead answered with her siren. A Communist landing craft opened up with machine-gun fire and from the bank shells tore the water. *Amethyst* passed the *Kiang Ling Liberation* and this further confused matters. The

Red Army batteries took the merchant ship as their target; it caught fire and ran aground.

Full out at 20 knots the sloop passed Rose Island and then the boom at Chiang-yin; a guard vessel fired on them but missed. At 1.30 a.m. Kerans signalled 'Halfway'. An hour later she raced past another patrol vessel, missing it by feet; and at 4 a.m. she ploughed straight through an unfortunate junk. At 5 a.m., just before first light, the *Amethyst* passed the Woosung forts and their 6-inch guns. A searchlight swept past and swept back again, but the guns did not fire. Half an hour afterwards the Yangtse lay behind them and the destroyer *Concord*, which had come out to meet them, was seen ahead. Kerans made a final signal:

> *'Have rejoined the fleet south of Woosung. No damage or casualties. God Save the King.'*

Admiral Brind at Hong Kong replied with a warning:

> *'What you have gone through in the Yangtse is child's play to the publicity you are now going to face.'*

After three months penned up in the Yangtse, the ship had ceased to be newsworthy; indeed had been almost written off. Now her sudden, triumphant reappearance from the chaos of China's civil war seemed to have something miraculous about it. Her return to England became a triumph at every port where she called, ending in London with a ceremonial march to the Guildhall and a reception at Buckingham Palace. All the same, it was the last occasion on which a European power assumed automatic overlordship in China.

SELECT BIBLIOGRAPHY

Chapter 1

Rowse, A. L. (1977). *Sir Richard Grenville of the Revenge*, London: Cape.

Monson, Sir William (1902). *The Naval Tracts of Sir William Monson*, Vol. II, Navy Records Society.

Chapter 2

Powell, J. R. (ed.) (1937). *The Letters of Robert Blake*, Navy Records Society.

Chapter 3

Mordal, Jacques (1965). *25 Centuries of Sea Warfare*, London: Souvenir Press.

Lloyd, Christopher (1975). *Atlas of Maritime History*, London: Hamlyn.

Chapter 4

Cahill, Bob (Sept. 1964). 'New England's Saga of Sunken Subs', in *Skin Diver*, USA.

Horton, Edward (1974). *The Illustrated History of the Submarine*, London: Sidgwick & Jackson.

Chapter 5

Cuddy, Don (Sept. 1956). 'I've Just Begun to Fight', in *Saga*, USA.

Warner, Oliver (Sept. 1965). 'Paul Jones in Britain', in *History Today*, London.

Chapter 6

Henderson, James (1970). *The Frigates*, London: Adlard Coles.

Cornou, Jakez, and Jonin, Bruno (1988). *L'Odyssée 'Droits de l'homme'*, Paris: DUFA.

Chapter 7

Branigan, D. P. 'Basque Roads', in *War Monthly*. (Date unknown.)

Warner, Oliver (1953). 'Mr Midshipman Marryat', article based on his *Captain Marryat: A Rediscovery*, London: Constable, 1953.

Chapter 8

Gruppe, Henry E. (1979). *The Frigates*, New York: Time-Life Books.

Chapter 9

Horton, Edward (1974). *Op.cit.* Chapter 4.

Gray, Edwyn (1986). *Few Survived*, London: Secker & Warburg.

Chapter 10

Winton, John (May 1989). 'The Raider Alabama', in *Seascape*.

Guérout, Max (Nov. 1988). 'The Engagement between the CSS *Alabama* and the USS *Kearsarge*', in *Mariner's Mirror*.

Chapter 11

Drinkwater, William (1989). 'Outrage on the Dogger Bank', in *Seascape*.

Rodway, C. P. (Jan. 1959). 'The Russian Fleet before Tsushima', in *The Navy* magazine.

Chapter 12

Bennett, Geoffrey (1962). *Coronel and the Falklands*, London: Batsford.

Pitt, Barrie (1960). *Revenge at Sea*, London: Cassell.

Pakington, Cdr. Humphrey (16 Dec. 1954). 'A Famous Victory', in *The Listener*.

Camfield, Lt.-Cdr. Oscar (8 Dec. 1964). 'Vengeance of the Navy', in the *Evening News*, Portsmouth.

Chapter 13

Hoyt, Edwin P. (1967). *The Last Cruise of the Emden*, London: Deutsch.

Chapter 14

Gray, Edwyn (1971). *A Damned Un-English Weapon*, London: Seeley.

Shankland, Peter, and Hunter, Anthony (1978). *Dardanelles Patrol*, London: Collins.

Ripley, Basil (13 Mar. 1973). 'Heroes on Picket Boats', in the *Evening News*, Portsmouth.

Chapter 15

Macintyre, Capt. Donald (1957). *Jutland*, London: Evans.

Hough, Richard (1964). *The Battle of Jutland*, London: Hamish Hamilton.

Hoehling, A. A. (1965). *The Great War at Sea*, London: Arthur Barker.

'Jutland—by Ten Men Who Were There', in the *Sunday Telegraph*, 20 May 1966.

King-Hall, Cdr. Stephen (31 May 1964). 'The Dying Boy . . .', in the *Sunday Express*.

Chapter 16

Pound, Reginald (1963). *Evans of the Broke*, Oxford University Press.

Beesley, Patrick (1982). *Room 40: British Naval Intelligence 1914–1918*, Oxford University Press.

Chapter 17

Hashagen, Ernst (1931). *The Log of a U-Boat Commander*, London: Putnam.

Campbell, Rear-Admiral Gordon (1928). *My Mystery Ships*, London: Hodder & Stoughton.

Chapter 18

Pitt, Barrie (1958). *Zeebrugge*, London: Cassell.

Beesley, Patrick (1982). *Op.cit.* Chapter 16.

The C3 Archive (courtesy of RN Submarine Museum, Gosport).

Chapter 19

Agar, Capt. Augustus (1963). *Baltic Episode*, London: Conway Maritime.

Fock, Harald. (1978). *Fast Fighting Boats*, Nautical Publishing Company.

Chapter 20

Divine, A. D. (1942). *Destroyer's War*, London: Guild.

MacDonnell, J. E. (1957). *Valiant Occasions*, London: Constable.

Roskill, S. W. (1974). *HMS Warspite*, London: Collins.

Roskill, S. W. (1977). *Churchill and the Admirals*, London: Collins.

Kemp, Lt.-Cdr. P. K. (1957). *Victory at Sea*, London: Muller.

Chapter 21

Poolman, Kenneth (1985). *Armed Merchant Cruiser*, London: Cooper-Secker.

Krancke, Admiral Theodor, and Brennecke, H. J. (1975). *Pocket Battleship*, London: William Kimber.

Kemp, Lt.-Cdr. P. K. (1957). *Op.cit.* Chapter 20.

Chapter 22

Kennedy, Ludovic (1974). *Pursuit*, London: Collins.

Grenfell, Russell (1968). *The Bismarck Episode*, London: Faber & Faber.

Bradford, Ernle (1965). *The Mighty Hood*, London: Hodder & Stoughton.

Kemp, Lt.-Cdr. P. K. (1957). *Op.cit.* Chapter 20.

Ballard, Robert D. (Nov. 1989). 'The Bismarck Found', in *National Geographic*.

Chapter 23

Borghese, Cdr. J. Valerio (1950). *Decima Flottiglia Mas*, Italy; *Sea Devils*, UK, 1952.

Attard, Joseph (1980). *The Battle of Malta*, London: William Kimber.

Bradford, Ernle (1985). *Siege of Malta 1940–1943*, London: Hamish Hamilton.

Chapter 24

Woodward, David (1953). *The Tirpitz*, London: William Kimber.

Winton, John (1967). *The War at Sea*, London: Hutchinson.

Bekker, C. D. (1953). *Swastika at Sea*, London: William Kimber.

Cornish, Peter (1973). Reports and Correspondence unpublished at the time.

Vallintine, R. (Sept. & Nov. 1974). 'Sink the *Tirpitz*', in *Triton* magazine.

Chapter 25

Morison, Samuel Eliot (1960). *Victory in the Pacific 1945: History of US Naval Operations in World War II*, Vol. XIV, Oxford University Press.

Spector, Ronald H. (1985). *Eagle Against the Sun*, London: Viking.

American Naval Fighting Ships, Vol. I (1959), Vol. II (1963–77), Washington: Navy Department.

'The Ship That Wouldn't Be Sunk: Story of USS *Franklyn*'. Special supplement in *All Hands* magazine, November 1964.

US Navy Department Archives: *Franklyn*, 11 April 1945.

US Navy Department Archives: History of USS *Bunker Hill*.

Rowe, William, and Wukowits, John F. (Dec. 1988). 'Life on a Bull's Eye', in *Military History* magazine.

Chapter 26

Brice, Martin. 'HMS *Amethyst* 1949', in *War Monthly*, no.15.

Kennedy, Ludovic (29 July 1989). 'HMS Amethyst: The Great Escape', in 'Weekend Telegraph', supplement to the *Daily Telegraph*.